1995

THEORIES OF
HUMAN
NATURE

THEORIES OF

HUMAN NATURE

PETER LOPTSON

broadview press 1995

Canadian Cataloguing in Publication Data

Loptson, Peter
  Theories of human nature

Includes index
ISBN 1-55111-061-X
1. Philosophical anthropology. I. Title.

BD450.L66 1995   128   C95-931167-X

Broadview Press
Post Office Box 1243
Peterborough, Ontario, Canada, K9J 7H5

in the United States of America
3576 California Road, Orchard Park, N.Y. 14127

in the United Kingdom
B.R.A.D. Book Representation & Distribution Ltd.
244A, London Road, Hadleigh, Essex SS7 2DE

Broadview Press gratefully acknowledges the support of the Canada Council, the Ontario
Arts Council, the Ontario Publishing Centre, and the Ministry of National Heritage.

PRINTED IN CANADA
10 9 8 7 6 5 4 3 2 1   95 96 97

For Karen, Matthew, Joe,
Harriet, and Kristjana

Human nature will not change. In any future great national trial, compared with the men of this, we shall have as weak and as strong, as silly and as wise, as bad and as good.
—Abraham Lincoln

The only thing that one really knows about human nature is that it changes. Change is the one quality we can predicate on it.
—Oscar Wilde

[Human] nature, Mr. Allnutt, is what we are put in this world to rise above.
—Katharine Hepburn to Humphrey Bogart in *The African Queen*

Contents ─────────────

Preface ————————————————

THIS VOLUME, IF USED AS A TEXTBOOK, WOULD perhaps most naturally fit a one-semester course in theories of human nature. It would also lend itself for use in a course in western civilization, and could be well suited to a disciplinary location in philosophy, sociology, history, anthropology, political theory, psychology, women's and gender studies, and broader humanities or history of ideas programs. In a one-semester course in theories of human nature it would likely be best to complement this book with three or more primary sources. Since there are eleven theories discussed in the book, it would be impossible to attempt primary text accompaniments for every theory discussed. Of course, in alternate offerings of the course over a period of time the selection of primary texts could be varied. For some of the theories, no single volume naturally suggests itself, and instructors will in some instances have texts they prefer to those I recommend. However, I think the following are good options. I have not indicated editions; in the majority of cases a number are available, and all are in print in paperback form.

Aristotle: *Nicomachean Ethics*

Christianity: John Locke, *A Letter concerning Toleration;* Joseph Butler, *Five Sermons*

Liberalism: L. T. Hobhouse, *Liberalism;* J. S. Mill, *On Liberty*

Conservative Individualism: Bernard Mandeville, *Fable of the Bees*

Rousseau: *Discourse on the Origin of Inequality, The Social Contract*

Marx: Marx and Engels, *The Communist Manifesto*

Biological theories: Charles Darwin, *The Descent of Man;* Konrad Lorenz, *On Aggression*

Freud: *Civilization and Its Discontents, Character and Culture*

Non-self theories: J. O. de La Mettrie, *Man a Machine;* Daniel Dennett, *Consciousness Explained*

Feminism: Rosemarie Tong, *Feminist Thought*

Marvin Harris: *Our Kind*

I prefer to assign fewer rather than more primary texts in conjunction with the book, enabling a somewhat more detailed consideration of three or four theories in a given semester. In this way, lengthy books like Darwin's *Descent of Man,* Aristotle's *Nicomachean Ethics,* and Harris's *Our Kind* can be included (all or in part), together with shorter works. Instructors might be hesitant to use a large work like *The Descent of Man.* I can report from first-hand experience that it has worked quite well. Darwin's Victorian prose is engaging and accessible, and he manages from time to time to be stimulatingly controversial (some would say objectionable) in pedagogically creative or effective ways. Some instructors may want always to give primary treatment to particular theories—feminism, perhaps, or liberalism, or some other. This, of course, can easily be accommodated along the lines of the textual guide proposed, or by adopting some other primary text than those suggested. An anthology of shorter readings will also seem a good idea to many instructors. No one volume in print will fully correspond to the theories of my book, although there are paperback collections that have selections representing a majority of them.

I would like to acknowledge helpful reactions from a number of people who have read this book in whole or part, or from whom I have received valuable suggestions and, sometimes, dissent. These include Kevin Corrigan, David Crossley, Len Findlay, John Mills, Wayne Pomerleau (of Gonzaga University), Jene Porter, Ahmad Rahmanian, Martin Tweedale, Willie Watts-Miller, and three anonymous referees for Broadview. All remaining errors of fact or judgement are, of course, mine. Thanks also to Donna Fesser for typing the manuscript of the book; to Terry Teskey, editor, for thorough, professional, and extremely helpful work with the text; and to Don Le Pan for having suggested the idea in the first place, and for support and encouragement throughout its development.

Peter Loptson
Saskatoon, Canada
March 1995

Introduction ——————————

SCIENCE, BERTRAND RUSSELL SAID, IS WHAT we know, and philosophy is what we don't know. He apparently meant that inquiry leads on the one hand to results that are regarded as more or less settled and intersubjectively or publicly validated, and on the other to results that remain "theory" and speculation; and we designate these two as, respectively, science and philosophy. The significance of the contrast spans time, for areas once merely speculative have become anchored and systematically grounded. Philosophy, the subject that sheds its offspring, has given rise to science. This has happened to physics, once natural philosophy; and perhaps also— opinions differ—to logic, semantics, linguistics, and psychology.

One of the things inquirers have most wanted to gain knowledge of is ourselves. What, if anything, is most deeply and generically true of human beings? What are we like? What is central and fundamental in our make-up, as beings, in the universe, on the earth, in history? How deep does whatever is most deeply true of us go? Is there such a thing as a fixed, centrally lodged *human nature?* If so, what is it? How long have we had it? Is it alterable? Or, if there is no single unitary nature that humans have, common and generic to all societies they have formed, exhibited in all (or at least all characteristic) individual lives, are there then stable substantive natures that *subgroups* of us have—the old, the young, people of the West, the working poor, males, females, East Asians, heterosexuals, homosexuals, humans since the Industrial Revolution, since the last Ice Age, or other categories? Or are there are no significant commonalities at all, none that aren't ephemeral, or too plastic to be genuinely disclosing of humanity?

Conceptions of what human beings are like may be identified in almost any cultural artifact focused on people, that is, in any piece of literature, written or oral, or art object in which people are represented. More explicit notions are found in many of the works in the western philosophical tradition, beginning perhaps with Pythagoras, the first of the Greek philosophers to develop a theory of the human soul. However, only in recent centuries have sustained, secular accounts of human nature been developed. It is possible to bring a reasonable degree of precision to this task. Aristotle certainly formulated a theory of human nature that remains of importance to the present day. But apart from Aristotle, explicit attempts to identify the fundamental features of human beings and empirical explanations of those features date essentially from the seventeenth century.

"Portraits" of humankind stand out in the writings of Thomas Hobbes (1588–1679) and Benedict Spinoza (1632–1677), and deserve some discussion for their own sake—both are vivid and distinctive and have some degree of impress in the centuries that follow. But as with very much else in human culture, the year 1687—when Sir Isaac Newton's *Principia* was published—marks a watershed in the project of investigating ourselves. Ever since Newton, a succession of inquirers have dreamt the dream of something that would be not merely theory, speculative philosophical *vision,* of human nature, but rather a *science* of humanity. These inquirers—sometimes teams of inquirers, such as committees, traditions, or research units—have hoped for and worked towards something that would move the study of human nature into the category of knowledge, just as Newton (and his seventeenth-century colleagues) had moved speculation about matter and motion into the category of knowledge. In the later nineteenth century, this vision began to take very diverse forms, as what we now call the social sciences appeared in systematic and often rigorous fashion. The development has mushroomed. A plethora of theories of what we are vies for attention and assent, quite a few of them—though entirely incompatible with each other—claiming to be the realization of the post-Newtonian dream.

I want to stress that it may be true that one or more genuine sciences of humanity have arrived among us. In the recent past behaviourism, Freudian psychoanalysis, and Marxism all have spoken with a cool magisterial authority of having achieved definitive knowledge—scientific knowledge—of humanity's nature, and place in nature. Contemporary theories and models proclaim themselves in no less quietly confident, analytical, and scientifically measured a tone as providing information about humans that wholly supersedes the stumbling, fragmentary gropings of folk belief, common sense, or earlier scientific endeavour. There is no question that quite a lot is now known by human beings about human beings; and some of it at least is both systematic and wide ranging. Among the many candidates, one, or some amalgam of several, may be the genuine article, an objective scientific account of what or who we are. But if so, we do not yet know it. To the present hour, no theory of human nature has won wide or general assent, or taken its place as the acknowledged objective science of humanity.

That this is so, and so long as it continues, is the point and justification of the study of theories of human nature, above all from within the broad umbrella of philosophy. It is also the point of and justification for the present book.

My aim in the ensuing chapters will be to describe a series of conceptions of what we most deeply and most genuinely are; visions or, better, *images* of what sorts of beings we are, of what the world has in it by virtue of having us in it. There have been a great many models or images of human nature; they jostle and compete for our assent. Some once living no longer resonate, and new models, including hybrid conceptions that unite what would formerly have been thought antithetical elements, continue to appear. Many allegedly new images of human nature are in fact old wine repackaged in new bottles.

I will discuss only theories of our nature that still live, and command the assent of reasonably sizeable constituencies in contemporary western life.[1] As well, to be a candidate for the attention of the survey offered here a theory of human nature must be at least at peace with, if not an active proponent of, what I will call "modernity." By this somewhat vague term I mean primarily an informed acceptance of a broadly scientific outlook on the world, and some degree of openness to alternative and new ideas. This is not meant to imply a secular, naturalistic, mechanist, or liberal set of commitments. Modernity is compatible with religious convictions, and views holding that the world needs to be made over, possibly in quite dramatic and transformational ways.

Some of the theories I discuss have respectable followings in the social science community or communities. Others engage even wider scientific communities, for some contemporary images of humankind primarily identify us as animals—primates—most meaningfully and accurately understood within a larger biological framework; and indeed, some current images see us as fundamentally information-processing systems—naturally selected biobasic ones, to be sure, but linked most significantly with other actual or possible information processors, some of them non-living.

---

[1] Which must exclude many otherwise deeply interesting theories of the past. Among them may specially be mentioned the theory of David Hume—whose classic work is called *A Treatise of Human Nature* and who surely, if anyone did, aspired to realize the Newtonian dream, with enduring results for *other* areas of philosophy. (Still, a number of Hume's ideas do appear in this book, in two distinct chapters.)

In addition to broadly scientific or empirical—and usually naturalistic—models, what might be styled more purely philosophical images of humankind also have a large presence in the modern world. These include models whose chief parameter is agency—degrees of power or control or direction that people exercise personally, interpersonally, and within the wider social, national, and historical systems they find themselves in. Many such models are a feature of our age, and seem less prominent or wholly absent in older theories of human nature. At any rate, models that view human identity in terms of who has and who lacks "power"—life-leverage, in one's own circumstances or those of others—are currently richly abundant. It is often most difficult to see clearly or to step back from what is closest at hand, and this may be the case for the images of the hegemonic, and the empowered and disempowered, now so manifest.

Other models on the current stage deny that there is such a thing as human nature. For some of these models this has a decidedly metaphysical grounding: we are *conscious free agents*. Each of these three features may be held to be antithetical to natural systems. By virtue of our consciousness, our freedom, and our agency we are precisely what is *not* determinately a such-and-such, a specifiable content of boundaries and nature. Rather, we are potency, blueprint, form without content, creators of our "natures" as of our values and destinies. G. W. F. Hegel (1770–1831), still another important and original human nature theorist, formulates a large and particularly metaphysical version of such a conception. We meet with it also in existentialism, the philosophy that defines itself as the view that in humans existence precedes essence, that is, that we first exist, without a nature or essence, and then by our choices and our actions create the contentful realities of our lives. Someone could, of course, claim that conscious free agency is after all an essence, or else that once chosen and created, the life patterns we realize will constitute an essence. But plainly there will be something hollow about both ideas. Such "essences" as these are (in the sense meant) not essences at all.

Other models share existentialism's opposition to "essentialism," seeing what we become—and hence at particular stages are—as created out of circumstances and realities that are "not-us." Many such views do not, however, share existentialism's conviction of our absolute metaphysical freedom. More frequently, as they see it, what fashions our "natures" (more accurately, the varied and ephemeral personas we wear) are features of our circumstances—class, economic, or social power, social-location-assigning ideology—that we are typically unaware of and in any case powerless to direct or modify.

Theories, or their advocates, tend to distort or simplify their (real or imagined) opposition. What is it to be an "essentialist" in matters of human nature, and which human nature theories are accurately so described? This theme will be taken up in the next chapter.

All of the theories discussed in this book have significant contemporary representation and advocacy. I would argue further that all of them have at least something to be said for them. All reflect and advance a set of intuitions and a body of data that, minimally, correspond to a genuine sector of human life and experience. All deserve to be taken seriously; each is a contender that might, quite legitimately and plausibly, convince an intelligent, fair-minded person initially of strongly opposing inclination.

Let it be said, too, that the truth is by no means necessarily going to please us or confirm our value judgements, whatever these latter be, including judgements of human dignity or equality. Some of the theories to be discussed in this book will have unflattering implications, or offer only dismal prospects for possibilities of change. The truth could conceivably be still darker than any of our theories holds. We could turn out to be a distinctly unpleasant species overall—murderous, short-sighted, aggressively cruel, hopelessly quarrelsome, or worse—and we could turn out to be significantly differentially endowed. The truth might be dangerous, unwelcome, politically incorrect, offensive. It might corroborate or reinforce the prejudices or power of people who may be viewed as already having too much of both. A view isn't necessarily mistaken if it issues from people whose interests it will most conveniently serve, just as it isn't refuted just because it diminishes our self-esteem. On the other hand, of course, the truth may well do none of these undesired things. If we really want to know what people are fundamentally like—and we might rather not know, especially if the realities are unsavoury or disappointing or threaten to undermine some modest bit of progress that has been made—we will be willing to accept what we think honest inquiry shows.

In this volume eleven major theories of human nature are surveyed. There are several interesting and substantive theories beyond these, and I would have liked to explore a number them as well.[2] Considerations of space made a wider range impossible. A compendium or encyclopedia of modern human nature theories would in any

---

[2] Of particular value and interest would be, in my view, the human nature theories of G. W. F. Hegel, Friedrich Nietzsche, Ferdinand Tönnies, Emile Durkheim, and Max Weber.

case be alien to the spirit and intent of the present book. The eleven chosen are, I think, significantly representative of a diversity of philosophical visions of humankind. And in the course of setting each one out I have sketched or referred to other theories.

One of the theories presented—Aristotle's—is from long before the modern period. Another is a modern version of an old theory, namely Christianity. All of the other theories were developed in the course of the three centuries since Newton, and are presented in more or less chronological order. Several were formed over the course of many years, so some historical overlap occurs.

The idea of a theory of human nature is an eighteenth-century notion, and is met with most explicitly in writers of that period. Of our eleven theories, only Enlightenment cases or versions thereof talk directly, using these terms or close synonyms, of a theory of human nature or human beings as the theory's central project. Otherwise what is found is either a scientific project located within a life science or social science disciplinary matrix, or a critique of other theory and of culture, along with notions of a practice. In the case of our one pre-Enlightenment theory, Aristotle's, a theory is assembled from discussions of human goals and of certain notions of rational functioning in a community. Nonetheless, in his and in all of our cases, the ascription of an image or conception of what human beings are is readily justified; what is more, it is important to know and to conceive of in precisely these kinds of terms.

This last claim may certainly be challenged. Some of the theories surveyed are more obvious choices than others. Possibly least obvious of them is a religious perspective, particularly in light of the generally guiding ideal of a science of humankind. And why, if a religious perspective is to appear, should it be Christianity? Ecumenicity, tolerant pluralist values, ought to provide a place for others as well, or else for none. Perhaps there ought to be a rainbow pastiche of "spiritual" conceptions of humanity. However, the fact is that Christianity was the religious framework that, for good and ill, shaped and helped create the western world. The members of western societies—as most readers of this book will be—come from and dwell within a cultural reality that is probably unintelligible without reference to Christianity. Even the term "Judeo-Christianity" blurs and misrepresents the fact that the formative matrix of western culture has been Christian. Christianity itself, of course, rests on prior cultural traditions, but that is another matter.

Further, despite confident predictions, religious views of the world in general and Christian ones in particular have not withered away. These anticipations began to appear with the very first flowering of the Enlightenment, in the early eighteenth century. They were expressed by Enlightenment social theorists and philosophers and by nineteenth-century liberal and socialist thinkers. They came to state power with the French revolution of 1789 and all Marxist revolutionary victories in the twentieth century. They appear in Nietzsche's prognostications for the twentieth century. But through all developments religion has survived, indeed generally thrived, although in western societies religion has, to be sure, largely been "privatized"—rendered individual, personal, private, not something enforceable on a state or social basis.

Christianity, alone among religious constituencies in the West, is independent of a specific historical cultural community—is in this sense "universal"—and has continued to claim the allegiance of large and disparate numbers of people, both in their private thoughts and in public, collective behaviour, for a very long time: Christianity has "legs." It endures particularly, and perhaps especially surprisingly, among the community most sharply disposed to probe and contest it, namely, professional philosophers. There is a sizeable and thriving community of Christian philosophers, consisting of both public advocates of Christian views and perspectives and individuals who are privately and quietly Christians. This total community is a minority within the aggregate of western philosophers, but it also shows no signs of going away.

Of course, mere longevity cannot be sufficient justification for including a view, nor can numbers, even if among them are many philosophers. Here we consider only what I call a modern Christian view of human nature—Christianity accommodated to modernity. Still, the view is Christian: it is a view that conceives human nature as involving participation—only potentially in perhaps even the majority of cases of human beings—in something divine. On this view humans have a capacity to imaginatively transcend their terrestrial bounds and their individual (relative) frailty and brevity of life, by virtue of a supposed relationship with a god who made himself a human being. Not just an uncertain metaphysics and philosophical history are involved in this idea. The self-levelling of God to humanity both reflects and creates a stature and an estate for human beings that is egalitarian, cosmic, social—we are brothers and sisters in this estate—deeply personal, and emotion engaging. This theory makes us creatures capable of self-elevation—more than merely moral or aesthetic self-elevation—from a darkness and a weakness we otherwise occupy and never escape, at least in this life. Love, Christian love, is a glue and the fuel for these realizations of our divine-like capacities. This is an image or vision of human nature, augmented or extended in different ways and directions by different forms of the theory.

To include feminism may also seem problematic. One view is that there are no distinctively feminist views of human nature—either because feminism is so diverse and multiform that there are just too many views of humanity there (most or all of them perhaps just variants of older human nature perspectives), or else because feminism is essentially a *critique* of other phenomena (western and other societies, institutional patterns, past history), without a positive body of theory of its own. Neither of these views seems justified, although the first is the more plausible. Feminism *has* given rise to a varied range of views; and certainly much feminist writing and thinking has analyzed and challenged existing or historical structures.

The proof, however, is in the pudding. Feminism in most or all forms comes to—usually strongly and actively enunciates—positions with regard to gender equality or difference, and this is a matter of a stance on human nature. Either males and females are at least approximately the same, across a continuum of human abilities, dispositions, and propensities, or there are significant differences between the sexes—differences that make a difference, affecting the conditions of well-being of large numbers of men and women. Equality (or equity) feminists take the first view, difference feminists the second. Of course there is more to the matter than just this, and some of that complexity will be explored. But this is a central feminist issue with respect to human nature.

The issue is not just one of structural or systemic critique. Attempting to argue otherwise, someone might hold that feminism doesn't take a stand one way or the other about human nature and simply wants to dislodge entrenched male power and accord women their due share of it. But this is insufficient to capture what is found in both equality and difference feminism. One thing all versions of feminism agree on is that women do not have too much power. Nor does any feminist position appear worried about the prospect of women having too much power in the future. For difference feminism in particular, this must reflect convictions about human nature, and male and female nature in particular. What difference feminism decries as "masculinism"—certain modes of thought and behaviour it associates with some or most males—is not just seen as what any group will succumb to if it enjoys lots of power for a long time. "Power corrupts," Lord Acton said; no feminist holds that power masculinizes. None seems even to consider female dominance as of hypothetical or theoretical concern. Difference feminists especially seem confident that women could do a better job of running the world than have men. Equality feminists do not share this confidence, but they too think the world's gender communities, in the persons of each of their individual members, can handle appropriate measures of social power, autonomy, self-determination, and adult interaction with the world's spiritual, economic, and other realities. These are views about human beings and their natures. In sum, then, there seem to be at least two substantive feminist views of human nature.

Another way to think of the investigation of the major theories of human nature, and another reason why it is a distinctively and importantly philosophical (rather than scientific) project, is as providing a set of imaginative blueprints—deposit accounts in the idea bank—for empirical investigation. Of course, science produces such blueprints too. As I see it, the two are not rival or even altogether distinct enterprises. But philosophy has wider boundaries and fewer methodological constraints; all options are potentially up for consideration. And since it is we ourselves who are the target of study, it is uniquely important that theory not be made to conform with anybody's gridlock idea of what a respectable theory had better be like. These various models or images are not going to go away. Even those judged implausible or off the wall stay around—and it is important that they continue to stay around—as reminders of what can return to the forum for reconsideration if currently favoured, respectable "normal science" images of what we are become in tension with what we dredge up from the well of self.[3]

The aim throughout this book is to present the theories under discussion in reasonably brief, accurate form, with special attention to aspects that seem to me particularly to engage a contemporary mind. Although there can be no substitute for reading the original works of the thinkers discussed here, in several cases a theory of

---

[3] As well as constituting blueprints or models for human reality, human nature theories reflect features of those who are drawn to them. While it is plainly fallacious to suppose that a theory is refuted or explained by virtue of the appeal it may have for a certain kind of personality (or members of specific socio-economic or other cultural groups, or those who have been specially marked by distinctive sorts of experiences), something is revealed about people by knowing what human nature view they believe. As in other domains, the ontological telescope has two ends. This idea is explored in Lawrence S. Wrightsman, *Assumptions about Human Nature* (1992).

human nature must be pieced together from scattered parts of those works, or inferred from remarks on other topics. So I would claim a specially synoptic value in setting such theories out as I do in this book. Moreover, this volume focuses on distinctive, original, and currently influential—more than that, currently *believed*—images of who we are, or of what it is to be a human being. While I salute the genius of the creators of these powerful images, my emphasis here is the theory itself, the cluster of ideas (with or without acres of corroborative empirical data), and not particularly the intellectual legacy of the theory's creator. I seek to show, and to evaluate, what it is to see the human world as being like *that*.

It may provide useful advance signposting to say that the chapters to follow are intended to be expository essays on the theories they set out. A general account of the fundamental components of the theory is given, sometimes with selective, deliberately imbalanced attention to facets of the theory of special significance for a modern audience. Beyond that what is attempted is an essay on the ideas adumbrated; I seek here to respect and engage both the theory and the reader. There will probably in some cases seem to be too much of me in the discussion; in others I may seem to assume an awareness of the place of the theory in modern culture that the reader may not have (indeed, might complain he or she was reading this book in part to acquire). It may also appear that the objections and criticisms offered at the end of each chapter impose unequal burdens on the theories discussed: some will seem to get off rather easily, others to receive a heavy tide of adverse comment. This will reflect, in some cases, my own undoubted predilections or biases, but also a conviction that it is the views most congenial to a university reader that may most benefit from the nudge of critical scrutiny. Most of the objections expressed appear in the secondary literature discussing the theories; a few are my own.

Most concepts and terminology relevant for the theories that will be discussed are introduced and explained as they come into play. A few ideas are of such recurrent utility that I will bring them into view now. Of special importance is a distinction originally developed by the linguist Kenneth Pike and given a specially prominent place in the work of one of our theorists, the cultural anthropologist Marvin Harris. This is the distinction between the *emic* and the *etic*. Like many valuable concepts, the idea is simple and obvious—once pointed out. A description or perspective is emic when it represents a piece of behaviour or other human reality in terms that would be recognized and endorsed by the human beings involved in that behaviour or reality. An emic account, then, will be meant to correspond to an agent's point of view, and to make sense from that agent's perspective (or "phenomenological[4] stance"). A description or perspective is etic when it represents a piece of behaviour or other human reality from the stance of an external observer, especially an observer aiming to produce an accurate theoretical account, which may or may not correspond to or utilize the terminology or conceptual categories of the agent. The emic then is participant-relative, and the etic observer-relative. Emic and etic *can* coincide (that is, be identical), though they typically will not. There may be corresponding emic and etic descriptions or explanations of the same event or phenomenon, in which case both may be literally true or accurate, or just one may be, or neither. Or one of the perspectives may pick out or express something that the other one fails to. The utility of this distinction will, I think, become increasingly evident as we proceed.

Two other distinctions are useful and find employment more than once in subsequent chapters. The first is useful primarily for its abbreviative power. It contrasts the *synchronic*—events and phenomena of a single time—with the *diachronic*—those across times, over a period or duration. The second is due to Friedrich Nietzsche (1844–1900), an interesting thinker whose remarks on human nature might have justified a twelfth theory for this book. Nietzsche famously distinguished the *Apollonian* from the *Dionysian*. These ideas are intended to signify a note or mood or spirit in theory or the life of an individual or a culture, and an accompanying set of values. The Apollonian is named from Apollo, Greek god of light and reason (and other less philosophically relevant things). It betokens moderation, calmness, tempered rationality, open clarity, and justice. Dionysus was the Greek god of wine and intoxicated excess. The Dionysian is the spirit and the values of passion and emotion, of the night-time, of intemperance, of wildness, and the subterranean. These ideas are more evocative than exact. They also seem to capture something valid, and important, in human experience. A further subtle and valuable notion also comes from Nietzsche: *ressentiment*. This is simply the French word for resentment. However, it is used—kept in French—in a Nietzschean sense to signify a state of consciousness that appears distinctive: a state of negative feeling involving envy of

---

[4] By "phenomenological" is meant the felt quality of some experience. Thus, the phenomenology of eating strawberry ice cream, of first love, of death, of solving a calculus problem, being female, being underweight, being a horse or a bat, is what it is like to do, feel, or be those things.

the circumstances of a resented other, who is conceived, feared, and hated as in some way superior, and whom the victim of *ressentiment* would like to destroy or be rid of, partly because of the spectacle of their freedom, beauty, or power.[5]2 (Like many of the ideas that appear in vivid and subsequently influential form in Nietzsche, the concept of *ressentiment,* complete with its Nietzschean coloration and purpose, appears earlier. Hegel gives the idea full expression—though without applying it, as Nietzsche did, to Christians and Christian morality—in the *Philosophy of History* [1991, p. 32].)

One of my aims in this book is to convey a sense of how a particular human nature theory sees humankind that is at some remove from, or is not altogether couched in, the language and point of view of the theory itself. Our theories take themselves very seriously indeed; most purport to be science, and some, as we have said, may really be so. I want to respect these high purposes, and also to explain what these theories say about people without wholly accepting their framework of assumptions. Each of these theories has a coloration, an emotional tone, that is almost never an explicit part of the theory. It will be valuable to bring that tone or colour onto the table of our survey. Several examples from the theories we will shortly encounter may illustrate what is meant.

Marxism, for example, involves a certain combination of moral earnestness and a cold-eyed analytic detachment that—it might be said—allows no one (except proletarians and Marxists) to be a human being; rather, they are identified, classified, and dealt with (processed, one could say) as embodiments of particular class interests, or particular ideological factional locations. Doing so is seen, by Marxism, as a requirement of being scientific, of being objective. Though the way I have just put this matter will undoubtedly sound anti-Marxist, it is not meant to be, and objectively isn't. A Marxist can recognize and acknowledge that insofar as one is being scientific and objective, particular people are not supposed to be conceived in their particularity but as members of classes, and (unless victims/perpetrators of false consciousness) inevitably pursuers of their class interest. Marxism involves an insistence that all objective knowledge of people (except for objective knowledge of ruling-class exploitation of the proletariat) is etic knowledge, and specifically class-focused etic knowledge. It seems important that that fact be added to the

[5] Nietzsche's Apollonian/Dionysian distinction is developed in *The Birth of Tragedy* (1872); *ressentiment* is discussed in several works, perhaps most thoroughly and vividly in *On the Genealogy of Morals* (1887).

account, and factored into the reckoning, of Marxism. More: the account should acquaint the reader with a sense of omissions and prohibitions, in what would otherwise be held to be knowledge one has of particular people, one accepts by virtue of adopting a theory like Marxism. To be a Marxist is to be, one could say, a certain kind of *soldier,* where one is to have renounced particular kinds of attitudes and reactions to people (and of course to have adopted others). One is now to see a human world that is colour-coded along class lines.

Similarly, to be a feminist is to see a human world that is colour-coded along gender lines, that empower and disempower. And to know that someone is a feminist is to know that they have taken up a set of lenses that will be sensitive to what others' lenses see blurrily if at all and, perhaps, not sensitive to other ways we can see another person (for example, as someone who has had to wait a disagreeably long time in a line-up, or someone for whom swimming, or smelling enjoyable odours, has a particular nuanced pleasure).

Again, being a Freudian involves bringing to human experiences, of self and others, a somewhat tragic sense of life, with persons perceived—sniffed, smelled, smoked out—as resultants, carrying the outcomes of life trials that are themselves descendant-outcomes of trials from childhood, on the individual's shoulders, in the lines of their face, and their features. It also involves screens or lenses that are sensitive to the detection of facets of privacy in everyone, above all everyone's sexuality—not so much particularities of sexual preferences as what meaning their sexuality has for the person in question, and what degree of comfort they have with it. These lenses are coloured with the absolute conviction that no one is genuinely asexual (indeed, *far* from it) and that there is no such thing as "mature sexuality," sexuality that isn't eternally and forever adolescent or pre-adolescent in its real, that is, undisguised, emotional tonalities.

Being an Aristotelian is in some ways harder to capture. Taking Aristotle on his own, and discounting the long centuries of his influence and the somewhat peculiar idea of what it does or could mean to be an Aristotelian in the 1990s, I would say that to be an Aristotelian is to hold to the very model of a scientific approach and understanding, where science is viewed as a striving for knowledge of the world, conducted by a rational inquisitive animal (i.e., ourselves). It is largely armchair, not hands-on, science, of mannerly, natural-historian type. Nonetheless it is wide open to the largest and smallest of queries, imaginative, organized, methodical, comprehensive, and detailed. Aristotle certainly had prejudices and limitations, but there is no reason to think he would refuse the exploration of any topic, including his own prejudices and assumptions.

But what does being an Aristotelian (and not being Aristotle) mean *now?* Contemporary Aristotelians are mostly in flight from or negation of other stances and currents of contemporary thought. But the weight of the sophistications (and pseudo-sophistications) of the last three centuries and more cannot be thought away. One cannot simply find an Aristotelian approach the most convincing way to think of things. The contemporary Aristotelian (if that is centrally what someone is) is, it seems plausible to believe, someone yearning for simpler or more wholesome things; someone wanting it to be the way it used to be, the way it's supposed to be, when we knew what a thing was, or could hope to. This is not to deny the very real surviving value in Aristotelian insights, or the amazing continuing contribution and intelligence of an Aristotelian perspective. It is perhaps to wonder whether it is still possible in full authenticity and good faith to be (*tout court*) an Aristotelian, as one can be, authentically and in good faith, a Freudian, Marxist, feminist, or Rousseauist.

I will not fill the complement of these impressionistic portraits. They have been offered in advance of the fuller accounts to come, to illustrate an angle of response to these minds and the powerful theories they have produced. The reader may be able to sketch further such portraits as the book progresses.

An old contrast drawn in Europe since the eighteenth century or earlier distinguishes two kinds of souls to be met with in the world—and this too is a piece of folk human nature theory—distinguished by reference to geographic provenance: there are what are called Northern souls and Mediterranean souls. This is a division drawn and articulated by "Northerners," and also conceived by them as a "Germanic"/ "Latin" partition. It differentiates reserved, formal, Protestant, abstract-conceptual people from passionate, imaginative, earthy, expressive, southern Catholic people (with the religious identifications more cultural than doctrinal). This is, of course, the (approximate) territory of national character generalizations, widened to clusters of nations, and subject to the very severe limitations—in fact, real hazards—of such generalities. Like other unscientific generalities, and other folk conceptions, this contrast will have a certain degree of fit with empirical realities and a great deal of vaporous imprecision and mythic content.

At any rate, a comparable New World polarity has, less frequently, been discerned. This one, specific to the United States, contrasts Californian and New York/New England souls. The idea here is that the Californian is without roots or even, except quite haphazardly and contingently, family. Attachments to individuals, communities, material surroundings, geography, and ideological and spiritual identifications, are chosen, and may well be reconsidered. This is the dream of a permanent frontier, and life as a smorgasbord where one may dine—would be a fool not to—à la carte. One may even opt, as currents and trends dispose, for rootedness and family, and then, as bestsellers, talk-show themes, or other features of popular culture or one's own creative initiative incline, turn tomorrow elsewhere. The New Englander (Woody Allen is a clear, obvious example), by contrast, is an Old Worlder, rooted, sentimentally and more than sentimentally bound to particularities of neighbourhood, culture, and background. This is in part an axis of freedom/unfreedom (and what are believed to be presences and absences of both). It also points to marked cultural differences. The New Englander has a sense of the authority of cultural background, and that background extends dimly and vaguely, or quite explicitly, across the Atlantic to western Europe. The New Englander is a card-carrying member of western civilization, even when of a proudly divergent and innovative and egalitarian branch. The Californian may also be, one or two days of the week, but transplantation is felt to sever the cord. There is for the Californian no canon.

Californians, then, are modern, or postmodern. They are drawn to other than DWEM (Dead White European Male) models. They might have interests in science fiction, contemporary Latin American literature, "classical" music composed after 1920. They may be information highway people, not deeply interested in history or tradition: what matters is now and what lies ahead. They are pluralist, egalitarian, democratic, not hostile to the natural sciences: they don't particularly believe in genius, or wisdom, or the classic, or are only somewhat impressed by them when they do (except perhaps two or three days a month, some months). Geniuses or sages have more appeal for Californians simply as celebrities.

New Englanders, by contrast, do have a sense of a canon. They may feel apologetic about it (or not), but they find themselves continually returning to and renewed by the creative voices and minds of western civilization. They do believe in genius and wisdom, and in art, civilization, and history. Sometimes they worry about science and technology (environmental Californians may also, but chiefly politically). They seek to drink at the wells of aggregative wisdom, like Odin in Norse mythology.

I won't continue this theme further, but I do think these notions, in their impressionistic, vague, and of course culturally dependent way, may assist us in the quest for illuminating images of ourselves.[6] They give focus, unanchored but imaginative and powerful, to the kinds of appeal the theories and theorists we are considering have, to the kinds of minds drawn to them in their diversity.

Freud, for example, is clearly a thinker of New England and not Californian appeal. Freud was a very learned man, widely acquainted with the western cultural tradition as well as the science of his day. What is more, he loved that tradition. He valued and sought both to learn from and to contribute to the pools of human understanding. The views we will be calling the non-self theories, by contrast, are plausibly taken as Californian. These views do not attempt to situate humans within a cumulative endeavour of exploring human nature. There is no regard here for forerunners or pre-scientific or even early scientific projects. One starts new, fresh, without baggage, above all cumbrous diachronic baggage.

I will not attempt a wider taxonomic alignment of our theories within the California/New England polarity. Like the earlier impressionistic portraits, this contrast may be explored, and insights generated, if the notion resonates for a reader.

The reader might like to hear what the author's own preferences, leanings, or commitments are, particularly in an area of inquiry as charged as ours. I have already indicated that I mean only to discuss human nature theories that seem to me "serious" ones, currently embraced and defended in intelligent, thoughtful ways by reasonably significant numbers of people. This way of describing a selection procedure is of course itself not neutral; indeed, it is openly normative. I have also said that I think that there is something to be said for each view this book will explore.

Matters could just be left there. Given a statement of respect for all theories under review, the reader could wait and see whether I am equally fair, accurate, or sensitive to all of them. I will try to be. And this will include airing objections, usually including some fairly formidable ones (or ones that seem to me formidable) to every theory. These objections occupy the final section of the chapters, each of which presents a distinct theory. Certainly, I do find some of the views presented more persuasive or plausible than others. My own

[6] This contrastive model would by no means be confined to the United States. It captures something universal, I think, which would be locatable by other terminology in non-western cultures as well as western ones.

view is *not* that the truth is to be found in some amalgam of all of them, even though I believe all have at least a case. On the other hand, there is no one of these theories that by itself seems to me the right one, or even the best among several.

A cardinal error of so many of these theories is a failure to recognize how many hats we wear. That is, humans have an extraordinary diversity of roles, very many of them of great importance to the player and other people, and we seem adept at moving among these several tasks and identities with astonishing fluidity as occasion, inclination, and need dictate or dispose.

At the end of each chapter are bibliographic references. The aim here is to itemize the principal writings setting out the theory or theories discussed in the chapter, together with secondary accounts that expand or contest the theories in distinctive and accessible ways. The intention above all is that these references be useful. That end is not served, in my view, by aspiring to be encyclopedic, so it is certainly possible that many references specialists think important are not included.

Bibliography

Hegel, G. W. F. *The Philosophy of History*. Translated by J. Sibree. Buffalo: Prometheus Books, 1991. [1857]

Nietzsche, Friedrich. *The Birth of Tragedy*. Translated by W. Kaufmann. New York: Random House, 1967. [1872]

————. *On the Genealogy of Morals*. Translated by W. Kaufmann. New York: Random House, 1967. [1887]

Pike, K. L. *Language in Relation to a Unified Theory of the Structure of Human Behaviour*. 2nd ed. The Hague: Mouton, 1967.

Wrightsman, Lawrence S. *Assumptions about Human Nature*. 2nd ed. Newbury Park, CA: Sage, 1992.

CHAPTER 2

Essentialism, Materialism and Idealism ─────────

MUCH RECENT DISCUSSION OF ISSUES OF HUMAN nature has turned on so-called essentialist themes, particularly though not exclusively in some feminist discussions of human nature.[1] Basically, the idea here is that there is a fixed unchangeable nature or "essence" that human beings have. Sometimes this is regarded as a normative view according to which humans *should not* behave other than as the claimed nature or essence directs. In other cases the supposed essence or nature is a *telos* or ideal condition in which (it is alleged) humans thrive, or the essence imposes limiting conditions beyond which it is supposed to be impossible to advance. Originally the model may have been biological: giraffes, bats, and salamanders will have an essence or nature, what it is to be things of their sort, and so too should humans. On all such views—according to those who discuss essentialism and human nature—the putative essence is independent of culture, history, class, sexual orientation, and other aspects of the human condition. I do not add sex (or gender) to the preceding list because essentialism and anti-essentialism particularly show up in contemporary feminist discussion, where claims of *gender essentialism* are affirmed and denied.

Essentialism is not the same thing as determinism—not even the same as hard (or freedom-denying) determinism. (Many philosophers now argue that determinism as such is compatible with free agency.) This is easy and straightforward to see. Hard or incompatibilist

─────────

[1] Thus, for example, Alison Jaggar (*Feminist Politics and Human Nature,* p. 32) asserts that "it is evident that liberal theory rests on the assumption that all persons, at all times and in all places, have a common essence or nature" and again that "liberal feminists seem to conclude that women and men may vary in their 'accidental' properties, both physical and mental, but that they are identical in their essential nature" (p. 38). Jaggar goes on to affirm that the Marxist concept of alienation "is a somewhat problematic concept for Marxists because it may be taken to presuppose a human essence from which people under capitalism are alienated, and the concept of a human essence seems quite at odds with the conception of human nature as a product of history" (p. 57).

determinism implies that we are powerless to modify or alter our life history, a background of causal factors in place from our births and earlier, ensuring that we will do what we in fact do. But the determining background could vary from individual to individual, or by generation or culture. Less metaphysically, economic, historical, geographic, cultural, psychic, and other determinisms have been formulated, which deprive us of agency but make the determinations of our destinies, at least partly, and quite significantly, external to ourselves. This kind of determinism, then, is compatible with *our* providing no significant enduring common content, that is, having no group essence.

Biological (hard) determinism would, it is true, imply that we turn out as we do, and have histories within a range of restricted possibilities, because of factors more narrowly confined to the human being as such. Some ideological stances on human nature seem then to qualify as essentialist.[2] But the quarrel that at least present-day anti-essentialists have with biology is not a quarrel with determinism, biological or otherwise. (Many anti-essentialists seem to regard the conditions of dominant culture as virtually controlling and dictating destiny.) The quarrel is with a nature that is internal to us, prior to culture, enduring, and that trumps the possible operations of culture or politics.

Some versions of essentialism would, it seems clear, permit or imply genuine free agency—further indicating the distance between essentialism and determinism. Liberalism, for example, which Alison Jaggar castigates as essentialist, is certainly a theory that regards people as capable of free choices.

For these reasons the character of contemporary thinking on these themes bears only a relationship of cousinhood to earlier Sartrean (and anti-Sartrean) dialectic formally on the same topic. Jean-Paul Sartre (1905–1980) developed, and became famous for, conceptions according to which a human is the being that creates, through choices and acts, a nature for himself and herself. Thus the formulaic idea was put together that in humans existence precedes essence—the defining idea of existentialism. Actually, some additional ideas are involved in the historical existentialist position, whether in Sartrean or non-Sartrean form, notably ideas about the solitude of each human individual and the absence of values without

---

[2] This is part of the thesis of R. C. Lewontin, Steven Rose, and Leon J. Kamin, *Not in Our Genes* (1984). This book's chief aim is to combat biological determinism.

acts and choices that (allegedly) create values. Further, this so-called defining formula expresses views that antedate Sartre. They appear in Heidegger, and before him in Hegel. They in fact express a kind of dualism, although other parts of Sartrean philosophy are supposed to repudiate this. Thus, the free self, without content or nature until choices, some of them value-creating choices, are made, is conceived here as antithesis to determined, non-active, natural material bodies. Problematic for this conception are non-human animals, especially so-called higher ones. Do dolphins and dogs partly, at least, create their own natures through their actions? If not at all, there would seem to need to be a component in us that is wholly lacking in the beasts, something (perhaps) ethereal or spiritual.

Current discussion of essentialism and anti-essentialism may be said to have two primary roots. One is a cluster of stances and perspectives chiefly found in strands of American sociology and anthropology, and cultural currents they have influenced (or, to some degree, reflected).[3] According to this way of thinking, we do not need to assume an immaterial, nature-transcending component in us in order to account for our escaping essentiality. Rather, life within culture (or "society") achieves this condition. Culture, whether material, ideal, or both (more on these themes presently), creates and fashions us. Even if this creative activity operates upon a biological content, the latter is something like Aristotelian matter: it cannot exist except as formed in some manner or other, and all possible forms for human matter are inherently and almost indefinitely variable socio-cultural ones. We are then like varieties of onions, with layers of cultural accretions the removal of which, were it even possible, would not reveal an inner core, still less one we all shared. Culture in this sense, and with this formative role, might or might not accord us meaningful degrees of free agency. Some versions of social constructionism—for that is what this theory is—will see us (or some of us) as meaningfully free, and others will see all that we are as formed in direction-determining ways that make free agency an illusion.

Again, the higher mammals seem to pose at least ground for pause. If dolphins, chimpanzees, and dogs do have an essence, and humans do not because they have culture, it is difficult to see how

---

[3] Probably the single most important and original of the thinkers whose ideas shaped this background was George Herbert Mead (1863–1931); but several other thinkers are also important or representative. These ideas, cousins of pragmatism, seem in some ways specially to fit features of American historical and cultural experience.

culture would achieve this nature-transcending alchemy, or even to understand what it could mean to assign culture this power. On the other hand, if the other higher mammals are deemed also to lack essences—because they have crude "proto-cultures," or for some other reason—it becomes difficult to see how this can be a very interesting fact about them or us.

Part of the appeal of social constructionist views seems to lie in their spirit of tolerance about cultures other than the dominant western (or still more specifically, American) one, coupled perhaps with guilt over real or imagined sins of that western (or American) culture. In geopolitical terms, this may be said to have originated in a self-dethroning of a disenchanted sector of an otherwise hegemonic imperial culture; or, one might prefer to say, a de-centering. The fruit of these currents has been varieties and degrees of cultural relativism, perspectival pluralism (both normative and descriptive), and social constructionism. Collectively these views may be said to constitute much or most of what is called postmodernism. Some of these ideas will be elaborated below.

The second root of current anti-essentialism is feminism, just as a predominant form it continues to take is feminist, as already noted. Feminist analyses became quickly sensitive to and (justifiably) rejecting of views, some purporting to be scientifically well-grounded ones, consigning, relegating, excluding, or marginalizing women in (or from) particular roles or favoured (or disfavoured) social or personal locations, on the basis of alleged male and female natures. Women, such views held, couldn't do *that*—because it was against nature, or their nature—and they had better do *that*—because nature or their nature required it of them: they couldn't be fulfilled or happy unless they did. (See, for example, Rosemarie Tong, *Feminist Thought,* p. 135.) Once these boundaries were contested, then rejected, the dialectically natural movement was towards more broadly social constructionist views, as with those rooted in social science.

In fact, though, there is good reason to believe the essentialist/ anti-essentialist issue a red herring, or at any rate not the central or pivotal matter so many take it to be. No one supposes there aren't at least *some* constraints that nature imposes on us. For example, even if our genes don't determine everything about us, it seems clear that they have *some* bearing on our destinies. And virtually everyone thinks there is at least some measure of plasticity in our possibilities. A continuum between positions of maximal and minimal human elasticity is the real character of the situation human nature theory confronts, not an either-or polarity between advocacy of frozen or lodged natures (for all or special subgroupings of humanity) and utterly blank-slate conceptions. To be sure, some human nature theories think our destinies are fairly sewn up, and others see almost boundless open-endedness, if the right (or wrong) circumstances are in place. But everyone will agree that there is such a thing as what human beings for the most part currently seem to be like, and that there is no reason to believe either that much earlier humans were exactly like that or that humans of remote futures will be. And some have more and some less interest in modalities of transformation, whether engineered through political action, through hastened attempts at "natural" selection, or through scientific technology; and whether of hopeful or nightmare motivation (ideas of genetic engineering, for example). It is not obvious that someone—even when the someone is a theorist—who doesn't care or profess to know very much about what humans might be like in a dramatically reordered world is an "essentialist," or that someone whose eyes and analyses are focused away from the human Here and Now is thereby automatically an "anti-essentialist."

Many, possibly most, human nature theorists see their views as empirical: factual, contingent accounts of how human beings are found (now) to be, in biological, cultural, psychological, or historical circumstances that prevail with, undoubtedly, a certain stability or anchorage. So understood, it is not clear that such theories are committed to believing that human nature, however they conceive it, is unalterable. Humanity (they say) is found to be thus and so—at a deep and stable level, to be sure, and the theory doesn't actively or explicitly envisage it as changing. But the theory may be silent, and in fact genuinely agnostic, about what degree of plasticity humanity may have, about what, we might say, humanity's modal options are. Evolution (cultural as well as biological) may well—some theories would say certainly will—take us in new, quite different directions as the future unfolds; and for some of these theories a considerable role might be played in such developments by our own active self-altering agency. In sum, it is not clear that many theories that anti-essentialists might want to describe as essentialist merit that (pejorative, and usually dismissive) label. Some biological, more specifically sociobiological, theories may. But feminist and postmodernist anti-essentialist views by no means limit their opposition just to these. Nonetheless, human nature theory *can* undertake to tell us merely how we *are,* and not necessarily how we *must* be. (And most anti-essentialist theories will also have a good deal to say, and most emphatically will want to speak, about how we are.)

The essentialist/anti-essentialist polarity becomes, too often, a matter of rhetoric and polemic. "Essentialist" is for many a piece of accusatory invective, not a serious characterization of a position. As such it tends to be double-edged, as erstwhile allies start to suspect one's own view of harbouring essentialist tendencies, if not in the out and out grip of this sin. The stance of being less essentialist than thou is not a helpful one, if one wants genuinely to try to understand humankind (either as a whole or in part).

A particular variety of anti-essentialist thinking that has been prominent in discussions of cultural life in recent years, and that some would regard as in itself a significant stance on human nature and theorizing about it, is what is called postmodernism. I shall make just a few remarks about this view.

Although it may sound banal or a merely academic philosopher's thing to say, postmodernism as a movement or current of cultural perspective mostly seems like a bunch of reasonable ideas pushed to unreasonable extremes. Many things are plausible to believe: that we ought to be tolerant of other views; that distinct communities (including communities of gender, class, ethnicity, age group, religion, sexual orientation, and others) have different kinds of experiences, in some cases extremely difficult or impossible to share; that power is inequitably apportioned in most societies; that cultural and other priorities often—too often—reflect differential degrees of social or other power; that a modern pluralistic society is in many ways a "Babel" of differing and sometimes incompatible or mutually contesting points of view and value systems; that all ideas come from somewhere, have a setting or context that ought to be made an explicit part of advancing, opposing, or trying to understand the idea; that the ways we see things are to some degree functions of our cultural locations; that much supposedly objective and value-free discussion or theory is highly normative or value laden; or that the ideas and writings of a rather small number of dead white European males have had a cultural centrality and authority that may have crowded out significant alternatives. However, contrary to what sometimes seems implicit in recent discourse, every one of these is an old idea, identifiable in writings spanning different times and places of the last century and more. Quite a lot of postmodernism is indeed old wine in new bottles, which might be alright if the wine were quite good. Unfortunately, most postmodernisms take these reasonable views and affirm unpersuasive extensions of them (among these, claims that adverse assessments of other cultures' practices are always unjustifiable, and that all theory about anything is normative). Moreover, these extensions of reasonable views are very rarely argued for or defended. They are offered as a perspective to adopt, rather like hors d'oeuvres from a tray, their chief allure apparently a certain contemporaneity and perhaps also their affording a reserve stance following the death of Marxist faith.

It will be quite reasonably felt that claims as general and sweeping as the preceding need lengthier discussion and defence, and that in any case some of the actual content of postmodernist thought should be set out for the reader's own evaluation. A movement as widespread and influential, and current, should, it may be held, engage some part at least of our attention. Foucault, Derrida, and other postmodernist thinkers are significant voices in contemporary cultural life, and one might argue that they deserve a place in the survey undertaken here. My response is that postmodernism is diverse and somewhat amorphous; that the theses listed above are all implied by postmodernist stances, but in virtually all cases stronger versions of them are affirmed (with relevant quantifiers typically going from "some" or "many" to "most" or "all"); and that the very currency of postmodernism, its being "of the hour," may justify waiting to see if it endures for a more extended period (the term, coined, it seems, in 1959, only became a constituent of cultural discourse in the late 1970s) before according it a place among older views; and finally, that while postmodernism is an anti-essentialist position with respect to human nature views, it appears to offer little more than that as an image of humanity.

I have argued that the essentialism/anti-essentialism issue is mostly unreal, a red herring. What is not a red herring, an artificial or merely semantical issue, is whether a broadly *materialist* conception, or a broadly *idealist* conception, is more deeply accurate about human beings. Many contemporary thinkers view positions on human nature, including those we will be investigating, in these terms.

Although this issue is a real one, it is enormously difficult to characterize (cultural or historical) materialism and idealism in accurate and plausible, or in clear and explicit, ways. These terms are borrowed from metaphysics, and they already lose some of their original meanings with the loan. In metaphysics materialism is the thesis that everything real is material or physical in nature (where "material/physical" is understood in terms of the kinds of substances, states, and processes to be met with in the "hard" physical sciences, i.e., such things as sound waves and gravitation as well as resistant corporeal objects). Some contemporary metaphysical materialists believe that mental states or phenomena are actually physical (brain) states or phenomena. Such a materialist as this could well turn out, surprisingly, to be an *idealist* in the historical/cultural sense (if they thought certain mind/brain states were significantly causal). Further complicating things is the fact that historical/cultural materialists don't usually dispute that mental and cultural phenomena are *real*. Typically, they hold that mental and cultural phenomena, though real and non-physical in nature, don't have any causal power: they don't explain what happens in the human world. These phenomena have, according to historical/cultural materialists, material causes and generally no significant effects. They are mere epiphenomena. Indeed, the position called epiphenomenalism (the dualist view that the mental is a spin-off, a causally inefficacious by-product of ongoing material processes) is arguably closer to the metaphysical position implicit in historical/cultural materialist stances than is a strict or proper materialism.

Similarly, metaphysical idealism—the view that everything real is a mind, mental state, or dependent object of one—does not accurately convey or suggest what historical/cultural idealists think. Actually, historical/cultural idealists would have been better called dualists, since hardly one of them would deny that material phenomena, including brute extra-human facts or developments of nature, quite often have major effects on human life and on human nature. But they also, and chiefly, hold that cultural, mental, and spiritual realities—"meanings"—also have major effect on what we do and are; for example, that codes of values, religious ideologies, or developments in art, may be necessary parts of the explanations of much human behaviour.

We might say, summing things up, that the so-called materialists (cultural/historical materialists) and the so-called idealists (also of cultural/historical stripe) are really both of them operational or methodological dualists. That is, they may be metaphysical dualists or they may have no opinion about such arcana; but in either event they both differentiate between two classes of phenomena in the human world, and they disagree as to the causal or explanatory importance of one of those classes, the one that is a matter of "meanings." The materialists think meanings don't matter, or don't matter very much, and the idealists think meanings matter quite a lot, that they have often been crucial in what we do and what we are.

Now, the foregoing has been rather vague. The position I want to advocate is that the materialist/idealist split is a genuine one, that is, that there is a significant difference of view involved in this contrast; that it is possible to spell out that difference, but difficult to do so with precision and accuracy. It is sufficiently difficult and complex, in fact, that I will not aim here to fully articulate the contrast. The task is difficult partly because there seems to be no way to describe or explain human beings with any completeness or plausibility that doesn't take account of the fact that we *interpret* and *represent* (or at least do things that we have a long record of describing in that way). Even if humans are driven to maximize their own genetic success, or to assuage hungers or metabolic imbalances, they still must, it seems, *recognize* situations as ones conducive to doing so. If we are utterly selfish, or self-interested, or are pawns of class interest, we still must, it appears, recognize, interpret, and represent—we must, in sum, behave *symbolically*. And if this is so, it already appears to establish a secure beach head for what seems to be the core idealist idea: that we operate in accordance with meanings, with what we take to be happening and what significance we attach to it.

On the other hand this seems too easy, a victory that appears to both miss the materialist point and fail to register what idealists really have in mind. But how to characterize the issue, if everyone will agree that we do behave symbolically or representationally? At first it might seem that the issue is one of contrasting views of our autonomy or powers of agency. But this isn't right either. Some materialist views insist that we have genuine freedom of action, that the material conditions of life that constitute us and fashion our directedness also include prospects for self-direction and self-creation. And some idealist views hold that much or most of our vaunted free agency is illusion, that the symbols under whose aegis and prompting we act are coercive for us, that we are helpless puppets on a stage of preconstituted meanings our lives will "mindlessly" enact and re-enact.

Perhaps the best brief characterization of the materialist/idealist contrast that goes at least a little beyond the account given so far says that according to idealists, significant amounts of human behaviour cannot be explained or understood without reference to values, ideals, or identifications felt subjectively to have emotional or valuational importance. Materialism will deny this claim and try to show that effectively all human behaviour can be accounted for in terms of non-valuational physical states of human individuals and groups. And with this still quite skeletal understanding, we may proceed to make acquaintance with eleven interesting models of our nature.[4]

---

[4] Some further exploration of materialism and idealism will be found in Chapters 8 and 13, on Marx and Harris respectively.

Bibliography

Harris, Marvin. *Cultural Materialism*. New York: Vintage Books, 1979.

—————. *The Rise of Anthropological Theory*. New York: Harper Collins, 1968.

Jaggar, Alison M. *Feminist Politics and Human Nature*. Totowa, NJ: Rowman & Allenheld, 1983.

Lewontin, R. C., Steven Rose, & Leon J. Kamin. *Not in Our Genes*. New York: Random House, 1984.

Sartre, Jean-Paul. *Being and Nothingness*. New York: Washington Square Press, 1966.

Tong, Rosemarie. *Feminist Thought*. Boulder, CO: Westview, 1989.

CHAPTER 3

Aristotle ————————

OF ALL THE THEORISTS OF HUMAN NATURE who predate the modern period (which we may date from about 1690), only one arguably has the stature of a living mind rather than a mere influence, however significant. That is Aristotle (384–322 BC). However great the debt we owe to the creative genius of Plato, the ancient Stoics, Machiavelli, Hobbes, and others, there are no Platonists, Stoics, Machiavellians, or Hobbesians today. But there are Aristotelians. There will be qualifications made, provisos, deference paid to the weight of the passage of 2,300 years. But these reservations registered, a number of contemporary thinkers would see themselves as having a view of the human world that is in its core features Aristotle's. And many more, while refusing the label, would accord an Aristotelian perspective on human nature a profound respect and contemporary relevance.

An important part of Aristotle's surviving stature—but definitely not the whole of it—stems from his significance, historical and authoritative, for the Roman Catholic branch of Christianity. Aristotle was "the Philosopher" to St. Thomas Aquinas, and St. Thomas is "the Philosopher" to Catholicism, so by a sort of transitivity of authority Aristotle's thought is canonical for Catholics, and much studied by students and practitioners of Catholic philosophy. If I may put this a little tendentiously, Catholic thinkers need to try to find relevance and plausibility in Aristotle, so they do try, and because there is so much in Aristotle that is relevant and plausible for human life in any time, and certainly still very much in our time, they succeed in rediscovering and extending Aristotle's ideas as active realities. Whether this degree of effort would be made but for the intellectual traditions of the church is of course doubtful. But no matter: Aristotle was a genius, of quite extraordinary creative and enduring range. Why someone dips into the well of that source matters less than that they do, and what they are able to find there when they do.

Aristotle lives also in contemporary social, ethical, and political theory, owing to considerations independent of Catholic intellectual life. Dissatisfaction with different features of modern ethical and political theory has led many philosophers back to Aristotle. Among these discontented are thinkers whose partly or wholly abandoned prior allegiances were liberal, Marxist, and feminist.

The brief and selective account of Aristotle's theory of human nature offered here seeks chiefly to convey a general conception, from a certain distance, and with an eye half open to other theories of the last few centuries. This may be misleading or inappropriate in some respects. It certainly does take Aristotle out of his time, and is therefore in an etymological sense, at least, anachronistic. Aristotle operated with considerably different assumptions, and in an altogether different world of thought, than thinkers of the eighteenth, nineteenth, and twentieth centuries. Aristotle also developed detailed, sophisticated, and interesting analyses of the emotions, the will, memory, and other aspects of cognitive and affective psychic life that will mostly be ignored in the present discussion.[1] He had a notion of rational agency—of judgment and deliberation expressed as a pattern of reasoning, the "conclusion" of which is not a statement but, interestingly, an action—that remains unique and arresting. Part of its appeal resides in a merger of thought and action, the mental and the physical, logic and bodily movement, that exhibits just the sort of unitary, non-dualistic notion of the whole, non-bifurcated person that so many twentieth-century theories avow but generally fail to provide content to.

The present account focuses primarily on Aristotle's understanding of the human being as a social and public creature, one among the many species of the animal kingdom, and interesting and distinctive as biological, political, and interpersonal entity. There is so much in the Aristotelian account just in these regions that Aristotle's investigations of the inner workings of mind may reasonably be omitted from an account that is in any case necessarily both general and brief.

What is Aristotle's view of human nature, that it would have the power and revivifying content claimed above? First of all, for Aristotle we are—as much as we are anything else that we are—animals, a component part of a natural order of living beings. Hence we are bodily beings, unitary living things even if we exhibit complexities of structure and aspect. Understanding us requires placing us within the wider web of living creatures and identifying our commonalities with, as well as our differences from, the other animals. Further, that

[1] Aristotle's classic short treatise *De Anima* (*On the Soul*) is the first and remains still an impressive investigation of these and other topics in rational and perceptual psychology.

understanding needs to be species-specific. We have species-being: we are human beings, a certain sort of thing that is constituted in the world with a discernible nature.

Scientific rationality—which for Aristotle includes common sense or "manifest" rationality—can analyze and explain a great deal of what it is that we do and are. There will, however, be a considerable residue that will have a certain accidentality, for which no deeper understanding will be obtainable. We will find that we are thus and so—the rational animal, the animal that can reflect, and act with conscious deliberation. That nature should contain such animals as these is not to be explored or explained, nor are other, quite contingent features of ours, such as our sociability or our capacities for friendship and for government. Zebras, or bald eagles, or timber rattlesnakes will equally well have discoverable natures, and accompanying contingencies.

A quite fundamental part of Aristotle's view of every species of living thing (indeed, of every existing object) attaches, accordingly, to human beings. This is the idea that a kind of (living) substance has a purpose or goal or function—in Greek, its *telos*. This is a problematic notion for the modern mind. We readily think of *artifacts*—things made on purpose for some aim intelligent creators had—as having a *telos,* and also of the bodily organs or other constituent subsystems of living things as having a purpose or function. It is harder to accord a clear sense to the idea of the living plant or animal itself having one. Moreover, the empiricist naturalism so distinctive of the modern outlook (though originally formulated by the ancient atomists) seeks to uproot and eliminate teleology even in biology.

Still, Aristotle's idea is of an objective condition of *well-being,* or *thriving,* for each living thing. Since the individual living things are found in kinds, or species, of shared nature, this will point to a common ideal condition of flourishing, of what it is to be a healthy well-functioning living being of *that* sort. This way of thinking of living creatures seems inescapably normative. Aristotle, however, seems not to have thought of it in this way. For him this is what natural science—biology—aims to disclose, as facts about creatures that do not depend on an observer's (or designer's) perspective or purposes. This animal, or plant, is *doing well,* living in a way that is in accord with its nature and conduces to what for it is vigour and vitality, over what for it is a natural span of life, with that profile of development, plateau, and decline natural to it; or else the animal or plant is not doing so. A thing's *telos* is what makes for such thriving, what fulfils and realizes its nature as what that thing is.

Specifically for humans the *telos* is, according to Aristotle, an active life of reason. In this lies fulfilment and happiness for us. The several subordinate conditions, or instrumentalities, of living an active reasoning life are the *aretai,*[2] or "excellences." A life of virtue, in this sense, is not a life of pious conformity to some moral code. It is a life engaged in skilled and satisfying deployment of the right measure of the attitudes and activities that go with being a human being, a natural living creature of *our* sort. (There would be analogous "virtues" for giraffes, squirrels, and orchids.)

There are then for Aristotle states and activities natural for us. They are not quite universal because circumstances unconducive to human flourishing sometimes obtain, and produce humans or human behaviour that is "unnatural"—antithetical to the flourishing of a human being. (This part of Aristotle's legacy has perhaps more appeal now to Catholic than to non-Catholic admirers.)

> There are three things which make men good and excellent; these are nature, habit, reason. In the first place, every one must be born a man and not some other animal; so, too, he must have a certain character, both of body and soul. But some qualities there is no use in having at birth, for they are altered by habit, and there are some gifts which by nature are made to be turned by habit to good or bad. Animals lead for the most part a life of nature, although in lesser particulars some are influenced by habit as well. Man has reason, in addition, and man only. For this reason nature, habit, reason must be in harmony with one another; for they do not always agree; men do many things against habit and nature, if reason persuades them that they ought ... we learn some things by habit and some by instruction. (*Politics* VII.13)

> Some things are naturally pleasant, and of these some are pleasant absolutely and others pleasant only to certain kinds of men and animals. But there are other things that are not naturally pleasant but become so, either through injury or through habit or through congenital depravity. Now corresponding to each of these types of unnatural pleasures we can observe abnormal states of character. I mean those that we call brutish, such as the female human who, they say, cuts open pregnant women and devours their babies, or certain savage tribes round the Black Sea, some of whom are said to have a taste for raw meat and others for human flesh, while others take turns in supplying children for the tribal

---

[2] *Aretai* (singular *arete*) is sometimes (misleadingly) translated as "virtues."

feast ... These states are brutish, but others result from disease (and in some cases from madness ...); and there are other morbid states that are the result of habit, like pulling out hairs and nail-biting, or eating coal and earth, and male homosexuality; because although these come naturally to some people, others acquire them from habit, e.g., those who have been victimized since childhood. (*Nicomachean Ethics* VII.5)

Among the features of natural human life are family and social life:

In the first place there must be a union of those who cannot exist without each other; namely, of male and female, that the race may continue (and this is a union which is formed, not of choice, but because, in common with other animals and with plants, mankind have a natural desire to leave behind them an image of themselves) ... (*Politics* I.2)

The family is the association established by nature for the supply of men's everyday wants ... (*Politics* I.2)

It is evident that the state is a creation of nature, and that man is by nature a political animal. (*Politics* I.2)

A social instinct is implanted in all men by nature. (*Politics* I.2)

Calling the family and the community institutions may obscure their biological significance for the Aristotelian view—the fundamental or essential role these structures have in what it is to be a human. We cannot make sense of ourselves, in respect of our origins or of developed civilized life, without reference to our position within these structures.

So, for the Aristotelian social contract theories,[3] whether intended to account for the origins of societies or the state or to provide a reconstructive rationale for ethical life or ethical rationality, are mistaken in principle. We only discern ourselves as creatures who

---

[3] Social contract theories appear in Plato and Lucretius, and in the work of a number of thinkers ever since. (The best known are Hobbes, Locke, Rousseau, and Rawls, the last three of whom will be encountered in subsequent chapters.) These theories hold that societies developed, or are usefully viewed as having developed, from rational agreements among people who had been living in a pre-social condition often called a "state of nature."

have had protracted childhoods in the care of guiding adults who are themselves within the framework of a social order or structure, and that social order itself involving, normally, other people who are relatives. We become, finally, the animal who lives in the *polis,* or (city-)state. The state grows out of the tribe, and it from the clan, and the latter from the family.

Later theories were to make more of the idea of a Folk, or national people, than Aristotle does. Here as in so much else, he aims at and often achieves a middle ground, a navigation between Scylla and Charybdis. My society will be (usually) me and my relatives and others, doubtless more remote relatives though untraceably, but also resident aliens, sojourners, and others who have come into this shared polity. And societies come and go. They have no claim upon history, or the world, by virtue of their particularity. What does have claim, and purchase, is human species-life, and its highest, finest flower, reflection and inquiry—wanting to know and to understand, and meeting with some measure of success in that desire.

It is easy to caricature or misstate much in Aristotle, and there is a necessary place for critical assessment of his ideas and their limitations. Before that is undertaken, it is important more fully to convey what is, I think, not just Aristotle in "best dress," but a rendering of a central core of his ideas on human nature in ways that may help explain their continued appeal.

Man, Aristotle says, is the rational animal.[4] This is easily misconstrued as androcentrist and absurdly intellectualist. It gets

---

[4] Aristotle's word for us is, in Greek, *anthropos.* Greek has distinct words—*anthropos,* and *aner,* respectively—for human being and adult male human being. The same is true in Latin (where *homo* and *vir* are the corresponding words). It also was originally the same in English. In old English, "man" meant "human being" (the same as *anthropos* in Greek and *homo* in Latin) and *wer* (cognate with Latin *vir*) was the word for an adult male human. In English *wer* dropped out, and "man" came to be used for both ideas. In recent years many have questioned whether "man" ought to continue to be used as a term for humans in general. That is, many now confine its reference to adult male humans. This isn't exactly a matter of aiming for what is called *inclusive* language, since "man" in one of its meanings (and that the original one) already *is* inclusive. But something along these lines is clearly the concern; it is perhaps as though males somehow get counted twice if "man" gets used with both meanings. Still, the issue is complex as well as problematic, particularly for human nature theory, where so many writers use "man" in the disputed generic sense.

worse when we learn that he thinks only middle-aged gentlemen of leisure, thinking and talking about philosophy with their male friends in a small city, can or do achieve what most and best suits our species. There are indisputably gender-related difficulties in Aristotle—both biases and unthinking assumptions the philosopher displays. And his paean to the small urban community sits oddly, at least, alongside the reality he was himself part of, of large Greek or Macedonian kingdoms grown, under his pupil Alexander the Great, to a huge, pluralistic, imperial social order. There seems in any case something incomplete, something important missing, in neglecting what it is to contend with life lived among large numbers of people, and life involving regular encounter with strangers. It is difficult to escape the feeling that no theory of human beings can possibly be adequate that does not address what it is to live in a large city.

Still, let us seek to understand what Aristotle's fundamental idea is here, and distinguish that idea from what he took to be its paradigm exemplification. A life ruled and dictated by unchosen toil and drudgery cannot permit the flowering of human possibility, cannot be a condition in which a human can thrive or be happy. Aristotle knows nothing of the labour-saving technology that has transformed the quality of modern life. For him there is no possibility of civilization without the consignment of the many to conditions that amount to servile labour. This is so bald and patent a fact that it would be disingenuous and artificial even to lament it. For Aristotle, then, human flourishing can only be for some, given the logistics of social and economic organization.

Why *these* rather than others? Why are the small group of individuals (made up, Aristotle supposes, of middle-aged, reasonably prosperous Greek males like himself) to be the favoured ones? In Aristotle's view this is another of the bald contingencies. Part of happiness, for him, is happening to be at least reasonably good-looking, to have good health, to have children who survive to adulthood and don't shame or disgrace you. While you may be able to affect these outcomes, you cannot wholly control them. Part, at least, of your good fortune is precisely that—good fortune, luck, the accidental favour of circumstance. It could have been another than you in a position to realize human good; and if you have not been so favoured, you could have been that other.

Now, Aristotle had rather dim views of the capacities of women. He also had beliefs, some quite negative, about other categories of people, including particular nations, tribes, and peoples, and thought that various individuals had natural dispositions to be slaves. All of these, we may say, constitute an assemblage of attitudes, convictions, and prejudices not unlike those that a great many—perhaps even most—people have had over the course of human experience. Some of these views will have some foundation in the individual's observations, others will rest on authority, most are uncritical, many indeed deeply irrational. At any rate we can quite appropriately separate these views of Aristotle's from his ideas about what it is to be human as such, and his notions of human excellence.

> To say that happiness is the chief good seems a platitude, and a clearer account of what it is is still desired. This might perhaps be given, if we could first ascertain the function of man ... What then can this be? Life seems to be common even to plants, but we are seeking what is peculiar to man. Let us exclude, therefore, the life of nutrition and growth. Next there would be a life of perception, but it also seems to be common even to the horse, the ox, and every animal. There remains, then, an active life of the element that has a rational principle ... human good turns out to be activity of soul in conformity with excellence, and if there are more than one excellence, in conformity with the best and most complete. (*Nicomachean Ethics* I.7)

The *reason* that is supposed to be our highest excellence, and in which human fulfilment and happiness are said to be found, is partly so highlighted by Aristotle on the essentially taxonomic grounds that there has got to be—for him—a uniquely and distinctively human trait that supplies the content of our aim and good. Thus, pleasure or sensation couldn't be our good partly because other animals also experience pleasure and sensation, and what is most satisfying for us must, he thinks, be something we alone have. This is not a very persuasive argument: we could obviously find our highest good and most fulfilling state or condition in something we happened to share with other animals.

However, there is more to Aristotle's case. (And let me stress that my aim at this stage is primarily to give Aristotle's views on human nature, not the arguments he had for them.) The central Greek philosophical tradition in place well before Aristotle identifies mind or reason as what is most valuable in us. Aristotle is in part just continuing to affirm this view, on similar but in some ways interestingly more concrete, bodily, social, earthbound grounds than his predecessors (chief among them Plato) offer.

Aristotle distinguishes practical rationality from theoretical rationality and accords high value to both, if greater to the second.

And he indicates that he thinks of practical reason as a matter of skills relevant to, and processes of mind that will issue in, action—both in actual, particular cases (what do I do *now*, faced with these alternatives and constraints?) and in more long-term and general respects (skills of craft and of public or political life, for example). The highest and the best of our activities of mind is indeed, for Aristotle, theoretical rationality, above all when it is *not* utilitarian (hence, for example, applied science—technology—would be relatively inferior). Disinterested curiosity, just wanting to know or to understand, is our very highest state; and *it* is in highest operation when its objects are general, or universal, rather than particular.

Of course this is philosophy, and Aristotle is a philosopher—this is what *he* likes to do, how *he* likes to pass the time—and some measure of vocational bias, and faulty induction, is operative here. But his case is at least somewhat better than just this. *Wanting to understand* just so I can know and fit together into a reasonably comprehensive picture what is going on, what it means, how I and others I care about fit into the scheme of things that has importance for me: in some version this surely is something more than professional philosophers would attach great value to. Aristotle, for that matter, did not conceptualize this as wanting to figure out "the meaning of life" or anything so "post-Christian" as this. The kind of rational understanding he had in mind was not vague, or other-worldly, or sentimental. For him there would have been a lot of physics and a lot of biology in the package. But there would also have been an attempt to understand the social world, the personal and interpersonal world of agency, and freedom, and possibility and its limits, for me and the individuals I care about, and my society.[5] This is all to say, I think, that at least constituent parts of Aristotle's notion of theoretical reason were concerned with what is also of central importance to many and perhaps most contemporary conceptions of human life and human value. To be sure, many such conceptions would value even self-knowledge as more an instrumental than an intrinsic good; but the fundamental good identified, our happiness, will be much the same.

---

[5] For Aristotle there is a considerable gap between these two varieties of rational understanding. They have different characteristics for him—the first admitting of a precision and certainty quite impossible for the second—and they differ markedly in value. The point, though, is that both forms of understanding are incorporated into Aristotle's conception of a fulfilling life for a human being.

Aristotle's focus on rationality, and what can seem a very cheerful picture of what human flourishing consists in and how to achieve and sustain it, does not imply a global optimism about human prospects. Aristotle is under no illusions that things always do go well. "Man, when perfected, is the best of animals, but, when separated from law and justice, he is the worst of all; since armed injustice is the more dangerous, and he is equipped at birth with arms, meant to be used by intelligence and excellence, which he may use for the worst ends. That is why, if he has not excellence, he is the most unholy and the most savage of animals, and the most full of lust and gluttony" (*Politics* I.2). Humans have potentialities for harmonious life. They can genuinely be happy, individually and in social conjunction. Here education, the cultivation of socially effective and individually satisfying dispositions—above all satisfying our urges to understanding and agency—is crucial. Humans with natural aptitudes for such effective humanity may be trained wrongly and go to bad, that is, become mere pleasure-seekers or destructively antisocial. And always there are factors beyond human control, matters of individual, biological, social, and historical chance.

Aristotle's account of human nature has many merits and also a number of limitations. Among the latter may be mentioned, above all, its confinement to what may be called the surface of life. Things are for Aristotle largely what they seem. There is little in what he has to say about people that constitutes or contributes to "depth psychology"—motivations or meanings that are unknown or dimly known to the individual or the community, oblique dimensions of mind and experience that are nonetheless important components of who we are. Plato offers a good deal more (if only in scattered fragments) on "subterranean" (or "subcutaneous") awareness of our makeup and its aetiology and prospects. Also, there is little in Aristotle's account that contributes to deep understanding on the social, historical, or systemic plane. He does not see, or think to look for, underlying patterns in synchronic or diachronic social life. (Hardly any of this kind of analysis appears before the eighteenth century, in fact.)

Aristotelians of the present day, it may be said, are primarily but not exclusively professional or academic philosophers. Some non-philosopher Aristotelians are Christians, Catholic and otherwise; others are persons with interests in the natural world of living species and systems. Modern Aristotelians have what I would describe as a compartmentalized view of the world. The different compartments are realms, domains, or worlds that are disconnected from each other if not actually (as with some philosophical Aristotelianisms) mutually incommensurable. These are, as with Aristotle, domains of living systems and non-living systems in the first instance; then within the domain of the living, disconnected circles or structures of animal or non-animal and human being (or person) or non-human being. This will do much to explain why, for example, among Catholics vegetarianism tends to be a non-starter as a moral issue, while issues involving interference in the creation of human life—abortion, artificial insemination, fetal tissue use, and others—are of the utmost significance morally. *Some* overlap among the fundamental categories is allowed. For example, a rock, a radio, a tulip, a mouse, and a human being might all be—and be said univocally to be—in the same room. Likewise, as one ascends the hierarchy there will be common features at each level not shared below that level.

Apart from the finicky niceties of academic philosophical divisions of conceptual pie, as a living outlook Aristotelianism involves seeing a world of human agency as self-contained—Wilfrid Sellars' "manifest image"—and subsisting accurately, successfully, (allegedly) more or less timelessly, and perfectly compatibly beside a highly arcane and technical realm of physical science—Sellars' "scientific image." Questions that might place the two in interlock, to the potential refutation or revision of one (or both), are refused coherence; or simply not asked. There is the way one talks and thinks in the laboratory, during white-coated weekdays, and there is how one talks, thinks, and behaves when with the spouse and kids or over the back fence with the neighbours. One is a fool, on this general view, to deny the validity of either of the modes, spheres, or realms; and one is quite as much if not more of a fool to attempt to bring them into any kind of conjunction. Doing so would only manifest ill manners or reveal oneself as inauthentic or immature.

Doubtless this puts the matter tendentiously, and with insufficient sympathy. The Aristotelian would defend what is complained of as compartmentalization on the ground that there is simply no science (or general theory of any impressive dimension) possible of the "manifest image" and that there is no point in pretending otherwise.

I will conclude this discussion of Aristotle's theory of human nature by noting that he gives central place to a phenomenon that, perhaps revealingly, very few theories about human beings do: friendship. Aristotle offers a lengthy analysis of friendship, believes it can be genuine, and that it is the highest and best expression of being human apart from rational theorizing. I will not provide Aristotle's analysis here: it is a deservedly lucid and interesting part[6] of the *Nicomachean Ethics,* to which the reader is referred. I note only that, like some other human phenomena, friendship affords a certain sort of touchstone for a human nature theory. This is because friendship at least purports to be—and certainly Aristotle sees it this way—a human condition, and relation, that is neither entirely self-interested nor in a clear way altruistic; personal and passional, and yet reflective, calm (Apollonian!), and often highly sophisticated. (There is a peculiarly *rational* element in friendship, for Aristotle. Pure, true friendship, for him, can only exist between fully realized human beings. If you and I are friends, then, our friendship is a matter of my *recognizing* the excellence that you are, and vice versa.) One ought to ask of every theory whether it can accommodate friendship, and what the place of friendship is in the structure and dynamics of the self and the collectivity of selves. For Aristotle it is our deepest, most genuine social pleasure.

[6] Books VII and VIII.

Bibliography

Ackrill, J. L. *Aristotle the Philosopher.* Oxford: Oxford University Press, 1981.

——————, ed. *A New Aristotle Reader.* Oxford: Clarendon Press, 1987.

Aristotle. *The Nicomachean Ethics* (*The Ethics of Aristotle*). Translated by J. A. K. Thomson & H. Tredennick. Hammondsworth: Penguin, 1976. (Valuable for its introduction, bibliography, and appendices)

——————. *Nicomachean Ethics.* Translated by Terence Irwin. Indianapolis: Hackett, 1985.

Barnes, Jonathan. *Aristotle.* Oxford: Oxford University Press, 1982.

——————, ed. *The Complete Works of Aristotle.* 2 vols. Princeton, NJ: Princeton University Press, 1984.

Clark, S. R. L. *Aristotle's Man.* Oxford: Oxford University Press, 1975.

Sellars, Wilfrid. "Philosophy and the Scientific Image of Man." In Wilfrid Sellars, *Science, Perception and Reality.* London: Routledge & Kegan Paul, 1963.

CHAPTER 4

Christian Philosophy
of Human Nature ————

THE THEORIES OF HUMAN NATURE CONSIDERED in this volume have largely been developed by one or more particular thinkers at reasonably precise historical times. The present chapter departs from this practice. Here I identify an understanding of human nature whose roots go back to antiquity and that existed long before the period when I take it up. The doctrine through a very much more extended period has been so influential that our account would be importantly incomplete were it omitted. Nonetheless, the modern form of the doctrine has distinctive features, and a continuing presence and plausibility, that I think earlier forms no longer have.

I speak of a Christian theory of human nature; and I use the indefinite article "a" because there have been a number of Christian views of humankind. These views have only sometimes had sufficient content to count as a theory of human nature, nor have they always been consistent with each other. And unlike most of our theories, which are generally secular, this-worldly conceptions, Christianity is of course a major world religion, its founder's kingdom said to be "not of this world." Credence in a wide set of extranatural and supernatural occurrences is a necessary condition of adherence to this religion. Still, the Christian theory of human nature I discuss here will be identifiable, I think, as a theory for as well as of this world.

I might have labelled the theory a Protestant Christian theory of human nature, since it has been developed almost entirely by Protestant Christians. This would be somewhat misleading, however. The term "Protestant" is far too broad to capture the nuanced and developed view envisaged. There have simply been too many kinds and sorts of Protestants. Further, in the contemporary world many adherents of Catholic and Orthodox varieties of Christianity would share some version of this theory. This may be because of an arguable "Protestantization" of their Christian faiths; I suspect that it is. Nonetheless, Catholic and Orthodox Christians who see humanity as this theory does do not thereby conceive themselves as Protestants. Rather, they think the theory they embrace is a Christian view. And so it is.

Among the thinkers in whose writings one may discern what I will accordingly be calling the modern Christian theory of human nature are John Locke (1632–1704), Joseph Butler (1692–1752), and Immanuel Kant (1724–1804). Indeed, these three Enlightenment philosophers are perhaps the outstanding exemplars of this conception. In the post-Enlightenment period Christians of the kind intended are legion. A leading twentieth-century thinker who provides a splendid example is Dietrich Bonhoeffer (1906–1945).

Christian theology is a complex and nuanced field, with a long, varied, theoretically rich history. It is reasonable to ask what sorts of doctrine, in what theological traditions, are intended as informing or accompanying what is called here modern Christianity. What is the theological character of modern Christianity?

This query cannot, I think, have a very straightforward or informative answer. Modern Christianity is, among other things, the Christianity of Christian workers in Amnesty International and other human rights and altruistic movements; likewise, that of Jesuit liberation theologians; and of a host of people of diverse occupations and educational levels, the majority undoubtedly leading quiet and unobtrusive lives, citizens, producer/consumers, spouses, parents, in contemporary societies. Modern Christians will embrace a spectrum of political views and commitments or none at all. The paradigm cases envisaged will not be advocates of demythologized or post-modern Christianity. They will typically believe, at minimum, in a literal divine intervention in human history in first-century Palestine, involving the death and redemptive resurrection of Christ. They may have a much more fully literal or traditional conception of New Testament history and of a basic Christian creed than just that.

I am identifying John Locke as a good, clear, early case of a modern Christian. What stands out theologically in Locke is his rejection of the doctrine of original sin, that is, of the (curiously Lamarckian)[1] theory that an acquired trait of a foundational human ancestor, Adam—namely, his having chosen morally objectionable actions—became thereafter a hereditarily transmitted condition of all human beings.[2] In his essay *On the Reasonableness of Christianity* (1695) Locke argues that a just God could not have afflicted such a punishing stain on Adam's innocent posterity.

Many modern Christians will share Locke's view. However, it is sometimes said that a belief in original sin is part of what defines

[1] See Chapter 9, note 4, for a brief explication of Lamarck's theory.

[2] This is not meant to imply that the *mechanism* of such transmission was supposed to be biological.

the conservative philosophy, and many modern Christians are conservatives. None of them, though, will attach literal significance to original sin. For one thing, they cannot as moderns do so, since as moderns they will accept the antiquity of the human lineage, and will not suppose evolutionary hominid biology has anything to say about a gene for sin acquired by the actions of an ancestor mere thousands of years ago and transmitted thereafter to all humans. For Christians of this stamp, some different, subtler account of an innate predisposition to behave badly will be held to be true of us. In any event, conceptions of humans as fundamentally either good or with a plasticity of nature permitting that possibility, or as fundamentally predisposed towards malfeasance (as well, possibly, as good conduct), mark a basic division between the branches of modern Christianity.

I mentioned that the Christian view referred to is a this-worldly one. Part of what is meant by this claim is that Christians of the variety discussed here do not actively expect miraculous or supernatural occurrences in the world they function in. The formal possibility is not, of course, excluded: Christians, including these ones, believe that supernatural events occurred in the eastern Mediterranean area in the first century AD. God is omnipresent and could choose an intervention, but this is not only not to be counted on; it is vaguely regarded as primitive or unsophisticated to have it in view or in mind. (On the other hand, *after the fact* an apparently quite improbably happy or beneficent event could be suspected or even believed to have involved a divine intervention.)

These Christians, then, are opposed to superstition, and accept the world's operations in much the same ways that naturalist thinkers do. But their view is not naturalist: they do think human beings are quite special in the order of things, or have a significance that contrasts with the rest of nature. As they see cosmic history, God chose to become a human being, and it is not absurd that he should have done so (whereas, in their view—and most people would agree—it would be absurd for God to have chosen to become a donkey, or an aardvark, or even a chimpanzee). The incarnation shows that there is something special about us, a spark of divinity, in spite of our warts and flaws. On this Christian view humans are genuinely metaphysically free, in ways no other creature even partly is. (This is squared with divine creation of the whole of the world and with divine foreknowledge differently by more metaphysically disposed Christians, or not at all by others.) Twentieth-century Christians of this type will usually accept human descent from non-human primates; but a veil—sometimes just of lack of interest—is drawn over the transitions to modern humans, or the earlier stages of proto-hominid evolution.

Humans (that is, biologically fully modern ones) participate in things that are divine, cosmic, universal. They are free. And they are moral agents, capable of choices and actions that will be good or bad. (And not good or bad simply as pleasing or displeasing to the creator. Our variety of Christians will not be divine command moral theorists.[3] The deity is held to the same high standards that we are.) And as moral agents humans have an equality of condition.

Many philosophical influences unite in the background of these and other Christian views. Of the ancient positions, there is something from each of Plato, Aristotle, and the Stoics. The last of these is probably the most important, with that school's conception of a universal human community.

This Christian view sees the terrestrial scene—the world in *that* sense—as on the whole good. Not all do: there are what we may call Tory Christians and also Whig ones.[4] The Tories—Samuel Johnson was one—see more of the bad than do the Whigs. They believe in some version of original sin (whatever historio-theological account they give of it, if any), and suppose that there is something intrinsic to humanity that is malevolent or malignant, disposed to cruelty, short-sighted self-interest, and destruction. Still, these dispositions can be overcome if the will to do so is there, and it can be there: the spark of rational free agency in all of us ensures that it can. For the Tory Christian all of us have a will to sin, and all of us can transcend it (possibly only with unending struggle), though far too many, possibly most, will not do so. Thus Tory Christians have dark, somewhat pessimistic views of the human world and its occupants (though a formal optimism is secured by convictions of divine long-term purposes).

The Whigs, by contrast, are optimists. They believe in fundamental human goodness, even if it is too often impaired by

---

[3] Divine command moral theories hold that good and evil (and all other ethical properties or states) derive the meaning and content they have from God's wishes or commands: whatever he enjoins is good, simply because he enjoined it. For such views, usually, it is wholly uninformative to assert that God is good.

[4] "Tory" was the colloquial designation in British political life for what became the Conservative Party, and is still used in the U.K. and Canada for its surviving Conservative Parties; "Whig" was, similarly, the colloquial term for the Liberal Party—though in this case the usage has not endured.

circumstance or choice or character. (All Christians believe deeply in the idea of character. The *term* has fallen into disfavour in our grimly egalitarian times, since persons of character will constitute a moral elite. But Christians remain quite numerous, and like others they still *think* what the current world makes it impolitic to *say*.)

Whig Christians are archetypally liberal Protestant progressives: members of Amnesty International, supporters of human rights and at least some environmentalist issues. But the eighteenth and nineteenth centuries had Whig Christians too: thinkers of benign outlook who saw this as a good world, requiring, but permitting, sustained creative human action to make it and keep it so; people who were doing God's work in combatting social and other ills (slavery, substance abuse, social inequalities, unjust war) or applauding and supporting others who were.

Christianity manifested in what we now call social activist form, independent of specific intentions to convert souls, seems to date from the later eighteenth century in Britain.[5] Then and ever since, a quite significant component in this impulse, very much greater than their numbers would suggest, has come from Quakerism. Thomas Paine, Mary Wollstonecraft, and many of the early British antislavery activists had Quaker backgrounds or connections. It would be difficult to exaggerate the importance of the role of the Society of Friends in the evolution of what I am calling Whig (Protestant) Christianity. At the same time, their relatively small numbers, and the austerity and simplicity of both their cultural style and their theology, distance them from the main bodies of Christianity and its successive building upon earlier forms and stages.

For most Christians of most stripes the world has opacities, is a mysterious and unfathomable place. (This is the Christian expression, many students of religion would say, of the desire for and valuing of *sacred mystery*. It is something Freud has much to say about.) This

---

[5] This is not meant to deny that there were significant Christian attempts to ameliorate social conditions from the earliest Christian period and continuously thereafter. It is to claim that earlier efforts of this kind were characteristically either acts of charity or were linked to endeavours to save souls or promote or strengthen Christianity. What is striking about the Christian social activism that begins in the eighteenth century and continues to the present day is that it typically has "no strings attached," and that it is aimed at social "revision" (changing laws or institutions).

above all is why philosophical worries about the problem of evil[6] so rarely affect those who are religious. The *point* is that we can't fully figure it out, see how it all fits and works and what our place in it is, or what our nature and its possibilities and destiny are. Protestant Christians in particular take the view that we can perfectly well try to reconcile Christian theology with the world's evil and make sense of the world with us in it, but, the Protestant is cheerfully confident, we will fail. The world's meaning, our place in it, and God's large (and small) purposes are hopelessly opaque to us—not entirely unknown or indiscernible, but oblique, always seen partially and usually through distorting glass. And for the Protestant Christian, this is part of the glory of it all, why he or she *likes* the view.

At the same time we know much of God's purposes, and of the world and our place in it. It is God's world, he made it, and some parts of that reality and his aims are conveyed to us. Their being so conveyed constitutes what is meant by God's word—chiefly the Bible, interpreted rather literally (a twentieth-century Christian of our type would have considerable difficulty in being a genuine biblical literalist) or quite selectively and figuratively. At any rate: "He hath shewed thee, O man, what is good; and what doth the Lord require of thee, but to do justly, and to love mercy, and to walk humbly with thy God?" (Mic. 6.8).

Well, maybe he requires a little more than that—some of the articles of the Nicene Creed,[7] for example, and certain notions of family life and social organization. For the Christian it matters that God set things up, or guided humans to set things up, in ways that suit our natures and the terrestrial environment, and provide prospects of coming to good and to God. There is accordingly an inherent conservatism in Christianity that eventually embraces even the most radical Whig versions. There are Communist Christians, but there are not and cannot be Jacobin[8] Christians: people wanting to set up a republic of citizens, and a new humanity fit for that republic,

---

[6] The problem of evil is the problem of whether, and if so how, the existence of a perfect God can be reconciled with the evil that exists in the world.

[7] The Nicene Creed is the statement of articles of Christian faith originally developed in the fourth century, subscribed to by Catholic and most Protestant churches.

[8] The Jacobins were the "radicals" of the French Revolution, their leader Robespierre.

without roots in prior history and acknowledging no horizons but logistical or humanly imposed ones, corporately bonded together into a state (after the model of Rousseau) or set at liberty to fashion themselves individually *de novo* (after that of Jefferson). We can move gradually, in loving, prayerful, tentative steps, away from biblical blueprints towards alternative God-guided self-creations—or not: some paths will be at odds with the fundamental covenant (itself, for these Christians, a rational covenant, founded for the realization of human good). This will be a matter partly of Whigs and Tories again. But for all Christians the sin of pride remains inescapably sin, one of the deepest and darkest because, apparently, it is one we are most disposed to; indeed, it almost defines us and is especially hard to eradicate from our hearts, though a particularly destructive part of our make-up. Jacobinism (including liberal and socialist forms of it), in analysis and values, is the attempt to construct the Tower of Babel anew.

The intellectual roots of the modern Christian philosophy of humankind lie primarily in the foundational ideas of Protestantism, which is to say, essentially the ideas of Martin Luther. The independent Protestant philosophy of John Calvin, while not without surviving cultural residue, is no longer a living vision of the world. Calvinist national churches continue, but the once powerful and distinctive Calvinist outlook appears gone from active contemporary culture. It seems to have died an early-twentieth-century death, perhaps a fatality of the First World War.

Were this an essay in the history of ideas, rather than an attempt to delineate conceptions of human nature that have significant purchase for numbers of thoughtful people in our culture, Calvin and Calvinism would have a larger place in the account of modern Christianity in general and Locke in particular than these dismissive comments accord. A well-known theory of Max Weber's[9] (explored in detail by other social and economic historians) seeks to account for the rise of capitalism in western Europe by reference to a Calvinist social ethic, stressing frugality, temperance, hard work, and individual initiative. This thesis, in some form, seems persuasive (though if true, it refutes historical materialism—no inconsequential matter). There is a "Protestant ethic," and it surely has played a formative role in the development of capitalism in the Protestant western world; and that ethic descends lineally from ideas and practices instituted by John Calvin in the sixteenth century, and *not*, particularly, from

[9] See M. Weber, *The Protestant Ethic and the Spirit of Capitalism* (1950).

anything Luther said or implemented. Diluted forms of Calvinism entered English cultural life in the seventeenth century (unalloyed forms had earlier come to state power in Scotland) and helped shape Locke's outlook. His clear emphasis on the virtues of the far-sightedly entrepreneurial, in the *Second Treatise,* seems definitely to have roots in this background. Moreover, what we will in a subsequent chapter call conservative individualism may plausibly be argued to be, in significant part, a secularized version of a still more severe Calvinism than Locke's.

The problem is, however, that neither Locke's nor the modern conservative individualist's "Calvinism" has the theological underpinnings of the once-powerful Calvinist thought-world. Real Calvinists think they should work long hours, save, and invest in order to glorify God and because these are necessary (though not sufficient) conditions of salvation. Neither Locke nor conservative individualists think this. Lockean values have an ancestry in a Calvinist social ethic, but their rationale and justification does not. On the other hand, Locke's conception of religious tolerance and of individual conscience and its rights and burdens is a version of Luther's.[10]

The core Lutheran idea is that of individual conscience, the self as a moral citadel and a moral tribunal, which must then also face higher tribunals, imaginatively in the ongoing present and actually on a future occasion of life-surveying judgement. These notions are in some form part of Christianity from the beginning, but in Luther they

---

[10] A powerfully "Lutheran" note will be found in the theories of conscience and moral obligation articulated by the Cambridge Platonist school from 1640 to 1670. These thinkers, especially Ralph Cudworth and Henry More, defended a strong free-will position against Calvinist predestinarian views. More's conception of conscience was so strong that he believed someone not sincerely convinced of the soundness of a decree was to be excused for not complying with it, even if it came from God: "For the *Sincere* ... if he be not yet convinced, ... he is, I think, justly excused from any obligation to those Laws, or any guilt of transgressing them, there having been no promulgation of them to him, though he has with all attentiveness and desirousness endeavoured to receive the voice of them into his conscience" (*The Apology of Dr. Henry More, Fellow of Christ's College in Cambridge,* p. 555f.). The Cambridge Platonists had a significant influence upon Locke. Although its full extent is unclear, much of his "modern Christianity" may be traced to the so-called latitudinarian Anglicanism of thinkers like More and Cudworth. (More anticipated Locke, for example, in strongly advocating tolerance of religious dissent and the legal establishment of liberty of conscience.)

achieve a new and vivid articulation that continues to the present day. More than that: Luther's idea of a personal, symbiotic relationship between the self and God, and its implication that, independent of any formal code or rule book, I will *know* what I have done, what it was, what it meant, and so too will God—seems to be a genuinely novel contribution to Christianity.[11] It is the inwardness that is novel, the idea of "the buck stopping here," with the self and its acts and their inner moral meaning known immediately by the self. This is precisely why Hegel saw Luther as a world-historical individual, an unusual case, since most of Hegel's explicitly identified world-historical individuals are military conquerors.

So the modern Christian philosophy of humankind primarily identifies human beings as moral agents (and non-humans as wholly non-moral agents, though perhaps the modern Christian is not altogether precluded from seeing some portion of virtue or vice in a dog or a cat). It also conceives human selves as existing and functioning within a morally coherent habitat—the terrestrial environment, designed by God to be a *home* for human beings as well as a complex of living and non-living systems in some degree of harmony, subject to human moral effectiveness in managing it.

The modern Christian view is *not* at odds with modernity, not at any rate where the view is thriving and healthy, as is still widely the case in the western world, more so than might be supposed (even if there are far fewer modern Christians than religious demographic data might suggest). Tory Christians will quite possibly, in most western societies, think of themselves as living in Babylon, part of a beleaguered minority in dark times growing darker; Whig Christians will be brighter-spirited about the present, with prospects for the future still the prospects of collective humanity (and not just those of Christians). In neither case is there any fundamental quarrel with science (though there might be with particular new theories, especially in the social sciences).

The modern Christian also has a deep belief in the soundness of basic social institutions and their fit with the natures God gave us. Marriage, the family, a community of households or family units: these are natural to humans, and meet elemental requirements of our being. They reflect the wisdom and the purposes of God, and what is nourishing for a human being. What of homosexuals? Tory Chris-

[11] There are anticipations of this idea in St. Augustine; the Lutheran imaginative note, though, seems importantly new.

tians will see them as uniformly either inauthentic, or else stunted, defective human beings prevented by their morally problematic choices, or by nature's occasionally cruel operations (as with the handicapped), from achieving full and mature self-realization. Whig Christians can take this view also, but they sometimes see (and endorse) possibilities of homosexual marriage—mature, committed, loving, spiritual pair-bonding between individuals of the same sex.

Although Luther appears to be the most important single intellectual source for the modern Christian view of the world, including its human components, Luther is not himself a modern Christian. He is too filled with what a modern, Christian and otherwise, would see as superstition: beliefs in actual physical encounters with Satan, for example. In any case, there cannot be a modern Christian until there is a modern world-outlook to which Christianity can reconcile and accommodate itself, and this is not to be found in the world (save for extraordinarily exceptional cases—Galileo may be the only one) before the 1680s or 1690s.

John Locke is in fact a good early example of the modern Christian. Of his Christian commitment there is no question. He is not merely a sincerely believing Anglican Christian; his Christianity colours and shapes his views of the earth, his fellow human beings, and their place on it. In his day, and occasionally since, Locke was by some held to be a Socinian. Socinianism was a small movement of Christian ideas and practice developed by two Italians, uncle and nephew, in the sixteenth century. Although soundly and generally condemned as heretical by both Catholics and Protestants, its distinctive views are, with one exception, very close to those here identified as modern Christianity. The Socinians denied the literal metaphysical reality of transubstantiation in the Eucharist (or Lord's Supper), taking this celebration as only commemorative of the life and work of Jesus. Their emphasis was on inward Christian affirmation, and a code of values and conduct this should produce. They denied a central life-transforming significance to Christian conversion; their orientation was rationalist, anti-enthusiast, ethical, self-directing. They denied the dogma of original sin. All of these are notes or themes that appear in modern Christians, including many twentieth-century Anglicans. The one definite divergence lies in Socinian rejection of the Trinity, and the godhead of Jesus. Like the fourth-century Arians, Socinians viewed Jesus as merely the best human being who ever lived and God's pre-eminent emissary on earth, but not God himself. In every respect save their anti-Trinitarianism, and their historical location in advance of a fully developed modern world-view, the Socinians would qualify as modern Christians, so the Socinian charge, if true, would only slightly diminish Locke's status as exemplar of the modern Christian view of the world. In fact Locke explicitly denied the charge, in detail and in print, and there seems no good reason to believe these denials insincere.

Many twentieth-century criticisms of Locke's social and political philosophy—whose most important expression is in *The Second Treatise of Government* (1690)—are, I think, unfair or superficial for failing to take due account of Locke's Christianity. His doctrine of property, for example, is clearly theologically informed. The earth and everything (and everyone) on it is in the first instance God's property. We are his stewards or trustees, our property held on a kind of leasehold for which we are accountable. It is a good world—for God made it—and we can see that terrestrial logistics *permit* it to be a well-functioning world, morally, socially, and economically. Shrewd and effective husbandry will allow it to be so, even if greed, short-sightedness, indolence, or other culpable human failings have often made it otherwise. The economic model of the first acts of appropriation, of "a man" (as it turns out, it might be a man's servants, or other members of his household—a wife, for example) mixing his labour with the earth seems derived from an imaginative conception of the Old Testament Patriarchs, and their households:

> Whether we consider natural reason, ... or revelation, ... it is very clear that God, as King David says (Ps. 115.16), "has given the earth to the children of men," given it to mankind in common ...
>
> God, who has given the world to men in common, has also given them reason to make use of it to the best advantage of life and convenience ...
>
> It will perhaps be objected ... that "if gathering the acorns, or other fruits of the earth, etc., makes a right to them, then any one may engross as much as he will." To which I answer: not so. The same law of nature that does by this means give us property does also bound that property, too. "God has given us all things richly" (1 Tim. 6.17), is the voice of reason confirmed by inspiration. But how far has he given it us? To enjoy. As much as any one can make use of to any advantage of life before it spoils, so much he may by his labor fix a property in; whatever is beyond this is more than his share and belongs to others. Nothing was made by God for man to spoil or destroy ...
>
> ... God, when he gave the world in common to all mankind, commanded man also to labor, and the penury of his condition required it of him. God and his reason commanded him to subdue the earth, i.e., improve it for the benefit of life, and therein lay

out something upon it that was his own, his labor. He that in obedience to this command of God subdued, tilled, and sowed any part of it, thereby annexed to it something that was his property, which another had no title to, nor could without injury take from him.

... in that part of the world which was first inhabited, and therefore like to be best peopled, even as low down as Abraham's time they wandered with their flocks and their herds, which was their substance, freely up and down; and this Abraham did in a country where he was a stranger. Whence it is plain that at least a great part of the land lay in common, that the inhabitants valued it not, nor claimed property in any more than they made use of. But when there was not room enough in the same place for their herds to feed together, they, by consent, as Abraham and Lot did (Gen. 13.5), separated and enlarged their pasture where it best liked them. And for the same reason Esau went from his father and his brother and planted in Mount Seir (Gen. 36.6).[12]

Locke's general outlook is secular and enthusiastically consonant with, in fact participant in, the new science; he styles himself, in the *Essay concerning Human Understanding* (1690), "an Under-Labourer in clearing Ground a little, and removing some of the Rubbish, that lies in the way to" the knowledge largely brought to humanity, and consolidated, in the work of Boyle, Sydenham, Huygenius, but above all "the incomparable Mr. Newton." The theory of human nature developed or implied by the *Essay* itself deserves greater elaboration than it can be given here. It is commonsensical, or perhaps more accurately, it helped shape a set of commonsense understandings of "man in the world" that three centuries later still resonate.

In the *Essay* Locke gives what he takes to be proof of the existence of God[13] and discusses, briefly but informatively, skeptical positions in epistemology.[14] What is conveyed is a clear, quiet sense that—on some topic or other more or less every philosopher has this view—some objections are frivolous and not to be taken seriously, even if we don't succeed in answering them. Some things we know

---

[12] This extended passage comes entirely from the much-discussed Chapter V ("Of Property") of *The Second Treatise of Government*. There is frequent biblical citation and still more frequent reference to God throughout the *Second Treatise*.

[13] *Essay concerning Human Understanding* (1690), pp. 619–630.

[14] Ibid., pp. 634–636.

to be true, even where we can't altogether be sure how to refute naysayers, and even recognize less than airtight proof in our own case. The juxtaposition of these texts, and the facts of Locke's life and historical and cultural location, unite to make it clear that Locke regards the existence of God as a matter of public knowledge. For Locke, this is something that humanity knows quite certainly to be the case—more certainly, he says, than anything not immediately given in sensation or introspection. Locke may be viewed as a member of the last generation of educated west Europeans for whom theism has this secure cognitive position. From the next generation after Locke deism and freethinking are rife in England—Locke's own disciple and friend Anthony Collins (1676–1729) is a splendid exemplar of this new current—and the possibility that there just might not be a God after all is thinkable as a non-frivolous metaphysical view. This is not to say that religious commitment thereafter was insincere or inauthentic, or that many believers did not feel wholly confident that they knew that God exists. It is to say that Locke felt quite sure not just that he knew God to be real, but that everyone else did also;[15] and that ever since the early eighteenth century such a stance has not been authentically possible within western culture.

Locke's Christianity is tolerant and humane. He esteems, he says, "the mutual toleration of Christians in their different professions of religion" to be "the chief characteristic mark of the true church."[16] One would wish this toleration, of course, to extend also to non-Christians (including those wholly without religion); but in its day, and coming from a leading protagonist of the Protestant (and generally quite intolerantly anti-Catholic) victorious party of 1688, this is striking and impressive. In fact, the spirit and many of the claims of *A Letter concerning Toleration* do imply a complete withdrawal of state activity from ensuring religious conformity.[17]

[15] Hobbes and Spinoza, both viewed as atheists (the former, at least, quite incorrectly), seem genuinely to have been regarded, to the end of the seventeenth century, as something like freaks of nature; rather like we might think of someone we thought brilliant in some sphere of activity but whom we also knew passionately believed in Atlantis or flying saucers, or denied the occurrence of the Holocaust.

[16] *A Letter concerning Toleration* (1690), p. 13.

[17] Ibid., p. 36f., explicitly affirms the rights of Jews to freedom of religion in Christian societies. The same liberty is affirmed for Moslems (ibid., p. 56) and for "heathens" (ibid., p. 65). Locke explicitly denies toleration,

The care of souls cannot belong to the civil magistrate because his power consists only in outward force; but true and saving religion consists in the inward persuasion of the mind, without which nothing can be acceptable to God. And such is the nature of the understanding that it cannot be compelled to the belief of anything by outward force. Confiscation of estate, imprisonment, torments, nothing of that nature can have any such efficacy as to make men change the inward judgment that they have framed of things.[18]

The last two sentences express something close to the Lutheran spirit of Christianity and its conception of human nature. We find it augmented later in the *Letter concerning Toleration:*

A good life, in which consists not the least part of religion and true piety, concerns also the civil government ... Moral actions belong therefore to the jurisdiction both of the outward and inward court, both of the civil and domestic govenor; I mean both of the magistrate and conscience ...

Every man has an immortal soul, capable of eternal happiness or misery, whose happiness [depends] upon his believing and doing those things in his life which are necessary to the obtaining of God's favor, and are prescribed by God to that end ...

But besides their souls, which are immortal, men have also their temporal lives here upon earth; the state whereof being frail and fleeting, and the duration uncertain, they have need of several outward conveniences to the support thereof, which are to be procured or preserved by pains and industry. For those things that are necessary to the comfortable support of our lives are not the spontaneous products of nature, nor do offer themselves fit and prepared for our use. This part therefore draws on another care, and necessarily gives another employment. But the pravity of mankind being such that they had rather injuriously prey upon the fruits of other men's labors than take pains to provide for themselves, the necessity of preserving men in the possession of what honest industry has already acquired, and also of preserving their liberty and strength, whereby they may acquire what they further want, obliges men to enter into society with one another, that by mutual assistance and joint force they may secure unto each other

however, for atheists (ibid., p. 56). But all theists, whatever their faith, ought to enjoy "the civil rights of the commonwealth" as well as freedom of worship.

[18] Ibid., p. 18.

their properties, in the things that contribute to the comfort and happiness of this life, leaving in the meanwhile to every man the care of his own eternal happiness, the attainment whereof can neither be facilitated by another man's industry, nor can the loss of it turn to another man's prejudice, nor the hope of it be forced from him by any external violence.[19]

My singling Locke out as an early modern Christian theorist may be thought to sit somewhat ill, or at any rate ironically, beside his more usual identification as an early modern liberal (indeed, almost the defining figure for classical pre-reformist liberalism). Since liberals, libertarian or welfare, certainly can be and not infrequently have been Christians, there is of course no contradiction in locating him in both roles and traditions. On the other hand, Locke as liberal is supposed to embody a break from and a measure of opposition to traditional conceptions of authority and its bases. Hence, one would suppose, he should signal a new conception of what it is to be a human being in the world; whereas a Christian thinker should perhaps reaffirm the continuity of a tradition, and specifically a tradition of a human identity and a relationship to God established many centuries before.

Locke's liberalism is in fact, I would argue, a less theoretically developed matter than it is typically regarded as being. The *Treatises of Government* were written, in some haste it seems, as part of an ad hoc justification for the Glorious Revolution—the overthrow of James II and the setting up of a new sovereign. Locke is primarily seeking to refute proponents of a divine right of kings, and to depict the basis of any system of government as necessarily popular will and support. The myth of the foundation of civil society he tells is not unlike other similar models, from antiquity (in Plato and Lucretius, for example), and in the generations preceding Locke's own. Locke does, to be sure, build up a certain sort of picture of the civil (and economic) structure and the kinds of bases he sees it as having both in fact and in a rationale that justifies it; and in doing so he does, of course, reveal assumptions he makes, some of which he seems more aware of than others. The influence Locke had in the eighteenth century, in both his epistemological and psychological theories and those about government and its foundation (and the justification for replacing it), was enormous. It seems quite right, for example, to view him as the "grandfather" of the American Revolution, as is typically done. At the same time it seems quite wrong to conceive his project, or execution of

[19] Ibid., p. 46f.

it, in the *Treatises of Government* as though it were an early version of John Rawls' *A Theory of Justice* (the contemporary classic of moral and political theory partly modelled on Locke's *Second Treatise*).

The alleged "atomic individualism" in Lockean liberalism, for example, seems an unwarranted extrapolation from the evidence of Locke's writings on government, society, and people. He is writing rather on the fly; there is much he omits to address or is casual or hasty about. (There is little or nothing about children and child-bearing, for example, though elsewhere Locke has much to say about both.) There is a theory here, but it is in intention more what we could call Christian republicanism than Spencerian (or Nozickian) libertarianism.[20] He means to be sensible, temperate, and a spokes-person for well-intentioned members of a polity who, reasonably, seek an ordered society offering protection and security in life and property and in which the individual judgement of individual adult Christian souls can find expression in the polity's institutions and procedures.

Locke's account is unquestionably androcentric, and in favouring those who have been resolute to gather acorns—the far-sighted and entrepreneurial—Locke's tilt of focus is certainly towards the prop-ertied. But the accompanying and underlying rationale is far more Christian, and biblical, than it is innovatively ideological, supplying a value scheme for burgeoning capitalism or possessive individual-ism. The fundamental underlying Lockean query is, throughout, Is this not God's world? And did he not, in making it, work well? And—the Lutheran premise as query—are we not in his image, crea-tures of judgement and agency, able to answer to ourselves, within ourselves, as also to him that made us?

Locke is particularly impressive as a modern Christian, it seems to me, because he is a non-clergyman. Hence we are able to see someone with the relevant convictions expressing them in different facets of his work, but without a clergyman's or theologian's profes-sional interest in those convictions. Many leading exemplars of the modern Christian outlook have, of course, been clergymen or theolo-gians. An outstanding eighteenth-century case is afforded by Bishop Joseph Butler. As with Locke, we find here a very good philosophi-cal mind; indeed, while less brilliant and wide ranging, Butler is generally the more careful philosopher of the two, clear and sharp

---

[20] Herbert Spencer was a leading nineteenth-century advocate, as Robert Nozick has been in the twentieth century, of the minimal, but private-property-securing, state.

and precisely articulated. Like Locke, Butler is calm, moderate, sensible, this-worldly, no friend of fanaticism or superstition. He lives in his time, and of it. And he is a deeply committed Anglican Christian. The philosophical work of Butler's that has received most attention—indeed, still lives in a fresh and contemporary way—consists of his writings on morality, especially *Fifteen Sermons* (1726) and *The Analogy of Religion* (1736).

Three of the *Fifteen Sermons* had originally appeared as a unit called "Three Sermons upon Human Nature." In these, and to a lesser extent in others of the sermons, Butler explicitly undertakes to develop a portrait of humanity. It is a lucid and subtly formulated expression of what I here call the Whig Christian view: an optimistic, integrated account of individual selves and a natural mutuality among and between them. Butler argues "that there are as real and the same kind of indications in human nature that we were made for society and to do good to our fellow creatures, as that we were intended to take care of our own life and health and private good" (p. 21). He develops a psychological theory according to which we have, inherently, both self- and other-regarding impulses; the latter, which include dispositions to friendship, compassion, family affections, and every variety of altruism, he calls benevolence. These impulses, fundamental parts of our nature, cannot be reduced to or explained in terms of other constituents of our makeup. We also have other impulses and desires, particularly short-sighted desires for immediate gratification, and they lead us sometimes to actions at odds with benevolence (or, for that matter, self-interest and self-love). Throughout, there operates an inner faculty or principle by which we recognize transgressions against our (genuine and long-term) self-love and against benevolence. This faculty or principle is a cognitive constituent of our makeup by which we discern right and wrong (though not without occasional possibilities of error, for we are always and in everything limited and imperfect). This faculty is called conscience.

Butler's depiction of our nature will be familiar to all; it is a legacy of most of our childhoods. We know it as a simple encapsulation of ideas of the moral life, internalized and made part of our own agency and judgements of responsibility. In Butler's version it is a Lutheran Protestant Christian conception. At the same time, Butler makes much of his case that his theory of human nature does not rest on revelation, biblical authority, or even basic theistic assumptions. He argues that we see it to be correct in everyday life and experience, and moreover, that non-Christians also do (appropriately so, if the theory is to hold universally of human beings). Part of Butler's view is that self-interest, benevolence, and duty will coincide, or converge. This is an old position in moral theory, argued for by Plato. What is more distinctively Christian—optimistically, Whiggishly, social-action-tending Christian—in Butler's account is the idea that it is in our very cognitive and affective "equipment," how we have been endowed, and by the satisfaction of which alone one can be happy, that these things are so (rather than, say, its being something demonstrable by a calculus of the facts and logistics of the exterior world along with features of ours). Hence, there is an implicit (inductive) moral argument for theism in Butler's case for our nature, as there would not be in the comparable arguments that morality is just that which is rational to do of, say, Plato, or David Gauthier.[21]

> The sum of the whole is plainly this. The nature of man considered in his single capacity, and with respect only to the present world, is adapted and leads him to attain the greatest happiness he can for himself in the present world. The nature of man considered in his public or social capacity leads him to a right behaviour in society, to that course of life which we call virtue. Men follow or obey their nature in both these capacities and respects to a certain degree, but not entirely; their actions do not come up to the whole of what their nature leads them to in either of these capacities or respects; and they often violate their nature in both. That is, as they neglect the duties they owe to their fellow creatures, to which their nature leads them, and are injurious, to which their nature is abhorrent, so there is a manifest negligence in men of their real happiness or interest in the present world when that interest is inconsistent with a present gratification, for the sake of which they negligently, nay, even knowingly, are the authors and instruments of their own misery and ruin. Thus they are as often unjust to themselves as to others, and for the most part are equally so to both by the same actions.
>
> ... there is a superior principle of reflection or conscience in every man which distinguishes between the internal principles of his heart as well as his external actions, which passes judgment upon himself and them, pronounces determinately some actions to be in themselves just, right, good; others to be in themselves evil, wrong, unjust, which, without being consulted, without

[21] David Gauthier is a prominent contemporary moral philosopher who argues, as Plato did (though Gauthier's arguments are very different from Plato's), that being moral is essentially a matter of thinking and acting in a rational and self-consistent way.

being advised with, magisterially exerts itself, and approves or condemns him the doer of them accordingly; and which, if not forcibly stopped, naturally and always of course goes on to anticipate a higher and more effectual sentence which shall hereafter second and affirm its own.[22]

Immanuel Kant is a third major Enlightenment modern Christian philosopher. Although one of the greatest philosophers, with developed views in almost every area of philosophy—including accounts of human nature, rational agency, freedom, the moral life, and our relations to extra-human nature—and also a committed Lutheran, Kant is in many ways less representative of the Christian philosopher of humankind than are Locke and Butler. The noumenal/phenomenal divide in Kantian metaphysics and epistemology[23] brings with it a kind of dualism that is in some respects alien to the realism and the unity of the world (even with its deeply differing kinds of beings) of the fundamental Christian scheme. Kantianism and Christianity may be reconcilable (obviously Kant himself thought they were), but if so, his vastly more complicated and highly metaphysical (or meta-metaphysical) rendering of the order of things has to be factored into the overall conception of Christianity.

Quite distinct from the complexities of his critical philosophy, Kant's account of morality, though ingenious, original, and with its own considerable plausibility, seems to be somewhat at odds with a fully Christian ethical conception, at least of the modern Christian kind. The Kantian ethical human is a kind of logician, doing the right thing because he or she has calculated that it is right, and not out of a sort of love, which is at least supposed to be the basis for Christian ethical life. Perhaps these complexities too are reconcilable. Some of the expressions of feeling Kant gives vent to suggest that he thought so. Alternatively, there may just be inconsistencies in his account.

Why then include him in this tally? Certainly other modern Christians can be found. I would say that Kant belongs here, in spite of the complications of his philosophical theories, because his own heart is clearly here. He revised the *Critique of Pure Reason,* in its

[22] From Sermons 1(15) and 2(8) of *Fifteen Sermons.*

[23] Kant holds that all human knowledge is limited to *phenomena* that are partly functions of our minds, even though we know that there are *noumena*—things in themselves somehow giving rise to the phenomena we experience. Even so we rationally *postulate,* for Kant, noumenal selves who are free moral agents.

second edition, largely to make room for faith. He produced a moral argument for the existence of God requiring stages in its reasoning that render it almost ludicrously implausible: surely the expression of a species of wishful thinking, in one otherwise so skilled at spotting difficulties above all in theistic argumentation. The Kantian heart is deeply Christian, and many features of the moral theory strongly reflect and express that fact, in ways that importantly enlarge and deepen the modern Christian philosophy of humanity.

The idea of each human being—each rational being—as an end in itself, and the idea of a kingdom of ends, a community of souls, who recognize and acknowledge each other's autonomy and person-hood as something of intrinsic value and inviolable, is an intensi-fication of Christian theory. There is a dimension of austere aesthetic to Kant's account, in the coloration his language provides, that goes beyond what the base theory would have required, and conveys the student of Kantian morality to the plane of the sacred.

Kant's Christianity is not in an obvious way either Whig or Tory. Politically he is a liberal, and the first prophet of the idea of an end of history (considerably discussed in recent years) through other instrumentalities than a return of Christ. But his psychological portrait of humanity is without commitments like Butler's, to a natural and deeply placed altruism or the inevitable ringing voice of the faculty of conscience in our everyday operation.

Kant is a Christian, and a Lutheran Protestant one, his outlook peopling a moral world of individual agents of conscience, united in a community of self-reflective and mutually reflective moral and personal recognition. He is also fully attuned to and accepting of the modern world, modernity itself, and the sciences. And his philoso-phical and cultural influence, most of it not specifically Christian but much of it so, has been immense.

I will offer just one more example of a modern Christian, this one also a German Lutheran, but of the twentieth century: Dietrich Bonhoeffer. Like Butler a clergyman, Bonhoeffer's destiny was alto-gether different. While Butler had a highly successful and increas-ingly comfortable ecclesiastical career, Bonhoeffer, early recognized as having very great promise, fell a victim to Nazi repression, imprisoned then executed as part of the reaction to the 1944 attempt on Hitler's life. Bonhoeffer's work survives in a number of mostly posthumous publications, outstanding among them *Ethics* and the *Let-ters and Papers from Prison*. In this work emerges both the biogra-phical image of a modern Christian of moral and intellectual strength, indeed heroism, and a set of reflections and perspectives that augment this philosophical stance and contribute to its vitality in contemporary life.

Bonhoeffer is perhaps a better exemplar of the modern Christian than are the several English academic or literary Christians, the best known of them perhaps C. S. Lewis. However influential and sometimes eloquent Lewis and others of these English Christians have been, they appear essentially to be mediaevalist romantics, with hearts yearning for older and more rural times. They have, in short, quite problematic relationships to modernity, expressed in attractions to pseudo-science and active hopes of miraculous interventions, hostility to cities and industrial civilization, and bifurcations in their own work, between dense mediaevalist scholarship and over-smooth, prettified, disguised Christian myth.

Bonhoeffer is, first and last, a Lutheran pastor and theologian. Indeed, he is sufficiently serious in that vocation that he sees himself without hesitation as needing to be in the present world and not a nostalgia-induced one. This leads him to a clear recognition of the centrality, and ineliminability, of scientific rationality and technology in the contemporary and any foreseeable world. As a result, Bonhoeffer is strikingly affirmative about oppositional periods, phenomena, and individuals, among them the Enlightenment, Nietzsche, and the fact of technologically informed modernity itself.

> Intellectual honesty in all things, including questions of belief, was the great achievement of emancipated reason and it has ever since been one of the indispensable moral requirements of western man. Contempt for the age of rationalism is a suspicious sign of failure to feel the need for truthfulness ... We cannot now go back to the days before Lessing and Lichtenberg. (*Ethics,* p. 34)

> The age of technology is a genuine heritage of our western history. We must come to grips with it. We cannot return to the pretechnical era. (Ibid., p. 35)

Bonhoeffer frequently cites Nietzsche, not always as opponent. Throughout his work Bonhoeffer strikes one forcefully as Christian through and through, intellectually as well as morally robust, with a sense of irony as well as high courage, and engaged with modern life; but even more as imbued with a deep sense of the common clay of humanity, not merely its Christian portion, the others not just enemies or fields to sow.

Bonhoeffer does not add substantively to a modern Christian image of humanity. He exemplifies fundamental conceptions to be found in earlier Christian writers, among them Butler. He is less cheerily optimistic than Butler, though clearly also of Whig rather than Tory Christian persuasion. This accords with the fact that the modern Christian *leadership,* at least in its creative cases, has tended more to a liberal and social activist stance, just as the followers, the large flock of the faithful (by which I do not mean to imply a necessarily supine or unthinking faithful) has tended, more often at least, to Toryism.

To sum up, and partly restate what is distinctive and plausible in the Christian philosophy of human nature: perhaps most striking is its idea of the incarnation, of God choosing to live in the flesh of humankind and experience reality as we do. And what is most compelling about this idea is that even if not empirically supportable, even if blasphemous (as some of non-Christian religion think), and even if arrogantly speciesist, still *it is not conceptually absurd.* The Christian analysis makes a claim about our ontic seriousness, one that is, curiously, a kind of cousin of the aspiration to science. The very idea that we might get it right, might sufficiently transcend the causal forces that produced and condition us, to stand in even partially accurate cognitive relation to reality; this fundamental, motivational assumption of the scientific enterprise parallels the Christian notion that we occupy a moral location that transcends the specifics of our biochemistry or positions in time or space, that elevates us to inter-identifiability with any other possible variety of consciousness in the universe. A moral identifiability alone is meant by this Christian analysis; it does not preclude impassable boundaries of kinds of experience different from or higher than our own. There is implicit in this analysis the notion of a deep—in fact a cosmic—*tragedy* in the human condition, if this transcendent jewel of our being in the universe were not to achieve its potential of existential seriousness, and secondly, were it to do so and this be confined to the seventy or so years of the human lifespan. This is part of what is meant, and what is so deeply Christian, about Kant's moral argument for the existence of God (however implausible it is as an actual *case* for the deity).

Time now for the posing of difficulties for or objections to the modern Christian view of human beings:

There are what we might call dialectical difficulties—problems, personal or inward—for the modern Christian, a continuous and unrelenting threat of falling into bad faith and defensiveness. What is the believer to think and to do, seeing, as he or she must if honest and awake, the tide of surrounding and ever-new theories, conceptions, models, and data that enlarge, enrich, and complicate understanding, almost none of which is Christian or even religious in the most extended sense? How can Christianity be, as it is supposed to be, final or definitive or a framework for understanding the world in the face of so much else that is so different, so clever, so good? And what about all the lower and lesser forms of Christianity—premodern, fundamentalist, evangelical, and other versions—that crowd public cultural space, not to mention one's doorstep, the TV airwaves, and politicians' not credible remarks? Doesn't one have, too often, to cringe with embarrassment? What prevents the believer's position becoming inwardly beleaguered, inauthentic, unintelligent, or at best only selectively intelligent? Bonhoeffer's writings and career show him to have been reasonably impressive in these respects, but Bonhoeffer was a hero and a martyr, and those times had the morally simplified bracing air of struggle against obvious (and intellectually shallow) evil. How can a serious or interesting modern Christian perspective be sustainable, really practicable, in non-heroic circumstances?

Many contemporary Christians achieve what is at least possible in this regard within the community of Christian churches and other (for example, human rights) organizations. There is strength, always, in numbers, and seeing others whom you respect and take seriously in like case with yourself can—clearly, for many does—consolidate and fortify a continuing Christian perspective in the contemporary world. But the problem still remains of moments alone. Christians are supposed to pray, and for modern Christians, as for Protestants broadly, this is supposed to include and involve not just ritual collective action or forms of a shared spirituality, but a private, immediate relationship with a non-human imperceptible being who— not to put too fine a point on it—a serious, intelligent, scientifically informed person living in and through non-heroic circumstances simply cannot believe is *quite certainly there.* That is, beliefs about probability are surely achievable, but no wide-awake person in the modern world with any brains at all can authentically, inwardly, believe he or she knows wholly for certain that God exists. And if there is necessarily some measure of doubt as to the reality of the being on the other end of the telephone of prayer, it is difficult to see how personal (as opposed to social, or communitarian) Christianity is sustainable. Again, it is obvious that some people do sustain this. One has to have a sense, though, of a juggling act that must often require more energy in the exercise of the gymnastics than in daily adherence to the perspective itself. Many modern Christians are, we might reasonably surmise, what we may call *cultural Christians:* people for whom Christianity is a personally meaningful or significant framework of values (and in many cases also of art, architecture, and music) and a social and communitarian focus, but where there is no personal prayer-involving relationship with God, nor much of deep-level metaphysical commitment to God's reality. (Hegel may have been one of the first fully developed cultural Christians.[24])

Other objections to Christianity as a perspective on human nature involve the claim that it is too simplistic or one-dimensional. In all its forms, it takes humans normatively, with notions of basic metaphysical freedom having been deployed for (depending on the variety of Christianity) good or bad over a lifetime. Or if modern Christianity is held to have a greater subtlety than this, with notable saints and sinners at extreme ends of a continuum of evaluable lives (the deity's complexity and opacity, for us, summoned to licence the more sophisticated judgment options), still much—too much—in the human range seems unable to find a non-negative place in a Christian reckoning. Christianity's central prized virtue is innocence: "Except ye ... become as little children, ye shall not enter into the kingdom of heaven" (Matt. 18.3). Jesus, in saying this, definitely does not anticipate Freud. He thinks children have a one-dimensional simplicity, a basic playful benevolence, and the highest human hope is to recover it. Critics say he is wrong about children, and wrong to think a human best would occupy so one-coloured a plane, even if it could. What of fantasy (including fantasies involving "inappropriate" or prohibited fantasy objects), ribaldry, biting satirical wit, black humour, ultra-cool style in personal adornment or the presentation of self in everyday life? What of body language, subliminal messages, subtextual analysis, the unconscious, love/hate relationships, inclusive fitness, feminism, Jacobin republicanism, art for the sake of art, and so much else? There seem to be such large and textured slices of life that Christianity has nothing to say about; so much more, in both heaven and earth, than this philosophy even dreams of.

[24] The character of Hegel's religious views is differently interpreted by students of Hegelian philosophy. There are indications that Hegel thinks that religion—even Lutheran Christianity, for Hegel its highest form—is at best approximation to and metaphor for the absolute and literal truth only achievable in philosophy. Since Hegel is also a historicist—someone for whom ideas are only intelligible within their historical location—and a thinker for whom human nature (apparently) makes institutions like an established church and hereditary monarchy necessary for optimally functioning civil society, though a philosopher would not need either, it is natural to see him as something other than a literal believing Christian.

Still other objections: many critics think Christianity over-flattering of humanity and at the same time over-severe in its portrait of us. The notion of our participation in divinity—not just that God makes us in his image, but that he *is* for some thirty years or more a human being, and our condition is shown thereby to involve a capacity for an eternity of knowledge and being—is held by many to inflate our particular primate species implausibly and (the appearance of humility notwithstanding) megalomaniacally. One is put in mind of the pre-Socratic philosopher Xenophanes' earliest formulation of the error of anthropomorphism:

> If oxen and horses and lions had hands
> and were able to draw with their hands
>   and do the same things as men,
> horses would draw the shape of gods to look like horses
> and oxen to look like oxen, and each would make his
> gods' bodies have the same shape as they themselves had.[25]

Xenophanes is in fact giving expression to theistic piety, but our end of the ontological telescope should perhaps disclose us to ourselves as ourselves, and not something so anchored in being that a God, if there were one, would want for a while to be one of us. That conception also doesn't allow us to be ourselves, for we are condemned by it to self-castigation, as falling short of what cannot but be an externalized and ultimately self-alienating expectation of being fit company for God.[26]

In this regard, some critics hold that in fact the most serious case against theism of anything like the Christian type is not the arguments of philosophers like Hume, Kant, and Russell—devastating as those arguments are—but rather that of Freud. Freud argues that the impulse to religious conviction and commitment is a species of infantilism. We want a God—those of us who do—as an authority-figure, an eternal watching father, whom we can lean upon and to whom we can devote our moral energy in attempting, both lovingly and fearfully but never

---

[25] Richard D. McKirahan, Jr., *Philosophy before Socrates: An Introduction with Texts and Commentary* (1994), p. 61.

[26] Much of the content of these objections, and still more, may be found in Lord Rochester's superb poem "A Satire against Mankind" (1680), to which the reader is referred for verse exposition of and comment on at least three theories of human nature discussed in the present book.

quite successfully, to satisfy and placate. The worst thing, these critics say, about accepting such a view of the world and our identity and place within it is not that it is false, but that it is immature.

Bibliography

Bonhoeffer, Dietrich. *Ethics*. Translated by G. N. H. Smith. London: SCH Press, 1955.

——————. *Letters and Papers from Prison*. Enl. ed., edited by E. Bethge. New York: Collier Books, 1971.

Butler, Joseph. *Fifteen Sermons*. In W. E. Gladstone, ed., *The Works of Joseph Butler*. 2 vols. Oxford: Clarendon Press, 1897.

——————. *Five Sermons* (Sermons 1, 2, 3, 11, 12 of the *Fifteen Sermons*). Indianapolis: Bobbs-Merrill, 1950.

Elshtain, Jean Bethke. *Public Man, Private Woman*. 2nd ed. Princeton, NJ: Princeton University Press, 1993.

Kant, Immanuel. *Religion within the Limits of Reason Alone*. Translated and with an introduction and note by T. M. Greene and H. H. Hudson. La Salle, IL: Open Court, 1934.

Locke, John. *An Essay concerning Human Understanding*. Oxford: Oxford University Press, 1979 [1690].

——————. *A Letter concerning Toleration*. Indianapolis: Bobbs-Merrill, 1983 [1689].

——————. *The Reasonableness of Christianity*. Reprinted in *The Works of John Locke,* vol. 7. Darmstadt: Scientia Verlag Aalen, 1963.

——————. *The Second Treatise of Government*. Indianapolis: Bobbs-Merrill, 1952, [1690]

McKirahan, Richard D., Jr. *Philosophy before Socrates: An Introduction with Texts and Commentary*. Indianapolis: Hackett, 1994.

Penelhum, Terence. *Butler*. London: Routledge & Kegan Paul, 1985.

Rochester, Earl of. *Selections: The Complete Poems of John Wilmot, Earl of Rochester*. Edited by D. Vieth. New Haven: Yale University Press, 1968.

Weber, Max. *The Protestant Ethic and the Spirit of Capitalism*. New York: Scribner's, 1950.

CHAPTER 5 /

Liberalism —————

WHAT I HAVE CALLED TORY AND WHIG FORKS
of a Christian branch of human nature theory, though in origin and
for many still Christian, in the nineteenth century took pronounced
secular forms. These remain prominent conceptions of human beings
and their possibilities. In the present chapter I want to sketch and
explore a central (secular) liberal view of humanity, and in its successor a corresponding conservative picture. A considerable part of the
ground for both has already been laid in our exposition, as it was historically, by their Christian antecedent.

What I am calling the liberal theory of human nature underlies
what is frequently termed reform liberalism or welfare liberalism, a
theory of political life and political action that arose over the past
century and a half. Its roots lie at least as fully in Enlightenment
conceptions as in Whig Christian ones. Indeed, modern liberalism is
probably the most direct and complete surviving embodiment of
Enlightenment views and values that there is. At the same time, there
are real and substantive contrasts between Enlightenment and modern
liberalism. Most accounts of liberalism have tended to minimize and
sometimes to wholly ignore these, so we will need to place special
stress on them.

Since liberalism has frequently been misrepresented to the point
of caricature by its opponents, a considerable degree of care is
needed in setting out the theory. Misrepresentation is partly encour-
aged or allowed by the extreme elasticity, synchronically and dia-
chronically, of the term "liberalism."

That elasticity notwithstanding, and outside of recondite books
and articles by professors of political philosophy, the world at large
has a reasonably clear understanding of what it means by liberals and
liberalism. A liberal, for the position's numerous enemies, is a moderate compromiser with a bleeding heart, unwilling to support fast-
track pathways to social reform though committed to a wide range of
improvements social, economic, and moral, which the liberal tends
to support by throwing money around (or advocating that others do
so). Liberals favour free speech and other individual rights. They are
champions of concerns about civil liberties and human rights abuses,

but chiefly in practice, and always in theory, where specific individuals' liberties or rights are involved.

There is considerable truth to this portrayal; but we want greater precision, and historical location. And we mean to depict a view of human beings, not primarily a moral stance. Reasonably so: there is a liberal view of humankind.

I should make explicit that by "liberalism" I primarily mean—as likewise with "Marxism," "feminism," "psychoanalysis," and "Darwinism"—a theory that would be self-ascribed by advocates and adherents. That is, I take liberalism to be what those who call themselves liberals take it to be. In general this seems justified procedure (and accords as well with liberal theory, which holds that people are, *ceteris paribus,* the best and most reliable judges of their values, desires, and beliefs). In rare cases it might be appropriate to view an individual or theory as really liberal (or anything else) even though he, she, or it does not profess to be; but this ought to require argument, the mounting of a sustained case. I don't wish to attach particularly critical significance to a mere label, but the point of departure really should be with those who do use the label self-referentially, and with figuring out what *they* seem to have in mind by it. Only then should we look to see whether it also fits some who don't use that label (or perhaps even some who self-consciously disdain it). All of this I take to be obvious, needing saying only because some discussions of liberalism don't conform to it. The most glaring example of departure from it, and of a resulting nearly pernicious confusion, is to be found in the authors who describe the seventeenth-century English philosopher Thomas Hobbes as a liberal. This seems to me perfectly bizarre, and not only because "liberalism" is not a term Hobbes would have used or recognized for anything he believed. Hobbes was English, and non-technical and plain spoken in his work, and his views disclaim the authority of tradition, and liberalism did primarily develop in England among thinkers whose work is also generally not obscure or technical, and their views too accorded no justifying authority to tradition; but there is otherwise little to link Hobbes to liberalism.[1]

---

[1] Hobbes and liberalism are often said to share an *individualist* view of human nature. I will be arguing that this idea is not as clear as often supposed. In any case, many other theories are as individualist as either without being labelled liberal. Moreover, as I will also argue, reform liberalism at least is *not* a wholly individualist theory.

It is also obvious that terms often change in meaning over time, and that what may have been meant by a term in one period may have only an overlapping sense, or no shared sense at all, with its meaning in another. Generally reasonable practice seems to be to go with current usage unless one is writing a history of another time. The term "liberalism" first appears in English early in the nineteenth century (certainly by 1819; Bentham uses "liberalist" in 1801). "Liberal" appears with something like the political sense we attach to it, in French, from 1750. Earlier eighteenth-century uses, in both English and French, appear just to mean "ample, generous, or free" (a meaning the word still bears).

Modern liberalism—reform or welfare liberalism—developed in the second half of the nineteenth century, especially in Great Britain. To a certain degree its evolution may be traced in the development of the social ideas and theories of John Stuart Mill (1806–1873), as he emerged from the shadow of his father and the Locke-Bentham tradition in British public life and social analysis.[2] The fully matured Mill is plausibly seen as the first fully formed modern liberal. And yet the liberal theory of human nature is only somewhat elusively, and not particularly uniquely, attributable to him. It is a development or extension of Enlightenment liberal theory, and others than Mill, some earlier than him, come to much the same conception. Most notable among these was Wilhelm von Humboldt (1767–1835), in Germany, whose writings give almost as full an articulation of this view as Mill's. (Mill in fact cites Humboldt as an important influence on his thinking.[3])

---

[2] Jeremy Bentham (1748–1832) was the founder and central figure of the utilitarian school in British moral, social, and legal theory. One of his leading followers and supporters was James Mill (1773–1836), J. S. Mill's father.

[3] Humboldt expresses clearly and fully what we will identify as the perfectionist strand or component in the liberal view, with its normative focus on the particular life of each human individual (more on this below). Indeed, by his own account, Mill came to this idea by encountering it in Humboldt's writings, notably *Ideen zu einen Versuch die Grenzen der Wirksamkeit des Staats zu bestimmen*. This essay, written in 1791–92, was published posthumously in Germany in 1852. An English translation appeared in 1854, titled *The Sphere and Duties of Government*. It is under this title that Mill refers to the book. The contemporary English version of the essay translates its title as *The Limits of State Action*.

Whether or not Mill's hand was crucial for the formulation of late-nineteenth-century liberalism, certainly his creative presence in that phenomenon was considerable. Directly influenced by Mill were two other English social and moral theorists, T. H. Green (1836–1882) and, slightly later, L. T. Hobhouse (1864–1929). The latter's little book, *Liberalism* (1914), is in many ways the single most perfectly realized textual expression of the liberal view of humanity.

As a political philosophy liberalism emerges first as advocacy of minimal governmental restrictions on trade, movement, and ideas. It was natural and appropriate, therefore, to identify, as nineteenth-century thinkers quickly did, eighteenth-century currents that prefigured such advocacy of *freedom* as liberal. Central Enlightenment positions in Britain and France favouring freedom from state controls came to be viewed as liberal. There is an immediate conceptual step from such liberalism to opposition to the weight of tradition, since west European traditions accorded governmental and ecclesiastical authorities very extensive control on trade, movement, and ideas. Of course traditions differ; there are, even now, liberal traditions. Liberalism wasn't (and isn't) necessarily opposed to tradition as such, or even to the weight and authority of tradition, provided it is the right tradition: a freeing, tolerating, liberating tradition.

One could be in favour of freedom from interference of various kinds for different reasons. One reason might be a self-interested desire that one be left alone oneself, in confidence that one would thrive however things might go for the rest of the world. Or that view might be held for self and kindred, or self and cultural group (a religious or linguistic or ethnic community, for example). World-renouncing religious communities—Amish or other Anabaptist Christians, for example—have sometimes taken this position (though, when they do, they rarely accord the freedom they wish for the community to individual members of that community). Some libertarian positions seem to have similar, if rarely stated, motivation: the position taken is that I and numerous like-minded people are willing to take our chances, and regard it as our right that we forge ahead on our own, making or breaking our own destinies and conferring like rights and responsibilities on all within our ken and power; but where there is no particular belief that this policy will in fact conduce to the thriving of all other human individuals.

Unless strongly inegalitarian views, morally or empirically, can be successfully defended—and there seems no good reason to believe any can be—this is too slender a base to support a genuine moral or empirical view about people. A liberal *theory* emerges only when the freedoms liberalism seeks are held to benefit and accord with the natures of all or at least a considerable portion of the human community.

In fact, the eighteenth-century French *philosophes*—Voltaire, Montesquieu, Diderot, and still more fully the later figures, supremely, Condorcet—are plausibly assigned such a theory. Although they didn't use the term "liberalism," they self-consciously believed in the possibility of substantive human progress, moral and economic, through the repudiation of priestly authority, and its replacement with institutions that would respect ideological diversity and implement rights to non-interference held against government as well as other individuals. They believed that this progress would be brought about through the study, development, and application of science, and of learning broadly. Their conception of human nature was of something chiefly formed through socializing processes; along with this they held that the human base, from which the socialized result was mounted, was fundamentally similar in all times and places. There were, to be sure, widely held conceptions of national character, and beliefs, many of them developed in quasi-scientific form, of the formative role of geography on national or regional typology. By their very character, these views too were mostly nurturative or environmentalist, even if they led to convictions of marked human differentiation. Typically, the *philosophes* had still more pronounced views on sexual distinction, usually regarding gender typology as deeply placed and justifying male socioeconomic superiority. The one outstanding exception to this pattern was Condorcet, most enlightened and progressive of the Enlightenment philosophers, a clearly enunciated anti-racist and the first thinker to publish fully formulated feminist views.

Contemporary evaluations of the Enlightenment thinkers vary widely. Some are still highly admiring, others quite severely critical. Some see all that has followed in western culture as a reaction to and extension of eighteenth-century cultural initiatives; others see the long Enlightenment shadow as a base, requiring—and capable of receiving—self-conscious repudiation. Certainly not all eighteenth-century developments were admirable or had much result. At any rate, much modern criticism of the Enlightenment conceptions and projects is, I think, unreasonable (just as some of it is entirely sound). What is most unreasonable of all is to ignore the fact that the Enlightenment thinkers were creating blueprints for what they saw as possible and better societies than the ones they lived in, where these improved social orders were not a utopian leap beyond the known order but a development from it, which in any case none of the theorists lived to see even partly implemented (except, in a modest and unsatisfactory way, Condorcet, who died during the Terror phase of the French Revolution). There is something artificial and formulaic in these blueprints; and much that is not foreseen, that would and did follow their putting into practice as the nineteenth and twentieth centuries unfolded. How could it have been otherwise? This is not just to say that no one has a very complete or impressive social prescience, now as then. Rather, western societies *have* implemented Enlightenment blueprints, and most of their members cherish the results and would not reverse or replace them. One should ask, of any new social policy or institution that one thinks is valuable, how well one would have anticipated its lived feel and impact on other facets of social and cultural life when it was still just an idea.

At any rate, liberalism in the wide historical sense has had two great phases: first, when it mostly consisted of ideas, only gradually and in the face of much opposition being implemented; then second, when not previously seen complexities occasioned in part by that implementation, and in part by advances in social knowledge (or what was supposed to be so), led to a rethinking of the first version. The first or classical phase of liberalism appears self-consciously in the mid-eighteenth century in France and Britain, from sparks held then and since to have been ignited by Locke. We might date this classic phase, very approximately, from 1725 to 1875. The second stage—reform, welfare, or perfectionist liberalism—first appears fully self-consciously in the work of T. H. Green, but was embryonic and half articulated in the earlier writings of Mill.

The differences between the two phases are considerable. They are most briefly discerned by reference to the distinction later drawn (by Isaiah Berlin) between positive and negative liberty. Negative liberty is the absence of formal bars and encumbrances; positive liberty is a genuine empirical possibility of availing oneself of something one has formal entitlement to. Everyone might be (negatively) free to become prime minister, or a mechanical engineer or university professor, or to come to own a Rolls Royce, but none of these things are genuine empirical possibilities for, perhaps, the majority of people. The political goal of reform liberalism is to secure positive and not merely negative liberty for ever-larger proportions of the population (ultimately, all of it), for the obtaining of goods that further human self-realization as creative, autonomous, integrated, socially conscious rational agents. Politically, this led to a complete reversal in liberal attitudes to the state: from suspicion and the favouring of a

minimal state to a developed conception and advocacy of a benevo-
lent, thermostatically interventionist state.[4]

With respect to ideas of human nature, this change reflects a
greater belief in human interconnectedness: our origins, development,
and well-being are thought to be bound up with close, mutually nurturing relations with those who share our society. It also involved the
incorporation of more explicit and detailed conceptions of a human
good or end. Hobhouse expresses this clearly and emphatically:

> The real man is something more than is ever adequately expressed
> in terms which his fellows can understand; and just as his essen-
> tial humanity lies deeper than all distinctions of rank, and class,
> and colour, and even, though in a different sense, of sex, so also
> it goes far below those comparatively external events which make
> one man figure as a saint and another as a criminal. This sense of
> ultimate oneness is the real meaning of equality, as it is the
> foundation of social solidarity and the bond which, if genuinely
> experienced, resists the disruptive force of all conflict, intel-
> lectual, religious, and ethical.
>
> But, further, while personal opinions and social institutions
> are like crystallized results, achievements that have been won by
> certain definite processes of individual or collective effort, human
> personality is that within which lives and grows, which can be
> destroyed but cannot be made, which cannot be taken to pieces
> and repaired, but can be placed under conditions in which it will
> heal itself by its own recuperative powers. The foundation of
> liberty is the idea of growth ... Liberalism is the belief that
> society can safely be founded on this self-directing power of per-
> sonality, that it is only on this foundation that a true community
> can be built, and that so established its foundations are so deep
> and so wide that there is no limit that we can place to the extent
> of the building ...
>
> ... freedom is only one side of social life. Mutual aid is not
> less important than mutual forbearance, the theory of collective
> action no less fundamental than the theory of personal freedom ...
>
> ... the organic view of society ... means that, while the life
> of society is nothing but the life of individuals as they act one
> upon another, the life of the individual in turn would be some-
> thing utterly different if he could be separated from society. A

[4] By a *thermostatically* interventionist state is meant one that does not
intervene in the social or economic worlds constantly and in principle, but
where interventions are judged necessary or desirable for preserving or
augmenting public good.

great deal of him would not exist at all. Even if he himself could maintain physical existence by the luck and skill of a Robinson Crusoe, his mental and moral being would, if it existed at all, be something quite different from anything that we know. By language, by training, by simply living with others, each of us absorbs into his system the social atmosphere that surrounds us ...

The argument might seem to make the individual too subservient to society. But this is to forget the other side of the original supposition. Society consists wholly of persons. It has no distinct personality separate from and superior to those of its members ... Thus, the common good to which each man's rights are subordinate is a good in which each man has a share. This share consists in realizing his capacities of feeling, of loving, of mental and physical energy, and in realizing these he plays his part in the social life, or, in Green's phrase, he finds his own good in the common good ...

... The good is something attained by the development of the basal factors of personality, a development proceeding by the widening of ideas, the awakening of the imagination, the play of affection and passion, the strengthening and extension of rational control ... it is the development of these factors in each human being that makes his life worth having. (*Liberalism,* pp. 65–71)

Official liberal theory—or rhetoric—has tended to be somewhat less expressive of semi-socialist commitments to social harmony and mutualism than Hobhouse's rather purple prose would suggest. Otherwise put, the "Humboldtian" note in modern liberalism appears most explicitly and fulsomely in liberal writings of the three successive generations of Mill, Green, and Hobhouse, and less openly or energetically since modern liberals have actually come to power. But the practice of liberal governments and administrations all over the western world since 1932 (when Franklin Roosevelt became U.S. president) has been to implement precisely the kinds of policies seeking to enlarge positive liberty that Hobhouse's views would prompt.

The liberal view holds that while biology, individual and that of our species, imposes certain constraints and boundaries, these are not great, indeed much exaggerated by other theories. Liberalism is conscious, and in fact a principal articulator, of so-called nature-versus-nurture questions. And for liberalism the nurture side almost always wins hands down. Such victory is by no means seen as guaranteed *a priori,* for liberalism views itself as empirically grounded. Experience, the facts of the matter, show that we are very malleable. Our nature has an extraordinary plasticity. This creates the immense potential that we have both for good and for evil. Again, let it be stressed, liberalism is not at the extreme pole of "nurturism" of, say, postmodernist and social constructionist views. For one thing, liberalism is objectivist: there are facts of the matter, independent of our wills, conceptual filters, or prevailing ideologies, and these include facts about people. *Some* of those facts about us will be biological and psychological givens, and will impose limits as well as creating possibilities for us. But for liberalism there is much less to these matters than conservatives, sociobiologists, radical feminist gender essentialists, and others make out. Liberalism will view the basic human clay as fundamentally similar; we are naturally or empirically approximately equal, as well as (fully) morally so.

On the liberal theory of human nature matters of social environment are central to how we will turn out. Parenting, kinds and degrees of affection, discipline, socialization, acculturation, formal education and its methods and norms—these matter, quite a lot. So too do physically nurturative matters. On the materialist/idealist continuum, as on others, liberalism is not emphatically at one pole. However, the weight given socialization in the liberal understanding makes the theory difficult to unite or reconcile with a pure materialism. If idealism is the position that ideas genuinely make a difference causally, then liberalism is an idealist stance.

Liberalism affirms human freedom. It will therefore contrast with some psychoanalytic, behaviourist, Marxist, and sociobiological views that doubt the reality or degree of free choice or action (at least, in the Marxist case, in existing societies). Mill, for his part, held that (genuine, metaphysical) freedom of action and complete causal determination are compatible, and both are true for us. That is, Mill was what in metaphysics and philosophy of action is called a compatibilist (someone who holds that actions can be both genuinely free and 100% causally predetermined). Few subsequent liberal thinkers were as philosophically wide-ranging as Mill, and liberalism as such takes no stand on such abstract questions. But it does affirm that capacities for free choice and self-direction are real.

Emphasis on social environment and individual freedom is what we may reasonably call an Aristotelian feature of a human nature view. There is a third such feature. Liberals, like Aristotelians (and many others, all of them doubtless deriving from a common Greek root), have a conception of human flourishing. We have a *telos,* a condition of being under which we thrive and deviation from which makes us wilt, or become ill, or non-human. The liberal *telos* is wider and less contentful than that of most other (and possibly any other) teleological or perfectionist theory. It is so wide and pluralistic that many critics of liberalism mistakenly suppose liberalism is non-teleological, or non-normative. At any rate, liberal humanity in optimally thriving condition is autonomous, self-directed, reality oriented, tolerant, and knowledge prizing. Green and Hobhouse would add "organic," or socially interconnecting, needs to this package. It is not clear that all modern liberals would fully share their view, though all envisage mutual support and nurturing as key components in any society that could achieve full human happiness. The liberal individual seeks exposure to a wide variety of human lifestyle models and needs. This needn't imply first-hand experience of them, but the liberal values diversity: knowing about alternative ways of living and valuing or at least tolerating a large number of these alternatives. The liberal views each individual human being as in an important sense a fresh start in the world. This is natural given liberalism's committed "nurturism," but not inevitable, for a nurturist could think, "All the more important, then, to get them while they're young and steer them to the one true faith and lifestyle." Liberalism, of course, does not take that view, being a philosophy of self-realization or self-actualization. We are all of us flowers of tremendous possibility, and markedly differing flowers. Some, from the experiences *they* have, might seek to crowd out the other flowers in the garden. This is non-thriving on their part and shouldn't be tolerated; it will be part of the social task that it not be.

Standardly taken to be almost defining of liberalism is commitment to a significant public/private distinction. It is not obvious how this might express features of a fundamental view of humanity, but in fact some important elements of the liberal view of human nature may be seen here. It must first be observed that this is another area of critics' distortions and caricatures. Some feminist critics, usually as part of finding fault with liberal feminism, even attribute to liberals the idea that the family, and all features of domicility, are parts of private life and therefore morally immune to state interference, whatever abominations take place there, typically through the actions of a domestic (usually male) tyrant. This is actually more or less the reverse of the liberal position, which is the first to authorize state interventions in domesticity to prevent just such tyrannies or abuse. Liberalism, if not quite anti-traditionary, accords no presumptive right or authority to individuals or institutions on the ground of long-standing exercise.

The liberal public/private distinction is indeed central for liberalism. It also historically has permitted, and morally and empirically does permit, shifts of boundary: some things once seen as private can in principle become public, and vice versa. There must, of course, be convincing ground provided for such boundary shifts, and they must rest on liberal principles; but they can and do occur. Just such shifts are at the heart of the development of reform liberalism from classical or libertarian liberalism, as the concept and the claims of positive liberty became articulated and applied.

The public/private distinction seems to go like this. (Mill's remarks in *On Liberty* are the chief textual basis for these claims.) An act is private only if all persons observing or participating in it consented to observe or participate. Since doing something implies having been able to do it, this will of course imply that if an act was private all involved were able—*genuinely* able—to consent, which is supposed to exclude minors, the deranged, and so on. As the idea of positive liberty is probed, and argued by many liberals to *expand,* a case can be made that someone might formally consent (say the relevant words, for example) but not really have been in a position knowingly and genuinely to consent. Reform liberalism here, as elsewhere, comes up against the charge or risk of paternalism, and here, as elsewhere, can avoid this hazard if care is taken.

We may plausibly see the public/private distinction as linked to a distinct set of liberal convictions about human psychology, and human nature broadly, namely that there is a world of difference between (mere) thought and action. As liberals see it, there are inner recesses for selves, where fantasy, imagination, uncritical opinion, prejudice, play, sport, and speculation may reign. The inner sanctum may be immoral, infantile, egotistical, embarrassing, or many other things. Though there are obviously *relations* between what people think and what they do, as liberals see it the world is safe, or safe enough, from what goes on in those inner private places, kept such. There are both empirical and moral dimensions to these liberal convictions. Empirically: liberals doubt that inner-sanctum contents are likely to lead to invasive or coercive acts directed against others. Morally: it is what people *do,* their actions or inactions, that justifiably warrant evaluation and sometimes interference.

Another expression of liberal optimism, or belief in fundamental human capacities for happiness and good, is involved here. In general, liberals hold that if broad social conditions are auspicious, human beings can be relied upon to develop and exercise autonomy, and sympathetic respect for the autonomy and personhood of others. They will not always or exceptionlessly do so; but liberal tolerance, and Millian strictures on the moral necessity of according unqualified private liberty where actions affect only oneself, rest upon or accompany a view of humans as capable of rational, intelligent, community-mindful lives.

It remains to make some comments on a particularly prominent contemporary advocacy of liberalism, that of John Rawls, most influentially in *A Theory of Justice* (1971) and quite recently in *Political Liberalism* (1993). These comments will be brief, since Rawls's project is one of attempting to argue for reform liberal moral, social, and political ends and values with a minimum of assumptions about human nature, and specifically without some key teleological assumptions we have viewed as central for liberal theory of humanity.[5] Rawls's moral theory is a sort of union of Mill and Kant, aiming to achieve the former's conclusions by the latter's methods.[6] Rawls does not argue for a human *telos,* and he assumes as contentless a notion of self-interest as he can and still derive political/moral liberal conclusions. In fact Rawls's political/moral liberalism is itself idiosyncratic, since it implies that no social inequality is justified except insofar as it tends to eliminate the disadvantages of the least advantaged members of a society. It is unclear that the reform liberal ethic as such holds to as stern and rigorous a code as this.[7] Certainly in political reality hardly any (if any) liberals have minded *some* unequal distributions of social goods, even where there is not even a pretence that such inequality helps the poorest. Indeed, one of the liberal values is diversity, a plurality of styles and options, more or less for their own sake. It is hard to see how a Rawlsian liberal state,

[5] In *Political Liberalism* (p. 18) Rawls indicates that his theory is conceived for *persons:* "It should be emphasized that a conception of the person, as I understand it here, is a normative conception, whether legal, political, or moral, or indeed also philosophical or religious ... As a normative conception, it is to be distinguished from an account of human nature given by natural science and social theory."

[6] This, of course, puts the matter somewhat too formulaically. That Rawls argues for something like Mill's conclusions (a social and political order aiming at pluralistic life-scheme realization for the greatest number of community members possible consonant with a modicum of autonomy) will probably not be disputed. But that he does so using Kant's methods may. By the latter I mean making an abstract case for a moral theory by reference to ideal models of rational agency. Rawls's version of contractarianism certainly attempts the latter.

[7] Though, in *Liberalism* (p. 70), Hobhouse takes a position close to Rawls's.

when it reached as near to its utopia as it could, could exemplify this value as abundantly as very many contemporary liberals would desire and value. If my distinctive lifestyle choice, for example, involved dressing up in particularly flashy ways, the absolute economic equality of all citizens—if I am living in Rawlsian utopia—might make this difficult or impossible to do.

This may seem a disappointingly brief discussion of the philosopher who for many is the most important and interesting liberal theorist of the present day. But Rawls's importance and interest come in significant part from the ambition of his undertaking in moral theory: to show how close to liberal goals and values it is possible to come from as universalist a position as is rationally defensible, making only such assumptions as all reasonable and fair-minded participants in moral theory (and not just those who from the outset will be liberals) can concur in. Even so, Rawls does make assumptions about human nature. Some of them are what I am calling modern liberal ones, such as that human flourishing is only achievable in autonomy and self-direction. Still, the Rawlsian human seems to need to be a kind of practical logician, who must determine his or her good in a set of calculations that will take account of the others in like case with himself or herself. This need not be the case for the modern liberal view, whose human being may make no efforts of this sort, or even need to be able to. A modern liberal theory of human nature can, for example, identify a faculty of *sympathy* as the basis for our mutual interest in our conjoint good. This would ground a modern liberal conception in positions more like those of Hume, Hegel, Schopenhauer, and Darwin than in the ratiocinative house, in Locke and Kant, that Rawls occupies.

The calculations alluded to in the foregoing are not, to be sure, computations that Rawls ascribes to or requires of actual individuals. Rawls is in *A Theory of Justice* endeavouring to determine what a just society would be like; he argues that its structure and institutions would need to be such that rational, self-interested, genuinely human individuals would choose those structures and institutions if they were constrained to make such society-forming choices from behind a "veil of ignorance" about their own life circumstances (including their talents and gifts). Some critics have argued (I think persuasively) that this "original position" is incoherent—that it either factors away traits and aptitudes without which the supposed chooser is not recognizably human or, if a real human is left, depending on that individual's actual traits the calculation in the original position could yield any of a number of incompatible social models, many of them anything but egalitarian or altruist. (I might, for example, decide—accurately or otherwise, but purely introspectively—that I am endowed with practical cunning quite sufficient to ensure my achieving favoured outcomes for myself, and so be quite willing to take my chances in an inegalitarian world.)

At any rate, Rawls's contractarianism seems alien in spirit to the perfectionist liberal view, which ascribes to human beings a more contentful nature than the occupiers of an original position can be assumed to have.

I have made much of inaccuracies and distortions in critics' accounts of liberalism. One might in turn wonder whether what I am claiming to be the real liberalism might not be so elusive or elastic that no objections or criticisms can touch it. Won't any expressed difficulty be dismissable with the immediate complaint that the critic has misunderstood, probably wilfully, his or her target?

There are problems in defining liberalism sufficiently specifically that it has credible alternatives. There *is* a sense, especially since the downfall of communism, that "everyone" now is a liberal, in at least a wide political sense. That is, there are no credible positions in the western (or ex-communist) world that would deny fundamental notions of human equality, autonomy, and basic rights, including some rights of adult conscience and judgement, even if the boundaries and full contents of these notions will be differently conceived and negotiated. Politically, and morally, there are perhaps several liberalisms, among them a wide liberalism whose embrace (even if with distaste for the label for many) few escape. Certainly the so-called communitarian positions of much recent discussion seem easily accommodated within this wide liberalism.

But of course we are, again, attempting to articulate and assess a specifically liberal image of humanity. I have argued that there is such a thing; indeed, that it is rich with content, and is or involves an interesting and plausible understanding of what we are. In this sense liberal theory of human nature is definitely not all-embracing or without major, plausible rivals (among them other theories discussed in the present book). For one thing, the liberal view is highly optimistic. It accords us the genuine empirical possibility of a quite large measure of self-knowledge, self-realization, and freedom, and holds that we can significantly escape or transcend both individual and collective pasts. And maybe we cannot, or cannot to the extent liberalism thinks, achieve any of these things.

The lines of the dubious form both to the right and to the left. Some critics, and advocates of alternative views of human nature, dispute the egalitarian claims liberalism makes. They hold that there may be or are deep differences, differences that matter, between some humans and others. Circumstances of early life, culture, class, biology, or logistical fortune may make for genuine prospects of autonomy, self-knowledge, and self-realization for a small minority of people and decisive exclusion from them for most others. These are views taken, from widely differing bases, by Aristotle, Spinoza, Nietzsche, Abraham Maslow, and sociobiology. The dim lot of the many may be regarded as a pity or not particularly mourned over; but substantive questions of fact are involved (some or most of them nonetheless difficult to decide on any present evidence).

Some positions deny even the serious possibility of an elite of happy self-actualizers. Again, some facets of sociobiology point in this direction, and the philosophies of human nature of Schopenhauer, Freud and, earlier, Hobbes emphatically assert it. Freud, like Spinoza, does allow the possibility, through the application of a certain rather specialized *rational methodology,* of a limited self-awareness and a correlative negative freedom. But all of these are philosophies that see the sunny liberal conception of the individual, who in a favourable setting will find or create his or her self, as a complete chimera. Freud thinks we all remain in a real sense lifelong children, and in any case never genuinely and stably happy; where Mill, Green, and Hobhouse suppose that we can grow up and be quite happy enough.

Other critics dispute whether liberalism's implied possibility of escape from historical, cultural, and class location is real or even meaningful. These objections are oversimplistic and distorting; liberalism does not need to hold that people are without these locations. Of course we are all born somewhere, in some setting of family, class and economic reality, culture, and history; and all of these shape and form us. Liberalism simply implies that we are nonetheless capable of rational agency; we can know what we want and who we are (including knowing some of the factors that formed us).

Another criticism accuses liberalism of diminishing or eliminating human responsibility. If only some of us have had earlier life circumstances permitting or encouraging genuine positive liberty, and still fewer a real flowering of our possibilities into a realized creative self, a considerable number of us—at least in most, not-yet-utopian societies—will be mired in some degree of unfreedom. Liberalism is egalitarian and nurturist and considers us, *ceteris paribus,* the best judges of our values and preferences. But the liberal tendency to see people as products of their background also tends to excuse, by explaining it, whatever someone may have done and however they may live. The Voltaire formula[8]—*tout comprendre, tout pardonner*—seems easily and frequently to fit liberals, in both their theories and in real-life practice. In this they differ from Marxism and some feminisms, which assign recalcitrant or retrograde behaviour to false consciousness, or inauthenticity. Liberals are paradigmatic multiculturalists (though some hesitate if they come to think multiculturalism threatening to the liberal society as such). Within their own culture or cultural group as in others, liberals will blame or censure, if at all, not a deviant or antisocial individual but forces and factors (including *other* individuals) that supposedly shaped the offending individual.

> Capitalism has severed the ties of personal dependence only to revive dependence under cover of bureaucratic rationality. Having overthrown feudalism and slavery and then outgrown its own personal and familial form, capitalism has evolved a new political ideology, welfare liberalism, which absolves individuals of moral responsibility, and treats them as victims of social circumstance. It has evolved new modes of social control, which deal with the deviant as a patient and substitute medical rehabilitation for punishment. It has given rise to a new culture, the narcissistic culture of our time, which has translated the predatory individualism of the American Adam into a therapeutic jargon that celebrates not so much individualism as solipsism, justifying self-absorption as "authenticity" and "awareness." (Christopher Lasch, *The Culture of Narcissism,* p. 218)

A strong indictment this, and eloquently worded. Much of Lasch's analysis seems acute and persuasive. There are grounds for qualification, however, and some degree of dissent. The vision of the therapeutic society condemned by Lasch is indeed set forth in many earlier versions of welfare liberalism, among them Hobhouse's *Liberalism* and some of Bertrand Russell's social essays. Liberalism, in its moral aspect, is not the same thing as democracy. The two embody distinct ideas, which have come into what now seems indissoluble conjunction over only about thirty years. Prior to this marriage, liberalism quite easily led to paternalistic intervention in private lives, and projects of rescuing people from themselves or their surroundings for their own good. Mill's *On Liberty* and the rights principles it encapsulates have always stood as a liberal bulwark against just

[8] From *Candide*.

such tendencies, at least applied to adults. This has historically been one of the dynamic tensions within liberalism; although it continues, the alliance with democracy has tipped the liberal scales in a Millian direction. At any rate, the liberal state now seeks, and finds, other than paternalistic grounds for its interferences with private choices. Mill condemned all state action directed at an individual contrary to his or her desires if motivated by the desire to improve or benefit the individual. The liberal state now justifies many such interferences not on this ground, but on the ground of social cost—excessive and unreasonable social cost—if the individual is permitted to pursue the contentious privately undertaken goals. Laws requiring seatbelt or helmet use and prohibiting "recreational" drugs (other than alcohol) illustrate the point.

Lasch is describing developments that did not go according to plan: a liberal paternalism that has affected population groups other than those involved in obvious victimization or self-victimization with consequent high social cost. This result is the "therapeutic" society, the "narcissistic culture" filled with self-absorbed people seeing themselves as victims and demanding compensation or rescue. Again, there seems to be some basis to his view.

Less clear is Lasch's contention that this development, or welfare liberalism itself, is some sort of inevitable dialectical expression of capitalism. Before the fall of communism in 1989, the (or a) capitalist economic structure was seen very widely by thinkers not only of left persuasions as much more external or peripheral or historically ephemeral than would now be held justified. It was common, then, to characterize current life as an embodiment of a "late stage of capitalism," clearly with the implication that this system had come to its sunset years. (One might easily imagine hopeful fourth-century anti-Christians before, during, or after the principate of Julian the Apostate, and aware of the three-century history of the hated system, referring to the Christianity of their day as a "late stage of Christianity.") Few would now feel so prescient. Doubtless capitalism will not endure forever, but its term seems now to be an exceedingly difficult matter to determine. It also seems more reasonable than formerly to think of competitive (more or less) free-market structures as endemic and internal to what the earth provides and permits and a convergence of the latter with human nature and human aspiration. There is a plausible Hegelian dialectical case for something resembling capitalism as inevitable and non-peripheral for socio-economic structures that could be satisfying for human beings.[9]

If this idea has merit it will make capitalism, because not so eliminable, less interesting for Lasch's kind of social and cultural analysis. It will provide capitalism with rather less aetiological work to do. Our narcissism, such as it is, will need another explanation. (Indeed, narcissism of Lasch's or comparable Nietzschean stripe seems easy to imagine in an affluent socialist economic order, with a life of bored abundance within a socially or publically owned, centrally planned system. People don't seem to need capitalism to be shallow, superficial, self-absorbed, or anomic.)

Still, Lasch's and others' central charge against liberalism withstands all of these qualifications. *Liberalism mollycoddles criminals.* It makes allowances, excuses, for people whom non-liberals think should have known better, could have refrained but chose not to, should be treated for once as responsible adults, made to answer for their deeds and misdeeds. The issues involved here are more complex than the permissive/non-permissive contrast suggests. For one thing, it is not altogether clear that liberal "softness" on malefactors reflects theoretical convictions that those misbehavers have less free will than other people. That doubtless covers some cases, both of liberals and of people they "let off the hook." But part of many or most liberals' view is that very severe punishment, no matter what the offense, is barbaric and unworthy of a truly civilized society. Liberals standardly oppose capital punishment, and not because they think those to whom it might apply always or usually had less control over their actions than others. Liberals want a kinder, gentler world and are willing to pay the price of an occasional monstrous misdeed, whatever produced it, not being visited with savage reprisal. In their zeal for such a world some liberals argue, in some cases it seems disingenuously, for lesser powers of self-control in the anti-social in general, sincerely

---

[9] This is, obviously, a large theme, and *many* will dispute the claim made or implied here. I note that a plausible case is not necessarily a sound or entirely correct one. I am thinking of the sort of case for capitalism—it is Hegelian—made by Francis Fukuyama in Chapter 8 of *The End of History and the Last Man* (1992). (Others have made similar arguments.) Briefly, the idea is that an almost or entirely centrally planned economic order cannot accord humans full autonomous adulthood, and also is logistically incapable of adequately utilizing or contending with human creativity (including market and consumer product creativity) and desires for consumer response to it.

believing (surely correctly) that *many* anti-social actions stem from less capacity for restraint.

I do not want to venture too far into the issue of the pros and cons of a liberal social ethic. As a view of people, liberalism does appear to "cocoon" humanity in a manner that many opposing spirits clearly do not like. They see a kind of inconsistency in liberalism's extreme nurturism alongside its indifference to the claim of nurturative culture and tradition, and above all the nurturative cultures and traditions of *majorities*. Liberalism also perhaps has too much to say about fair-weather conditions, how humans do or might flourish in the right (if necessary, socially and legally engineered) circumstances, and too little to say about what people are like when the going gets rough: when projects of social amelioration can no longer be afforded, during conditions of social stress or breakdown. "Liberty, as a principle, has no application to any state of things anterior to the time when mankind have become capable of being improved by free and equal discussion. Until then, there is nothing for them but implicit obedience to an Akbar or a Charlemagne if they are so fortunate as to find one," says Mill (*On Liberty,* p. 10), and the sentiment seems intended for other liberal goods than liberty. But the species didn't change when liberal programs and analyses first came into the world, about two centuries ago in two interesting but not peculiarly representative western societies.[10] Maybe there is more to learn and to know about human beings in conditions not necessarily conducive to the success of progressive liberal programs than liberalism can accommodate.

[10] Great Britain and France.

Bibliography

Elshtain, Jean Bethke. *Public Man, Private Woman.* 2nd ed. Princeton, NJ: Princeton University Press, 1993.

Fukuyama, Francis. *The End of History and the Last Man.* New York: Free Press, 1992.

Hobhouse, L. T. *Liberalism.* Oxford: Oxford University Press, 1964. [1911]

Humboldt, Wilhelm von. *The Limits of State Action.* Edited by J. W. Burrow. Cambridge: Cambridge University Press, 1969. [1835]

Jaggar, Alison M. *Feminist Politics and Human Nature.* Totowa, NJ: Rowman & Allanheld, 1983.

Lasch, Christopher. *The Culture of Narcissism.* Rev. ed. New York: W. W. Norton, 1991.

Manning, D. J. *Liberalism.* New York: St. Martin's Press, 1976.

Mill, John Stuart. *On Liberty.* Indianapolis: Hackett, 1978. [1859]

Rawls, John. *Political Liberalism.* New York: Columbia University Press, 1993.

―――――. *A Theory of Justice.* Cambridge, MA: Harvard University Press, 1971.

CHAPTER 6

Conservative
Individualism ——————

WE HAVE IDENTIFIED AND EVALUATED A LIBERAL
view of humanity. This stance was seen, with a number of qualifications, as a secularization of what we had called a Whig Christian
perspective, and in one line of development becomes the reform
liberal perfectionism of our century and the last generation of the
nineteenth. Within the formative period of modern Christianity,
understood for our purposes as approximately coinciding with the
"long" eighteenth century (1660–1820), we also discerned a Tory
stance. Its supreme Enlightenment exemplar is perhaps Samuel
Johnson (1709–1784), and acquaintance with its tones and textures
and many of its characteristic doctrines can best be made by reading
James Boswell's classic *Life of Dr. Johnson*.[1] This is not to make
any claim for Johnson's *influence* as a theorist, or location in a
particular intellectual tradition. Throughout our enterprise, the aim
is to delineate major views of humanity that numbers of at least
reasonably thoughtful contemporary people find compelling and accurate, and to draw upon the writings of someone who seems to have
expressed the view effectively. For this purpose Johnson seems ideal
as an embodiment both of Tory modern Christianity and of the theme
of the present chapter, conservative individualism.

We tread on ground rather more insecure in this case than perhaps in any other chapter. Though a good many writers and thinkers
of the past two centuries seem clearly to endorse the view of humankind we are calling conservative, no one stands out as promulgating
an explicit and systematic theory. Conservative theory tends rather

---

[1] Another conservative individualist text of importance is Bernard
Mandeville's *The Fable of the Bees* (1714–1732). This is the original and
classical formulation of the idea of private "vice" translating into public
"virtue"—later better known in Adam Smith's notion of the "invisible
hand" that achieves functional social and economic rationality from individual pursuit of self-interest. (Similar ideas, with different applications,
appear in Vico and Hegel.) The philosophy of human nature implicit and
sometimes explicit in Mandeville's work is a variant of the outlook explored
here.

to be implicit in the outlook of its adherents. Moreover, the conservative label will be found to collect together positions that are markedly at odds in *other* respects, indeed, that frequently hold their conservatism for apparently quite different reasons. Thus, the grounding of some conservatisms even of the present day is religious (and of non-Christian as well as Christian stamp); the basis of others is wholly secular and sometimes anti-religious and naturalist.[2] The latter is true, for example, of the philosophy of human nature developed and advocated by the novelist/essayist Ayn Rand (1905–1982). Rand's philosophy is politically libertarian, and I would identify most—not all—libertarian conceptions of human nature as conservative. (The exceptions are the *optimist* libertarians—the sunny-dispositioned folk whose confidence in their fellow humans is so great that they suppose that the removal of the boot of government, of police and tax collector, will lead to a broad thriving, material as well as moral, for humanity at large.) Other varieties of conservatism have Freudian, biological, and sociobiological bases. Some of these positions we discuss in independent chapters. In general, though, there is a tension between conservative and fully naturalist positions, for conservatives, even when non-religious, almost invariably believe in good and evil. (We might say, a little flippantly but not altogether inaccurately, that they may some of the time harbour doubt about good, but they are quite sure of the reality of evil. In this respect, as in others, they are a kind of mirror image of liberals, who tend to think of evil as a pre-civilized notion, something meriting relativizing and historicizing, but who have a firm conviction of good.)

Of course, good and evil do not always crop up in these theories under these names. The strongly normative tends in our time to appear in disguise. Thus *good,* for liberals, is to be met with as *positive, progressive, creative, constructive, enlightened, civilized, happy, advanced,* and *mature,* among other names. *Evil,* for conservatives, takes a variety of forms, among them *criminal, lazy, irresponsible, short-sighted, sadistic, psychopathic, frivolous, dark,* and *mean.* (This is not to say that these terms do not have clear empirical content in addition to the normative significance they have for liberal and conservative philosophies. Nor do either of these positions always refrain from explicit moral claim and commitment.)

[2] Naturalism, in the sense meant here, is the idea that there is only one universe, that it is the one the sciences explore, and that human beings are wholly a part of this universe.

Still, conservative views of human nature are by no means only or even primarily the expression of moral convictions. They are genuine positions on human nature. Even if lacking a leading systematizer, conservative philosophy of humanity involves a number of clearly discernible tenets. It is also extremely widely held in the general population. Both are very good reasons for including a conservative view as an important and distinctive contemporary vision of humankind.

For conservatism, in the sense intended here, is a way of seeing people. It believes that people have "natural" dispositions and qualities, whose origins may be regarded as unclear: traits may run in families or develop from signal early-life experiences, but mostly are just *there,* differentiating people into kinds, including inexpungeably hierarchical kinds, largely but not entirely somewhat negative kinds. Conservatism quite certainly "believes in human nature," believes it is something more or less stable, fixed, unchanging: a fundamental core characterizing human beings in general, then a range of typologies of humans, chiefly characterized in terms of clusters of disposition, temperament, and talent as well as gender profiles. These typologies and profiles tend to differ somewhat from conservative to conservative; their common feature is the affirmation of differences (within a common underlying psychological substratum), and the relative powerlessness of individuals, groups, or society at large to do anything, except harm, about these differences.

It should be remarked that major conservative political theorists, especially of the past, are typically not examples of what is meant here by (modern) conservative individualism. Classical political conservatism—whose outstanding representative is probably Edmund Burke—specially values the traditions and institutions of the culture's past, and (critically, for our purposes) never for wholly utilitarian or rational-prudential reasons. Classical political conservatism invests the cultural and institutional past with sentiment and imagination and, sometimes, the character of the sacred. A contemporary conservative individualist might or might not view his or her society's traditions and long-lasting institutions with sentimental or spiritual fondness. It will depend on what those traditions and institutions are. A century of life in a culture actively engaged in social engineering, were there a conservative individualist living at the end of it, would not inspire that conservative with spirited allegiance.

There is, I think, a good case for seeing the theory of human nature held by Hobbes and possibly Machiavelli as essentially of conservative individualist stripe. This outlook, then, is certainly not absent from the Great Political Philosophers; but neither Machiavelli nor Hobbes can be labelled classical (political) conservative theorists.

It seems particularly important to distinguish conservative individualist philosophy of humanity from conservative political ideas and programs, and perhaps especially from far right political views. To see the human world in conservative individualist terms is, as we have said, by no means necessarily to have any special hankering for traditional social structures or institutions. Nor need it be to yearn, secretly or otherwise, for a stern and forceful Leader, or nights of long knives to set matters right by clearing out degenerates, liberals, or the wrong kinds of ethnicity. Indeed, many conservative individualists actually have the courage of their convictions: they really believe that left-liberal utopianism won't work, indeed is so defective that it won't even succeed in gumming up the wheels and mechanisms of social, political, or economic life; that inevitably there are reversions to type, with the shrewd, the far-sighted, and the energetic maintaining the control of the heights they only briefly ever lose, and the indolent, the self-destructive, and the stupid, however they have been prodded, falling again by the wayside. And many conservative individualists are deeply convinced democrats: on Churchill's famous ground that, bad as democracy is, the alternatives are worse; or because they think that if people are determined upon folly, as they often are, they will engineer it whatever barriers are placed in the way; or out of a genuine commitment to, even sometimes love of, humanity. Conservatives typically think people are widely diverse in talent, energy, ethics, culture, and experience. Sometimes they cherish this human array, even if it does contain altogether too many knaves and fools. Often conservatives think they are realists, seeing the world and the people in it as they are, without the pink-tinted glasses—the (usually left-wing) wishful thinking—of other views. Conservatives frequently are cynical, even jaded, but on the other hand they can come to hope, and act on the hope, that—as they see it—intelligent, effective, directive, managerial leadership in political or economic life (though rarely in social or moral life) is possible. Certainly conservatives often are active and energetic participants in political activity; but sometimes it will be a formally liberal or even a social democratic party they support. And sometimes they sit altogether on the sidelines, entirely apolitical.

As remarked at the beginning of this chapter, no systematic thinker looms clearly as giving expression to the conservative individualist view of human nature. We noted also that Samuel Johnson may be regarded as an embodiment of the position, even if systematic theory will not readily be garnered from his writings and reported conversations. Further, Johnson is a Christian, and somewhat more aptly identified as representing what we have called the Tory modern Christian perspective than the conservative individualist stance familiar in the twentieth century. Still, among his voluminous writings and recorded conversations, on an immense range of topics literary, religious, historical, and anthropological, a considerable number might be cited as illustrating substantive parts of a conservative philosophy of humankind. Here is a representative sample, easily added to by dipping into Boswell. In many cases the view of humans expressed is implicit rather than explicit. It should also be noted that there is much more in Johnson than (as many will suppose) mere conservative philosophy of human nature, including views of humans that transcend this particular perspective.

> Human life is everywhere a state in which much is to be endured and little to be enjoyed. (*Rasselas* [1759], chap. 11)

> How small, of all that human hearts endure,
> That part which laws or kings can cause or cure!
> Still to ourselves in every place consigned,
> Our own felicity we make or find.
>> (Lines added to Goldsmith, *The Traveller* [1763–1764] [appearing also in Boswell's *Life of Johnson* (hereafter "LJ"), I.314])

> To be of no church is dangerous. Religion, of which the rewards are distant, and which is animated only by faith and hope, will glide by degrees out of mind unless it be invigorated and reimpressed by external ordinances, by stated calls to worship, and the salutary influence of example. (*Lives of the Poets* [1779–1781], Milton)

> Wickedness is always easier than virtue; for it takes the short cut to everything. (From Boswell, *Journal of a Tour to the Hebrides* [1785], Sept 17, 1773)

> I am a great friend to public amusements; for they keep people from vice. (*Life*, March 31, 1772 [LJ I.424])

> Life is a progress from want to want, not from enjoyment to enjoyment. (*Life*, May 1776 [LJ II.36])

Every state of society is as luxurious as it can be. Men always take the best they can get. (*Life,* April 14, 1778 (LJ II.203)

Most schemes of political improvement are very laughable things. (LJ I.374)

I would not give a half a guinea to live under one form of government rather than another. It is of no moment to the happiness of an individual. (LJ I.424)

There is now less flogging in our great schools than formerly, but then less is learned there; so that what the boys get at one end they lose at the other. (LJ I.589)

So far is it from being true that men are naturally equal, that no two people can be half an hour together, but one shall acquire an evident superiority over the other. (LJ I.318)

Providence has wisely ordered that the more numerous men are, the more difficult it is for them to agree in any thing, and so they are governed. There is no doubt, that if the poor should reason, "We'll be the poor no longer, we'll make the rich take their turn," they could easily do it, were it not that they can't agree. So the common soldiers, though so much more numerous than their officers, are governed by them for the same reason. (LJ I.374f.)

Raising the wages of day-labourers is wrong; for it does not make them live better, but only makes them idler, and idleness is a very bad thing for human nature. (LJ II.439)

The vulgar are the children of the State. If any one attempts to teach them doctrines contrary to what the State approves, the magistrate may and ought to restrain them. (LJ II.466f.)

Mrs. Knowles affected to complain that men had much more liberty allowed them than women. JOHNSON. "Why, Madam, women have all the liberty they should wish to have. We have all the labour and the danger, and the women all the advantage. We go to sea, we build houses, we do every thing, in short, to pay our court to the women." MRS. KNOWLES. "The Doctor reasons very wittily, but not convincingly. Now, take the instance of building; the mason's wife, if she is ever seen in liquor, is ruined; the mason may get himself drunk as often as he pleases, with little loss of character; nay, may let his wife and children starve." JOHNSON. "Madam, you must consider, if the mason does get himself drunk, and let his wife and children starve, the parish will oblige him to find security for their maintenance. We have different modes of restraining evil. Stocks for the men, a ducking-stool for women, and a pound for beasts. If we require more perfection from women than from ourselves, it is doing them honour. And women have not the same temptations that we have; they may always live in virtuous company; men must live in the world indiscriminately. If a woman has no inclination to do what is wrong, being secured from it is no restraint to her. I am at liberty to walk into the Thames; but if I were to try it, my friends would restrain me in Bedlam, and I should be obliged to them." MRS. KNOWLES. "Still, Doctor, I cannot help thinking it a hardship that more indulgence is allowed to men than to women. It gives a superiority to men, to which I do not see how they are entitled." JOHNSON. "It is plain, Madam, one or other must have the superiority. As Shakespeare says, 'If two men ride on a horse, one must ride behind.'"

(It should not be inferred from the fact that Johnson was what we may call a defender of gender inequality that conservatism as such is so. In the contemporary world there are many conservative individualists of both sexes who are gender egalitarians. Conservatives tend to favour only gradual change, where they favour change at all; many now will be of the view that western societies have over the course of recent decades become sexually egalitarian, and—so long as misguided efforts at implementing positive liberty from above are not attempted, and so long as the nuclear family preserves its social centrality and fosters lovingly raised children—this is altogether satisfactory.)

The conservative view of human nature has one thing going for it that is perhaps insufficiently appreciated: a considerable majority of western culture's folk sayings and bits of common wisdom (and, it appears, those of most other cultures) are pieces of conservative philosophy of humanity. This has huge significance: it suggests that conservative philosophy closely fits basic common-sense intuitions capturing what large numbers of people deeply believe about themselves and each other, and find confirmed by ongoing life, generation upon generation. Consider:

Hew not too high lest the chips fall in thine eye.

Before you trust a man, eat a peck of salt with him.

A fool and his money are soon parted.

When poverty comes in the door, love flies out the window.

Three may keep a secret, if two of them are dead. (Benjamin Franklin)

Experience keeps a dear school, but fools will learn in no other. (Benjamin Franklin)

When the well's dry, we know the worth of water. (Benjamin Franklin)

Misery loves company.

It would be a lot easier to become self-sufficient if someone would help you.

One could add to these a huge and evidently widely endorsed genre: the aphoristic quip that appears with unfailing regularity in most morning newspapers and many other mass media. Those of contrary persuasion—and they will include proponents of many of the other theories in this book—may smile, sneer, feel sorrow, anger, or knowing condescension, but these pieces of folk wisdom seem to express what a considerable majority of the general adult population think their own observations have taught them about human nature.[3]

A tacit human nature theory is discernible in these and countless other aphorisms. What is depicted is a world of fools and knaves, and rare individuals who have natural virtue, kindness, or heroism. On the whole, though, humanity is assigned a natural indolence, a difficulty in learning what is genuinely to human benefit except through slow and usually painful experience, with a predisposition to narrow (and typically only short-sighted) self-interest. Wanting something for nothing, or for as little expenditure of effort or resource as possible (and less than the thing is worth), vain, fearful, gossipy, back-biting, complaining, following the crowd, easily duped, slow to learn, even slower to gain wisdom or perspective, indifferent to if not positively delighting in the misfortunes of others, greedy, prepared to step on others to gain desired ends, dishonest, self-deceptive: this

---

[3] Assuming, of course, that newspaper editors and similar persons are correct in judging that their readers appreciate and tend to nod assentingly when they read these pearls.

is the, or a, conservative portrait of humanity, or at any rate of a very wide swath of it.

Of course, many other philosophies will assign such traits and character types, even if granted to fit most of the population, to class division, false consciousness, insufficient maternal love in early life, inadequate social planning, lack of affordable quality daycare, or other conditions emotional, physical, or structural. These conditions not only explain, exculpate, and excuse, but also offer promise of a transformed tomorrow if people would only resolve to do things as the philosophy in question advises. The conservative is skeptical about all such promises. He or she thinks human nature has a leaden constancy to it that invariably defeats the utopian designs of the do-gooders, reformers, and revolutionaries. Moreover, the conservative thinks, these interfering schemes will, more or less invariably, do more harm than good.

What may be said to be wrong, or problematic, for Dr. Johnson's view of humanity? Where do critics see difficulties for the conservative understanding of our condition?

Liberals, feminists, and "progressives" broadly tend to exhibit considerable impatience with conservative views, a contemptuous, slightly irritated peremptory dismissal of them as things one should not still need to talk about, old-fashioned, naive, rustic positions. But lots of people hold conservative views, and new believers—young, middle-aged, and old—return to or come round to them.

So why shouldn't they? What is the case against a conservative view of humanity? As elsewhere, we face the delicate need to differentiate moral and political from putatively descriptive or empirical positions. Conservatives think we are significantly free, and yet often make short-sighted, self-injuring—stupid—uses of this freedom. It seems odd that we would. One would think that evidence of human ineptitude should be also evidence of limitations and qualifications in human freedom, should diminish the meaningfulness and the blame-ability of human agency; or else this ineptitude should be viewed as something else, as cunning, a high degree of practical rationality, even if directed to ignoble ends. (This is sometimes, or in part, the conservative view—conservatism is, again, the systemization of the conviction that original sin is real, whether or not God is.)

There seems in both alternatives (which, strangely, conservatives don't seem to see as inconsistent with each other), to be an unwillingness or lack of interest in attempting to *explain* human conduct. *Why* do those urban underclass people behave as they do? Why does the "booboisie"[4] vote, year in and out, so foolishly on the basis of personalities or empty, superficial, ideological banalities? Explanation may need to come to an end somewhere, but conservatives seem too willing to abandon the trail of inquiry too soon. It is easy to suspect that there is a *fear* that the Voltaire maxim—to understand all is to forgive all—just might be true, and so one is going to make sure that there is not the slightest danger that one has understood all.

Yet of course there are enigmas, among them enigmas in people. Why might we not just be a crowd of rather porcine creatures, with better possibilities we *could* act on but just tend not to, predispositions we could and sometimes (rarely!) do overcome, but just don't typically *try* hard enough to? And, it may be protested, this will put the conservative account of human psychology too uncharitably. Conservatives believe that human beings generally *need* to go through a certain amount of struggle to gain things they seek and value, or attainment of those things will bring less satisfaction, and their own character will be worsened. We are like that, they hold: if things come too easily for us, we don't appreciate them. We gain not just morally but teleologically—in our thriving, our optimal condition—if we have worked, if some adversity has been confronted and overcome, if elements of doubt, toil, and tears were involved.

Some version of this view will probably be agreed to by more or less everyone. (Possibly some kinds of anarchists would be exceptions.) Most people will suppose that having to do practically or literally *nothing* for one's bread or gain or good or pleasure is not particularly good for human beings. That is, they do not thrive if this is their case: they wilt, falter, become mentally and physically not in good form. Doubtless this reflects evolutionary history. We are in general, at least, naturally selected for genuinely satisfying levels of satisfaction only after some expenditure of labour has occurred. Before Darwin provided a modern and scientific basis for this evident (if elastic and imprecise) fact about us, there had been an arguably not more stern biblical one: "In the sweat of thy face shalt thou eat bread, till thou return unto the ground" (Gen. 3.19) had been part of the divine penalty for disobedience, part of having lost Eden. Dreams of

---

[4] This was the term coined by the satirist, political commentator, and scholar H. L. Mencken (1880–1956) to denote the American populace at large. Mencken's general perspective on human beings shows him to be a very good case of a conservative individualist—with the qualification that his harsh strictures seem peculiarly limited to American humanity, not humanity in general.

something for nothing have been recurrent throughout human history in, it seems, most or all cultures (accompanied, usually, by stories of how undesirable it would be to have such dreams come true).

The conservative image of humanity sees us as needing carrots and sticks to act well, to create or achieve results of value, or even to do anything at all. (Simplistically, the liberal image might be said to hold that carrots alone will suffice. Conversely, some conservatives seem to have held that sticks—the right ones—are both necessary and sufficient for human results.) As intimated, some version of this idea can be granted while still leaving a great deal undetermined. For example, it is not at all obvious that our carrot-and-stick needs, whatever they may be, imply that such welfare provisions as medicare and unemployment insurance are not good for human beings, and impair their well-being. The boundaries of our needs in these directions seem in general exceedingly difficult to specify with precision.

It seems, then, that a conservative view of humankind, as well as being less curious and probing than it appears reasonable to be, is both vague and over-inexact in respect of fundamental and central features of its psychology. One can—and should—grant the conservative nugget, without needing to take along with it the accompanying surround and shell.

Bibliography

Boswell, James. *The Life of Dr. Johnson.* 2 vols. London: J. M. Dent and Sons, 1958. [1791]

Mandeville, Bernard. *The Fable of the Bees.* 2 vols. Indianapolis: Liberty Classics, 1988. [Reprint] [Originally published in several editions 1714–1732]

O'Sullivan, Noël. *Conservatism.* New York: St. Martin's Press, 1976.

CHAPTER 7

Rousseau ——————

JEAN-JACQUES ROUSSEAU (1712–1778) MORE THAN
any other single individual is regarded as having formulated the ideas
that usher in the so-called Romantic Age and end the Enlightenment.
There is, of course, something artificial about such claims even
where they have a considerable degree of truth; but Rousseau's
importance in the history of ideas would be difficult to exaggerate.
Many applaud and many regret his great influence, but few deny it.

Like other thinkers of the western European Enlightenment,
Rousseau identified the study of humanity as a unitary, focused intellectual undertaking, of high importance and with reasonably straightforward prospects of success. "The most useful and least advanced of all
human knowledge seems to me to be that of man," he begins the preface to the *Discourse on the Origins and Foundations of Inequality
among Men* (the so-called *Second Discourse*) (p. 12).[1]

As a theorist of human nature, Rousseau is important not just in his
age and for the generations immediately following his death, but as the
chief formulator of an image of humanity that continues to be extremely
influential and widely encountered. Indeed, there is a good chance
that the reader has views about humanity and its relations to nature
and civilization that stem at least in part from Rousseau's ideas.

Like all ideas, these have their own ancestry, and others besides
Rousseau gave expression to them or variants during the Enlightenment. Not so clear is that these views are in themselves particularly
obvious or "natural," though they now widely seem so.

As Rousseau saw things, there is for humans a natural condition
or state, in which they flourish and out of which they do not. So far,
this is a teleological conception of humanity with obvious resemblance to that of Aristotle and others.

Rousseau thinks there are two principles that operate in human
beings "anterior to reason" (*Second Discourse*, p. 15). One of these

[1] Citations are from R. D. Masters and C. Kelly, ed., *The Collected
Writings of Rousseau*, Vol. 3: *Discourse on the Origins of Inequality
(Second Discourse), Polemics, and Political Economy* (trans. J. R. Bush,
R. D. Masters, C. Kelly, and T. Marshall).

principles "interests us ardently in our well-being and our self-preservation." The other one "inspires in us a natural repugnance to see any sensitive Being perish or suffer, principally those like ourselves" (ibid.). Rousseau makes clear (ibid.) that the first principle has precedence, both empirically and morally, over the second. Both, however, are fundamental in us, and from their conjunction Rousseau derives human sociability. The second principle by itself makes the case for our inherent natural goodness. Indeed, all humans are actuated, unless and until civilization ruins them, by the maxim "Do what is good for you with the least possible harm to others" (*Second Discourse*, p. 38). A human being is naturally, moreover, "a compassionate and sensitive being" (*Second Discourse*, p. 37).

The *Second Discourse* traces human development from conditions of pure animality to those of complex modern state-societies. Rousseau speculates about and proposes explanations of a variety of fundamental features of human life—language, nationality, familial structures, various forms of economic organization, technologies, the relevance of geographical factors to cultural types, and other topics. His account is targeted upon the idea already highlighted, of a supposedly natural, changeless human mode of being in which we find our fulfillment, our *telos*.

For Rousseau the natural human condition is one of inherent goodness, and contentment in a life of simplicity, in small communities of somewhat rudimentary technology. The operative idea is one of harmony with a surrounding and nurturing natural and social habitat. As with Aristotle—indeed, more so—we are a species unable to be whole except in a web of relations to other humans. To this Rousseau adds the necessity of our integration into a natural environment of objects and processes whose reality and meaning for us is familiar and intuitive. In this integrated condition humans are largely benign, not particularly given to competition or aggression. This is a state of nature that—unlike those of Hobbes or Locke—is satisfying and happy, and, barring natural calamity, a sort of Eden. In this rustic simplicity the natural human lives in inner harmony and peace with his or her fellow members of the community. That condition, Rousseau supposes, is still to be met with in some "New World" parts of the globe (the Americas and the Pacific) where large state-societies had not yet significantly obtruded by the mid-eighteenth century (but which they were in the course of contacting and ruining, then and subsequently, as they had done in earlier cases).

The serpent in what once was Eden was the development of large-scale societies. (Rousseau usually just identifies "Society" as the villain,[2] but since he clearly exempts small tribal societies, and also the scale and pattern of life of a Swiss canton like his own native Geneva, this is evidently his meaning.) Society led to war, classes and class oppression, and a general condition of misery. These deplorable and anti-human results were not particularly a function of elemental human traits. Rather, they come about (one speculates—Rousseau himself does not say) partly from large population increases and other environmental stresses. One might think of the sorry condition of animals kept in zoos or other captivity, hothouse or cabin-fever circumstances that produce destructive (self-destructive or aggressive) behaviour that isn't "natural" to the creature, and would not obtain but for these deeply infelicitous conditions. But at least as much as from environmental stresses, our descent from natural virtue is due to our propensity to knowledge and technological skill: the cultivation of our inventive capacities, which lead to implements and methods of tyranny and war.

In *The Social Contract* (Book I, Chapter 1) Rousseau asks himself how a natural condition of liberty has given way to one in which the many are enslaved by the few. His answer: "I do not know." But in the *Second Discourse,* and elsewhere, some parts of a more informative answer are given or implied. In *Émile* (1762) Rousseau says: "What makes man essentially good is to have few needs and to compare himself little to others; what makes him essentially wicked is to have many needs and to depend very much on opinion" (p. 214). But whence comes many needs? Not, for Rousseau, from within, from a dynamic internal to the human species. Many needs arrive, it would seem, from systemic enlargement and complexity: from luxury and a plurality of options. This is an old idea, particularly to be met with in Rousseau's sources, in accounts of the corruption of original Roman republican virtue. For Rousseau the rot sets in much, much earlier.

> As long as men were content with their rustic huts, as long as they were limited to sewing their clothing of skins with thorns or fish bones, adorning themselves with feathers and shells, painting their bodies with various colors, perfecting or embellishing their bows and arrows, carving with sharp stones a few fishing Canoes or a few crude Musical instru-

[2] Late in his career, in 1772, Rousseau was to sum up his views as founded on the "principle that nature made man happy and good, but that society depraves him and makes him miserable" (*Rousseau, Judge of Jean-Jacques* [the *Dialogues*], in *Collected Writings of Rousseau,* Vol. 1, p. 213).

ments; in a word, as long as they applied themselves only to tasks that a single person could do and to arts that did not require the cooperation of several hands, they lived free, healthy, good, and happy insofar as they could be according to their Nature, and they continued to enjoy among themselves the sweetness of independent intercourse. But from the moment one man needed the help of another, as soon as they observed that it was useful for a single person to have provisions for two, equality disappeared, property was introduced, labor became necessary; and vast forests were changed into smiling Fields which had to be watered with the sweat of men, and in which slavery and misery were soon seen to germinate and grow with the crops.

Metallurgy and agriculture were the two arts whose invention produced this great revolution. For the Poet it is gold and silver, but for the Philosopher it is iron and wheat which have Civilized men and ruined the human Race. Accordingly, both of these were unknown to the Savages of America, who therefore have always remained Savage; other Peoples even seem to have remained Barbarous as long as they practiced one of these arts without the other. And perhaps one of the best reasons why Europe has been, if not earlier, at least more constantly and better Civilized than the other parts of the world is that it is at the same time the most abundant in iron and the most fertile in wheat. (*Second Discourse*, p. 49)

Men are wicked; sad and continual experience spares the need for proof. However, man is naturally good; I believe I have demonstrated it. What then can have depraved him to this extent, if not the changes that have befallen his constitution, the progress he has made, and the knowledge he has acquired? Let human Society be as highly admired as one wants; it is nonetheless true that it necessarily brings men to hate each other in proportion to the conflict of their interests, to render each other apparent services and in fact do every imaginable harm to one another. (*Second Discourse* [Rousseau's Notes], p. 74)

And of course these unfortunate developments are precisely what has occurred over most (and eventually, it is feared, all) of the globe. "Man is born free, and yet we see him everywhere in chains" (*The*

Social Contract, p. 5). State-societies have fostered systematic division and aggression, war externally with rival states and internally in civil struggles that invariably culminate in the domination of the miserable many by the privileged few. Our interim hope can only be in the creation of societies that will unify their citizens in conditions of equality and mutual identification (fraternity); this alone can yield the liberty that is our natural condition. Even so, ultimate salvation lies in a return to simplicity and harmony with nature: we've got to get ourselves back to the garden.[3]

From Rousseau's perspective civilization—with its legal codes and other institutions, and its increasingly encumbering creations, social and technological—is alienating to humanity. We are not meant to live in cities, not big ones, anyway, and natural life requires freedom from magistrate, police, and government.

(We see, then, the central importance of Rousseau in the intellectual ancestry of Marx as well as Thoreau, Baden-Powell, and Heidegger.[4] Marx, importantly, makes alliance with industrial technology, which is to be mastered and put to the betterment of life for all; in this he departs significantly from Rousseau.)

Rousseau's portrait of the "natural" and "original" human, as opposed to the "artificial" and "socialized" one, is painted repeatedly in his writings, and is a central and familiar part of his view of the world. It corresponds to the contrast he draws between the "Savage" and "Civilized" or "sociable" human—the savage and the citizen, he sometimes more briefly styles them. Even if it would be in many ways desirable, Rousseau does not think it possible to reverse history. He seems to intend to show just how bad that history has been, what it has cost us, and the value and importance of small-scale life

---

[3] I deliberately choose a "Woodstock generation" phrase to bring out Rousseau's resonance with many perspectives of that generation. Rousseau did not in fact think "savage society" could be recreated in the world, although it seems clear he viewed this as a great pity.

[4] Henry David Thoreau (1817–1862) celebrated and wrote about simple self-reliant rural life, in harmony with nature. Lord Baden-Powell (1857–1941) founded the Boy Scouts, a movement for educating the young to collective versions of such self-reliant harmony. Martin Heidegger (1889–1976) left a philosophical legacy attacking technological modernity, in favour of the model of an artisan's harmony with self and nurturative surrounding community.

and of preserving the surviving cases of it.[5] By implication, the possibilities of human happiness must, it is clear, be based on learning from and replicating these lessons. The investigation of the savage is explicitly intended to offer a sort of experiment, and to reveal aspects of human nature as such, which Rousseau does not see as eradicable or alterable in its core components.

Almost all of the features of the savage—the original and natural human being—are for Rousseau virtues. Among them is the fact that the savage is, in Abraham Maslow's famous later phrase, inner-not-other-directed. "The Savage lives within himself; the sociable man, always outside of himself, knows how to live only in the opinion of others; and it is, so to speak, from their judgment alone that he draws the sentiment of his own existence" (*Second Discourse*, p. 66).

Rousseau's depiction of the savage, original human may suggest a greater individualism in his view than he seems to intend. I have stressed the harmony with nature and other humans, our interconnectedness, in Rousseau's understanding of our natural condition. His idea of a society that would be humanly fulfilling for humans who have known civilization, implicit in that portrait, becomes explicit in *The Social Contract*. Here we learn of a "general will," that will be other than a majority preference in a society; it is, rather, a shared apprehension of social resolve, desire, and valuation, in which the citizen will submerge their individuality, or at any rate their individual perspective. It is left unclear—and is certainly politically problematic—how this shared social resolve will be arrived at. In this general will will be formed not only efficient, non-fractious government, but general happiness and fulfillment. It is this idea perhaps

[5] "Human nature does not go backward, and it is never possible to return to the times of innocence and equality once they have been left behind. This too is one of the principles on which he has most insisted. So that his object could not be to bring populous peoples or great states back to their first simplicity, but only to stop, if it were possible, the progress of those whose small size and situation have preserved from such a swift advance toward the perfection of society and the deterioration of the species ... He ... worked for his homeland and for little states constituted like it. If his doctrine could be of some utility to others, it was in changing the objects of their esteem and perhaps thus slowing down their decadence ... But despite these distinctions ... the large nations [applied] to themselves what had been intended only for small republics" (*Collected Writings*, p. 213; the passage is from *Rousseau, Judge of Jean-Jacques,* where Rousseau surveys his own work in the third person).

more than any other that has led some commentators to see Rousseau as a leading contributor to the development of totalitarianism.

The Rousseau depicted in the foregoing is primarily, it should be stressed, the Rousseau of the *Second Discourse* and other essays on nature and education. Although also brought into this account, the Rousseau of the *Social Contract* may seem not easily to fit into the picture of human nature these writings fashion.

The Social Contract (1762) sets out an ideal model for legitimate government, according to Rousseau: it depicts how things would work if they proceeded as they should, from the first formation of a state to a structure of institutions, and the basis and rationale with which they would bind humans together into a society of and for themselves. Because this model is ideal, it is not always clear how Rousseau thinks it relates to actual human history, or future possibilities for human social organization. The potential for confusion is augmented by the fact that in the *Social Contract* there appear to be just two conditions in which humans can find themselves, but the *Second Discourse* implies that there are at least three. The ideal model of the *Social Contract* distinguishes only the so-called state of nature and a state-society that has been formed by a social compact; but in the *Second Discourse* there are also societies that are not state-societies. These are the tribal societies of the New World (and, Rousseau supposes, originally also in the Old World): nomadic, hunter-gatherer, pastoral, or settled agricultural societies, somewhat loosely structured (it is not obvious that all or any of them are conceived as founded by a social compact) and that the *Second Discourse* regards as representing the happiest, most fulfilling condition human beings have ever known, or could know.

> This period of the development of human faculties, maintaining a golden mean between the indolence of the primitive state and the petulant activity of our amour-propre [self-love] must have been the happiest and most durable epoch. The more one thinks about it, the more one finds that this state was the least subject to revolutions, the best for man, and that he must have come out of it only by some fatal accident which for the common utility ought never to have happened. The example of Savages, who have almost all been found at this point seems to confirm that the human Race was made to remain in it always; that this state is the veritable youth of the World; and that all subsequent progress has been in appearance so many steps towards the perfection of the individual, and in fact, towards the decrepitude of the species. (p. 48f.)

To be candid, my own view is that Rousseau was a thinker who, characteristically, allowed himself to be seized with the theme and the mood of an occasion. So seized, he would deliver himself—sometimes brilliantly and sometimes not—of what that occasion called forth, without particular regard for what other occasions had elicited. The result is, I believe, formal inconsistency on a number of topics; or, where not quite inconsistent, Rousseau addresses topics in altogether different ways on two separate occasions. In the *Social Contract* Rousseau's topic is, more or less: "How would a legitimate and moral state have been set up, and how would it sustain itself, if there were such a state?" Here he engages in something like what some twentieth-century philosophers have called rational reconstruction, which, while it is supposed to apply to empirical realities, need not be particularly closely prompted or capable of monitoring by them. A rationale for a society that would exist *of right* (*de jure* and not merely *de facto*) is, perhaps, as distant from a survey of developmental stages of social organization, and assessments of each stage's fit with a supposed transhistorical human nature, as could be. In the latter mode Rousseau is normative philosophical anthropologist; in the former, abstractive political philosopher.

Whether Rousseau is in fact inconsistent, it seems not unreasonable to claim a higher consistency for his overall view of the human, social, and political worlds. If rational-reconstructive ideal models for *anything* empirical are feasible or sensible, they must permit some sort of mapping upon concrete empirical realities.

The difficulty in the present case is that *The Social Contract* seems to imply that a morally legitimate and humanly satisfying modern state-society is possible, whereas the anthropological ruminations of the *Second Discourse* seem to imply that it is not. The issue is whether nature and civilization can, for Rousseau, be satisfactorily blended or united.

The account of Rousseau's theory of human nature I have given has attempted to amalgamate some of the apparently conflicting thematic ideas just indicated, from what are acknowledged to be sometimes sparse clues. I take it that the central datum is Rousseau's vision of what a humanly fulfilling society might be like. He sees such a society as, above all, harmonious and egalitarian. I have also taken it that next in order of value is simplicity, for how else can one interpret Rousseau's paeans to Amerindian and Polynesian tribal life and that of the Swiss canton? The paradigm for a society that could *have* a general will is then—though Rousseau does not say this explicitly—just such a small-scale social order. Still, *The Social Contract* sometimes hints at the possibility that a large state might have a general will and be, presumably, capable of satisfying human nature.

Regardless of Rousseau's thoughts on the prospects of human happiness within state-society, his portrait of "natural humanity" seems to have a certain coherence, whatever its plausibility, and to be the theory sketched here. It is that portrait which has exercised continuous influence in the western world, from its first being penned to the present day. Rousseau's model for the just state, while it undoubtedly played a formative role in the philosophy and institutions of the first French republic (and *may* have a place in the ancestry of twentieth-century conceptions of total organic societies), otherwise has no current purchase even in political philosophy. Hence it seems wholly reasonable to accord the theory of natural humanity central focus in discussing Rousseau's view of human nature.

Twentieth-century western cultural life finds familiar and natural a deep polarity that we may identify by clusters of concepts. On the one side we group together analysis, logic, reason, the formal, and theory, and on the other emotion, intuition, the informal, and anti-theory. (The first is close to Nietzsche's Apollonian; the second might be characterized as a calm version of the Dionysian, if this is not oxymoronic.) Both lists are easily enlarged. Some feminist theory has seen this putative divide as signalling a gender contrast: either an unjustified male-posed polarity, male alleged superiority supposedly contrasting with female inferiority (the males typified by analysis, reason, etc., the females by emotion, intuition, etc.); or—standing the latter on its head and effecting a Nietzschean transvaluation—a justified expression of difference between the sexes, with women's putative empathic and contexual knowing at least as good as supposed male analytical rationality.[6] At this stage I don't particularly want to explore or comment on sex or gender dimensions to this alleged polarity. Instead, I want to make two *historical* claims about the polarity itself.

First, this contrast, in our culture so widely seen as natural and obvious, is difficult to find earlier than the later eighteenth century;

---

[6] This contrast has also been identified as *cultural,* marking a fundamental divide between a putative logocentric, analytical, and imperialistic West and an intuitive, empathic East. For this version of the contrast, its origins in the eighteenth-century West, its flowering in the nineteenth and twentieth centuries, and its refutation as bogus, see John M. Steadman, *The Myth of Asia* (1969). Sometimes this idea contrasts the supposedly ratiocinative West with Third World tribal or aboriginal societies.

sufficiently difficult that it is plausible to view the polarity itself as only appearing in the world in the European Enlightenment, and as *not* reflecting any universal way of carving up the realms of ideas or people. Of course, this historical claim, if correct, will have implications for gender theory: males who have thought their gender different and better because more rational, and females who have thought their gender different and at least as good or better because more contextual, are both wrong.

The claim itself should perhaps be enlarged upon. Normative contrasts between reason and unreason go very far into the philosophical past. The man—or, on Plato's view, woman—of reason is celebrated throughout Greek philosophy, very centrally and subtly in Plato. The opposing human type, the slave of irrational passion, makes the contrastive note. Plato's portrait of the appetite-driven bondage of the unphilosophical soul, sometimes achieving proto-Freudian colour and depth, is one of the literarily as well as intellectually impressive features of the *Republic*. Stoic and Epicurean thought, but especially the former, augments this polarity. Long before the end of antiquity, then, it has become an archetypal idea-complex, an identifying badge, of philosophy and philosophers. Thus we find it reappearing in essentially Stoic form in Spinoza's *Ethics,* and in Hume's insouciant, reason-denigrating reversal of the model with the famous slogan that reason "is and ought only to be the slave of the passions."[7]

But this antique duality is not the one that appears in the eighteenth century in Rousseau, and after him in several of the thinkers of the Romantic Age. Half of it is the same: the model of cool, dispassionate, analytical rationality, only now transmuted into something obtuse, clumsy, ham-fisted, and linked to commerce, war, and empires of various kinds. The opposing theme is not, however, irrational desire or emotion but a new kind of Knowledge: a form of intuitive knowledge unattainable via analysis, holistic anti-theoretical and anti-theory knowledge, direct, subjective, and empathic. Platonic rationality was not anti-emotional. The vision of the form of the good is passional, perhaps mystical; for Plato mysticism does not preclude mathematics, systemacity, providing a theoretical account, definitions, necessary and sufficient conditions, cutting up conceptual pie. For Plato they all go together. Similarly, Spinoza's intellectual love of God involves a passional attitude towards the universe, and knowl-

[7] *A Treatise of Human Nature,* II, 3, p. 415.

edge of it; a calm passion, to be sure, but one happily combining theory and feeling.

I cannot here pursue these ideas, their histories and inter-relationships, and their place in contemporary culture. I will leave it at a claim that, I think, the cultural record justifies: opposition between analytical intelligence and intuitive intelligence cannot be traced with any clarity or confidence before the generation of Jean-Jacques Rousseau.

The second historical claim I want to make is that Rousseau himself was chief architect of the reason-versus-intuition contrast. Certainly in him the contrast finds full expression. Rousseau distinguishes, in strongly valorized fashion, the natural from the artificial, feeling from reason, and the contextual from the atomically individual, throughout his work celebrating the life of intuition and anti-theory. This was a large part of his appeal: legions of readers then and since have been drawn to his speaking for the heart, and an ideal of natural empathic understanding that does not require and indeed will oppose technocratic expertise and rational structures of ideas remote from common, bodily experience.

Rousseau does have one important predecessor in respect of the reason/intuition divide. This is Pascal,[8] in whose *Pensées* a number of elements of our contrast may be found. There are, however, important differences. Pascal was above all in the grip of religious passion. He wanted deeply to have grounds for his Christian beliefs, but did not find the standard arguments persuasive, so his highly inventive intelligence was put to work to find other indirect bases for belief. Thus the celebrated wager argument[9] was engendered, and a theory of reasons of the heart that may be superior to reason, that is, to matters of argument and evidence.

Pascal aside, there is little theory of anti-theory before Rousseau, and nothing like the developed contrast of style and perspective that we find in, and ever since, Rousseau. Since him there has been a con-tinuous stream of mockers of Official Reason, who scold and denounce and deny scientific rationality, often in very shrill and dogmatic voice, and usually in the name of human integration and opposition

---

[8] Blaise Pascal (1623–1662) was a French mathematician and religious writer.

[9] Which argued that it is more rational, in terms of a calculation of possible gains and losses, to adopt religious belief than not to; even if (as Pascal held) reason is completely powerless to justify such belief.

to polarities. (And so we find the continual paradox, that those most opposed to bipolarity are those guiltiest of it.) Kierkegaard, Wittgenstein, Rorty, postmodernism, and much feminist theory are examples.[10] Doubtless new writers and thinkers will for some time to come "discover" yet again that analysis is falsification and the quest for general theory illusion, and evidence of character flaw.

Alongside Rousseau, other thinkers played a formative role in the opposition to the Enlightenment and the creation of the Romantic Age and irrationalisms beyond it, reaching to our own time. Most important of these is Johann Georg Hamann (1730–1788), who even more thoroughly and dramatically than Rousseau embodies implacable opposition to theory and reason and a passional commitment to intuition and feeling. He was little known beyond German-speaking Europe, but his influence was considerable, upon Kierkegaard as well as the German Romantic thinkers. Nonetheless, although a distinctive conception of human nature is also to be found in Hamann's work, it is on balance wholly right to see the Romantic legacy as most importantly due to Rousseau alone. Hamann is religiously preoccupied in a way and to a degree that is more backward looking than innovative; though a pronounced irrationalist, he seems more naturally conceived in the company of the reactionary aristocrats, like de Maistre and de Bonald, than with the new tide of simplicity and feeling that Rousseau represents. Still, Hamann has an important place in the fabric of creative opposition to the Enlightenment, and would have a yet larger significance had he lived and written three or four hundred miles further west and in French or English.

One might reasonably see some of the roots of Rousseau's view in primitive Christianity, both in the highly valorized ideal of the innocence of children expressed by the Jesus of the gospel narratives, and in the Protestant revivals of ideals of Christian simplicity in the sixteenth and seventeenth centuries. It is clearly no coincidence that Rousseau was a product of Calvinist Protestant Geneva: that is, Rousseau's advocacy of natural, rustic simplicity in a community of the like-minded is not unlike Anabaptist and Calvinistic notions of communities of the saints, who had sought to emulate the Old Testa-

[10] Søren Kierkegaard (1813–1855) was a Danish religious philosopher whose work celebrated both the existential solitude of the individual and the idea of truth as passional and subjective. Ludwig Wittgenstein (1889–1951) was an Austrian philosopher whose mature work attacks philosophical theory. Richard Rorty is a contemporary American philosopher and postphilosopher.

ment patriarchs in technologically simple and personally unadorned conditions of rural or small-scale wholeness of heart.

On the other hand, it seems mistaken to discern a very long or "natural" history for Rousseau's philosophy of humanity. He is quite importantly original, his ideas not quite like any that went before. Attempts to revive primitive Christianity above all sought methods of bringing Christian believers closer to God and to winning favour in his eyes. This is very different from the idea that nature made and meant humans for a condition of communal rural simplicity that contrasts with the artificial results of life in cities and with advanced technologies. Rousseau was a theist and a (certain kind of) Christian—Protestant, Catholic, then Protestant again—but his is a secular philosophy of human nature. Indeed, at least as important a source for his outlook as extra-episcopalian Christianity is the Enlightenment revival of selective parts of the Greco-Roman heritage, chiefly the Roman contrast (which now mostly seems to us sham) between the virtue of the early Roman republic and the sophistications and corruptions of the late republic and principate.[11] For Rousseau this will have been encountered especially in Livy, Tacitus, and Plutarch. Rousseau's natural, original humans are less like people of a recovered childhood innocence sufficient for entry into the kingdom of heaven than they are like the republican hero Cincinnatus, Roman patriot citizens of plain food and dress, moving comfortably between farm, senate, and defence of the homeland in the ranks of a citizen army. Yet here too we locate a source only, a stimulus and model, for what is principally Rousseau's own idea.

Rousseau's conception of the "natural" self gives rise as well to the idea of a true, core, inner self that may be hidden from view, undeveloped, still only potential, but nonetheless there to be discovered.[12] This would be the real "me," possibly at variance with how I behave and what I consciously believe about myself. This development is in part just a case of the old (possibly the oldest)

---

[11] These Roman notions seem unpersuasive to us because we know the scions of the early republic were slaveholding oligarchs with patriarchal powers of life and death over the members of their households. They were brutal, ignorant, and blindly patriotic. These Roman notions also don't impress us as they did eighteenth-century thinkers because we are aware of the degree of ideologically constructed nostalgia in the writers of the imperial period.

[12] The germ of this idea may be discerned in part in Rousseau's influential novel about education, *Émile*.

philosophical contrast between appearance and reality. How something appears to be may, but also may not, coincide with how it is. Rousseau adds here, however, the idea of a reality that is stable and constant.

Popularized diffusions of Rousseauism—*very* familiar in our day—particularize the idea of the core self: an important and perhaps the most important quest a contemporary human can undertake is to discover the being or person that they really are. My core self may be importantly dissimilar from yours. Indeed, it may be that each core self is qualitatively unique. The latter possibilities make Rousseau-esque conceptions of natural and real or core or inner selves not readily labelled "essentialist." Each of us may have our own "essence" in these terms, or there might be types or kinds of us (possibly your soul-mates will be those with the same or a similar inner self); but there needn't be a core self-nature common to all human beings as such, or even to all males and all females as such.

The Rousseau (or Rousseau-esque) conception of the possibly hidden natural or inner self should not be confused with the ideal of self-knowledge. The Socratic injunction to know yourself may presuppose that there is a self to know, but it doesn't assume that that self is stable or natural—a fixed changeless hard jewel to which one should remain true, or something not shaped by civilization or culture. The Socratic idea, in other words, is wider and makes fewer assumptions.

There are many conceptions of selves and identities that human thought has conjured up. A fuller exploration of these would take our inquiry into empirical cultural anthropology. I want chiefly to suggest that Rousseau's notion *is* just one of these peculiar cultural products, a piece of eighteenth-century folkways that has managed to persevere in our culture, and not something necessary or natural to the investigation of human identity and nature.

The ancient Romans had an interesting conception in this regard—yet another piece of cultural anthropology. This was the notion of the *genius* that was sometimes held to attach to a family or clan—a *gens*—and sometimes to the individual. The genius was a sort of tutelary spirit, personifying the distinctive traits of the family line or individual, including ideas of zenith and nadir—the highest and lowest that that clan/individual was capable of. One could and possibly *should* be guided by one's genius. It was a beacon and a totem, what one should be true to, have faith in; it also embodied one's fate or destiny. Attunement to one's genius (in some idioms one's *star*) implied that one could possibly (dimly) discern that fate or destiny, which one should then accept. Julius Caesar is described as having a pronounced and developed version of this Roman belief. The idea resurfaces in western Europe in the sixteenth century, doubtless through the "humanist" reappropriation of the pre-Christian classical texts that effectively defines the Renaissance; and we find it frequently in Shakespeare.

I mention this cousin conception to Rousseau's partly for its own sake, but more because no one would now take it to be literally true. It is a picturesque way of thinking of one's life and nature and their determinants, but no one literally has a genius in this sense. Many people do, however, think they have permanent core selves, which astrology or books from the self-help section of the bookstore might help them to discover and be guided by. How much of this fact of contemporary society and marketing should be laid to Rousseau's door is unclear; certainly some of it should be.

From a number of the foregoing remarks it will have become clear that I am unable to take Rousseau quite as seriously as some of his twentieth-century scholarly admirers do. At his best Rousseau writes quite well, with psychological skill and a penetrating sense of what, in our century, became styled the subtextual. It is hard to believe that there could have been a Hegel had there not first been a Rousseau, and without him there fairly certainly would not have been a Marx.[13] Moreover, the central idea Rousseau developed, of the natural core self discernible and recoverable for us by tribe as well as individually, was not just hugely influential; it evokes affirming response almost universally. It is obvious enough that there is a way someone is without cosmetic adornment, physical or non-physical, and this is a truer and more fundamental self. Affectation, disguise, simulation, self-deception, mannered presentation of someone one is not—these are all real and familiar experiential phenomena, as is the encounter in another (can one *encounter* it in oneself?) of what it is to be refreshingly artless, straightforward, natural. The dream of *honesty* is part of the same complex, the idea and the hope of being able to offer and meet with elemental honesty about oneself, about others, about human feelings. Tell me who you really are, what you really feel, and let me tell you the same things about me: lovers say they want this from each other, parents from their children as also children from their parents, and others from others. There is surely

---

[13] Some of the very considerable impress of Rousseau on Marx will be discussed in Chapter 8.

something here, something to this; and Rousseau is, among other writers and among other things he has to say, fastening sometimes compellingly upon this something.

The problems with Rousseau's view of humanity, and the many that stem from or resemble it, are multiple. There are difficulties of both content and methodology. The latter are more serious than the former, because they impede correction or revision of contents. As befits a "natural" philosophy of humanity, Rousseau's rests heavily on intuitions that are not felt to require much testing. Rousseau does, as was observed above, take (some) "first nations" societies—particular Amerindian and Polynesian societies he knew of from explorers' books—as models for and evidence of the characteristics of natural or original humans. It seemed clear to him that these people were both free and happy, and that most of his fellow Europeans were neither. This body of data, and the largely impressionistic response it produces in Rousseau, is a rather slender empirical base for the theory of human nature Rousseau develops. The chief enemy to the truth having been artificial theorizing, one is almost supposed to know elementally, from one's pores as it were, what being human is and should be. The obfuscating chains and the artificial polish of urbane rational culture having been dropped, primeval understanding is supposed to register itself, and guide individuals and collectivities more or less unerringly to their good. Rousseau himself, like other confident human intuitionists, certainly felt that this happened in his own case.

The results Rousseau was guided to seem in some respects reasonable, in others true only of some people, and in still others deplorable. Some of these results are notorious: his view of male and female natures, for example. It turns out that males alone were really born and meant to be free, Robinson Crusoes fashioning a rustic citizenry with nature and other males, and females were meant to be their thralls, living to please and serve them.[14] Rousseau's sexism is so pronounced and overt that it seems now almost a joke. Curiously, he is scolded and then the sin is rather quickly dismissed by the

[14] Rousseau's account of females, nature, and the natural is usefully discussed in Susan Moller Okin, *Women in Western Political Thought* (1979), Part 3.

many feminists who otherwise admire Rousseau and his ideas.[15] Yet his sexism has the same source as most of the rest of his philosophy of humankind: the ur-impulses and intuitions that did not have, and he never felt needed, any foundation in long or patiently developed observation of human life. It is difficult not to feel that Rousseau comes to the world not as its student but as its teacher.

In spite of the enormity of his impact, as a best-selling author in his lifetime and to the beginning of the nineteenth century, and to the present hour as a formative influence on a wide range of currents in both popular and theoretical culture, Rousseau's writings can now seem somewhat dated. The contemporary reader must often make considerable effort to enter into his pages with sympathy, respect, affection, or identification. He remains easy to read: chatty, conversational, spirited, epigrammatic, full of pointed remarks that rise, fall, and dash about the page. One knows he is Important, a big figure in the fabric of our culture, and it is easy to make something, adversarily or otherwise, of what he has to say about the sexes, education, the state of nature, and other themes. But there is also, frankly, a let down. Kant interrupted his routines for *this?* What could have been in the heads of the west Europeans that they found Rousseau so mesmerizing, so stimulating of thought and action that the Bastille fell and Napoleon rose to victory and power in part because of him? There is hardly a chance that he can *live* for us as he did for them. This may be said even as we acknowledge that there continues a huge and rich Rousseau scholarship and many individuals, some acculturated to the Enlightenment and others not, who find themselves drawn to Rousseau's writings and his ideas.

What I have said may seem grumpy, or insufficiently historically sensitive. But it does seem fair, and accurate, to say that the modern reader, new to the texts of Rousseau, will likely find a certain flatness, a valedictorian quality, of rhetoric, and few official themes that engage the modern mind. They will also find Rousseau's appeal to the heart and to the natural; and part at least of the reason he will seem stilted and dated, on so many topics, will be the extent and depth of his influence. He made themes and values we know well familiar, and internal; made it possible that they should become old

---

[15] Among feminist essays seeking to make a positive case for Rousseau may be noted Penny Weiss, "Rousseau, Anti-feminism, and Women's Nature," *Political Theory* 15 (1987), 81–98, and Penny Weiss and Anne Harper, "Rousseau's Political Defense of the Sex-roled Family," *Hypatia* 5, no. 3 (1990), 90–109.

hat, and also receive more sophisticated or at least better disguised redeployment. And some of Rousseau's non-contemporaneity clearly is mere cultural distance and difference. The nineteenth century is the day before yesterday for us, but the eighteenth is at a further remove. One feature of that greater remove is the significance, and its peculiar character and colour, that the ancient authors and models (above all Cicero, Horace, and Plutarch) had throughout the eighteenth century. We cannot easily don the mantle of Roman republican virtue as the *lumières* did.

One could share Rousseau's conception of the contrasting natural and artificial humans but disagree about what either or both were like. Rousseau's view of human nature includes, of course, both the contrast and what he imputes to each as contents. There is reason to disagree with both these parts of his view.

One does not have to be a social constructionist to find it implausible that there is such a thing as a single natural (contentful) condition or state for humans, all departure from which is artificial. Even a fundamentally teleological conception of humankind does not require Rousseau's view. How could the real human *telos* be so well hidden, and so rare, as Rousseau's theory implies? Why not suppose we ought to be able to find it in at least a wide array of the circumstances in which human beings are found to live? Can they have been that inept at securing the habitat and institutional structures that conduce to their good? If so, that very ineptitude, and not only a simple goodness, needs to be included in the portrait of our nature.

Humans, in fact, appear to be far more comfortably adaptable and adjustable than is supposed by Rousseau (and some other teleologists). Humans are omnivores, the creatures that if given lemons by life tend to find a way to make lemonade, beings that live in every terrestrial climate, and sometimes seem to like artificial things as well as "natural" ones.

Rousseau's image of us is one that would preserve, indeed enforce, innocence. Some views—the conservative, Freud's, some liberal ones—deny that there was that innocence in the first place to be preserved or enforced. Even if there was, we seem drawn as naturally to the bright lights of the city—which of course we created in the first place—as to the plain food and social and institutional contours of the rural canton or village.

Bibliography

Berlin, Isaiah. *The Magus of the North*. New York: Farrar, Straus & Giroux, 1994.

Horowitz, Asher. *Rousseau, Nature, and History*. Toronto: University of Toronto Press, 1987.

Hume, David. *A Treatise of Human Nature*. Oxford: Clarendon Press, 1978. [1739–1740]

Masters, Roger D., & Christopher Kelly, eds. *The Collected Writings of Rousseau*. Translated by Judith R. Bush, Roger D. Masters, Christopher Kelly, & Terence Marshall. Vols. 1–3. Hanover, NH: University Press of New England, 1992.

Okin, Susan Moller. *Women in Western Political Thought*. Princeton: Princeton University Press, 1979.

Rousseau, Jean Jacques. *Basic Political Writings*. Indianapolis: Hackett, 1987.

—————. *Discourse on the Origin of Inequality*. Indianapolis: Hackett, 1992. [1758]

—————. *Émile*. Edited by A. Bloom. New York: Basic Books, 1979. [1762]

—————. *The Social Contract*. New York: Hafner, 1947. [1762]

Steadman, John M. *The Myth of Asia*. New York: Simon & Schuster, 1969.

Weiss, Penny. "Rousseau, Anti-feminism, and Women's Nature." *Political Theory* 15 (1987).

—————, & Anne Harper. "Rousseau's Political Defense of the Sex-roled Family." *Hypatia* 5, no. 3 (1990).

CHAPTER 8

Marx ————————————————

KARL MARX (1818–1883) WAS A NATIVE OF TRIER, about fifteen kilometres east of the German border with Luxembourg. Of middle-class family, Marx studied at the universities of Bonn and Berlin. He is the first significant theorist of human nature who obtained a Ph.D., in 1841. (His doctoral dissertation was entitled "The Difference between the Philosophies of Nature in Democritus and Epicurus.") The philosophical climate of Marx's university days was heavily dominated by the ideas of Hegel, and Marx became and remained in a meaningful sense a kind of Hegelian. He worked as a journalist, newspaper editor, political activist, and voluminous writer. Only some of his writings were published in his lifetime, most notably the revolutionary tract *The Communist Manifesto* (1848), co-authored, as others of his writings were, with his colleague and friend Friedrich Engels (1820–1895), and two major works of social and economic analysis, the *Critique of Political Economy* (1859, the same year as Darwin's *Origin of Species*) and *Capital* (Volume I, 1867; two posthumous volumes also appeared). In the sixty-year period following Marx's death other notable work was published, most importantly the *German Ideology* (1932), the *Economic and Philosophical Manuscripts of 1844* (1932), and the so-called *Grundrisse,* or "Fundamental Outlines" (*Grundrisse der Kritik der politischen Ökonomie,* published in Moscow in 1939–41). Marx's correspondence is also a rich source for his views. Some discern importantly differentiated stages of development in Marx's ideas in the large body of his writings, from more Hegelian and philosophical foci in the earlier writings to more empirically grounded economic analysis in the later. Others stress a fundamental unity at all stages of his thought.

Marx, of course, was not just a theorist. Philosopher, moralist—though both of these labels he explicitly repudiated and scorned—economist, and sociologist, he sought to change world history, and, it is beyond dispute, he did. Marx is the single most important and original advocate of revolutionary socialism. He thought his historical and economic analyses showed that world-historical development was leading, in a lawlike manner, to the supersession of capitalist societies and their universal replacement with a socialist and ultimately a communist order. In the course of shaping these analyses—in the course, in brief, of creating Marxism—Marx developed a distinctive and significant account of human nature.

Marx's image of humanity was until 1989 one of the major conceptions of human reality. Few views have exerted a greater influence among so many people in so many countries, and few have been so widely and magisterially put forth as providing a science of human nature (as of human history, and economic processes). This view constituted a vision of what we once were; are now, in estrangement from ourselves; and can be in a transformed socioeconomic order. The Marxian vision had a power and a hold that were deep, compelling, and imaginative. This was true even for thinkers not living within communist societies, and hesitant to proclaim Marxism the science of human nature and human history. During much of the post–World War II period Marxism, pure and classical or in modified form, was the *Weltanschauung* of very broad segments of the intellectual classes of Latin America, East Asia, the European continent, and widely in the English-speaking world.

Few views have fallen as far as quickly. With the collapse of the communist regimes of Eastern Europe and the more or less total moral eclipse of communism in China (also definitively, in 1989) this faith, framework, vision has plummeted. It is, of course, completely non-rational if not irrational that it should have done so because of this collapse. Few Western Marxists were uncritical admirers of communist societies; it was commonplace to deny that any of these societies were good exemplars of Marx's views and values. Nonetheless, the energy and much of the life has gone out of Marxism since 1989.

Marx continues to be read and studied, but a more historical and fragmentary Marx now receives most of this attention. He always was food for scholars and scholarship; now he is little other than this. Influences, lines of ascent and descent, a place in intellectual history and the history of contemporary life from just the day before yesterday: these are the keynotes around which Marx-thought now clusters. Whether this remains the case will have to await future developments. There seems little reason to anticipate a large-scale Marxist revival, even among people employed by universities. Still, it seems unlikely that Marx's ideas will wholly disappear from the forum of contending and seriously considered views. There are still university Marxists, even if far fewer than formerly. And there is good reason to expect that among generations yet to be born Marx's outlook will evoke response. For even if flawed, even if more heavily dependent on predecessors—Rousseau, Hegel, Saint-Simon—than is often acknowledged, Marx offers a detailed and comprehensive analysis of our condition and its possibilities, one that unites earlier insights in novel ways.

Like Rousseau, Marx is an organicist and anti-individualist. One of the large issues in human nature theory is the extent to which individual identity is constituted by the individual, to some degree independently of the groupings and communities he or she is part of while developing, and the extent to which those groups comprise that individual without remainder. These ideas, of the relative roles of individual autonomy and of relevant enveloping social units, appear to exhibit a continuum that is not easily differentiated. This seems accurate in spite of strong claims made for marked contrasts between allegedly individualist (or "atomic individualist") theories and group- or community-based ones. Our formative human nexus of family and surrounding social order and culture matters immensely, essentially; and we do achieve meaningful individuality. (Generally, both a social and an individual component are important. Rare human cases appear to have drawn exceedingly little from early-life circumstances, or to never arrive at adult autonomy.) "Individualist" and "organicist" are best seen, then, as terms for *tendencies* in human nature theories, with those so labelled open to criticisms of a measure of blindness or insufficient attention to the role or the reality of the group or the formed human being in their picture of human life—a measure only, if we are not engaging in polemics or hyperbole.

"Organicism" seems more apt for Marx than "social construc- tionism." Strictly, a social constructionist could allow the creation, and the subsequent personal and social reality, of significantly atomic individuals, needing only to insist that social forces (for contem- porary social constructionists necessarily *hegemonic* social forces) would have constituted those individuals. But for organicism we never do or could escape or transcend the web of "social relations." The sixth and seventh *Theses on Feuerbach* give this view expression in Marx's terms:

> (*vi*) Feuerbach resolves the religious essence into the *human* essence. But the human essence is no abstraction inherent in each single individual. In its reality, it is the ensemble of the social relations ... (*vii*) Feuerbach does not see that the "religious sentiment" is itself a *social product,* and that the abstract individual whom he analyses belongs in reality to a particular form of society. (Marx and Engels, *Basic Writings on Politics and Philosophy,* p. 244f.)

This is given still sharper and more scientific form in *Capital,* where, Marx declares:

> Individuals are dealt with only in so far as they are the personifications of economic categories, embodiments of particular class relations and class interests. My standpoint, from which the evolution of the economic formation of society is viewed as a process of natural history, can less than any other make the individual responsible for relations whose creature he socially remains, however much he may subjectively raise himself above them. (*Basic Writings on Politics and Philosophy,* p. 136f.)

A theory like Marx's that sees human identity as socially constituted (with the details of the constitution supposed to be a matter of relations to modes of production), that denies a significant historical or socioeconomic role to individuals, above all in terms of their emically constituted projects and values, will easily lead to a conception of considerable human interchangeability, and a deeper ontic anchoring (i.e., fixed existential location) in the class or society than in the individual. It seems right, then, to see Marx as an organicist, without meaning thereby that he altogether neglects the individual. Critics of Marxism therefore do seem to have a point in their claim that authoritarianism is non-accidental to Marxism; that being a genuine democrat and a genuine Marxist may indeed be, if not quite impossible, something requiring art, self-discipline, and conscious attention to the claims of individuality. There is no conflict between Marxism and genuine compassion for and outrage about human suffering, especially when caused by capitalism or capitalists. But the fully democratic note is something else.

At any rate, for Marx the full formation of the human individual requires the reality of others and interconnection with them. There is no *me* unless there is a *we:* "Man is a species being."[1] That phrase is Feuerbach's, giving expression to a core idea of Hegelian philosophy. Hegel also conceives humanity as incomplete without community, yet he, like Aristotle, comes to a mediated position that preserves significant individual autonomy, even if within a web or network of social relations. In Rousseau and Marx we find a submersion of the individual within a social collectivity that is somewhat alien to Aristotle and Hegel. The latter pair are (in spite of the ana-

---

[1] Karl Marx, "Estranged Labor," in *The Economic and Philosophic Manuscripts of 1844* (p. 112).

chronism of the label) liberals. Theirs is the path of moderation, that characteristic liberal value; of acceptance of pluralist compromise, respectful of human diversity; their outlook is imbued with an admiring advocacy of polities and other transformations or stases that will (and can only) grow organically out of what has preceded. Unlike them, Rousseau and Marx want the world made over, and think it can be. They are radical, utopian, profoundly at odds with the world they find and disaffectedly live in.

In calling Marx "utopian" I mean that he envisages a future society substantially different from the present one, that will be as good as the present one is bad. He believes, of course, that it is possible to bring about this future order, and possible to sustain it indefinitely once achieved. Describing such a view as utopian is not meant to imply that these beliefs of Marx are untrue. Utopian visions have been realized in some cases. At the same time, the label "utopian" is a somewhat sensitive one for Marxism. As part of the process of distancing his ideas from mere philosophy so that they can lay claim to being science, and adding to this the novel dimension of *praxis*— seeking not merely to understand the world but to change it—Marx makes much of repudiating philosophers and speculative idlers, dismissing them as armchair utopians. Among the thinkers so viewed are Hegel and Saint-Simon. Nonetheless he owes much to both, and sometimes acknowledges both debts.

Like Hegel, Marx seeks to understand change, above all historical change—change that matters for human beings—in terms of dynamic evolutionary processes that have a logic and rationale that is universal. There are laws of history, and laws of human nature, even if—for some this is paradoxical—these include laws of freedom, which in turn involve laws applying to things without a fixed content or nature. Hegelianism is the first version of existentialism, though entirely without its radical and lonely individualism. In acting—in history, and by means of activity in history—a human being creates himself or herself. A blank shell of possibility gives itself (and is given) content, in interaction with other selves and with an enveloping natural habitat. Like Hegel (and Aristotle), Marx is a sort of naturalist: we are organic parts of an organic order; all that we can know in a systematic, theoretical, or scientific way is confined to that order. Also as with Hegel and Aristotle, for Marx there is nonetheless an irreducible chasm between the reality of conscious agency, the free ones who create, and inanimate nature. Marx's much-vaunted materialism is therefore somewhat hollow. Other evidence will show the same thing.

Marx's image of humanity is the Hegelian one of the essentially free being who creates a nature and a world for himself and herself through labour—the appropriation and refashioning of material reality. This is the Marxian view even though the causal order is inverted from Hegel's. For Hegel, ideas people have had find expression in the material world that they transform, implementing those ideas; for Marx it is material reality that fashions and shapes our ideas. Nonetheless, we are the creatures who fulfil ourselves—create ourselves—in work.

As with Rousseau, our condition became unhappy and unsatisfactory long, long ago, in the first formation of societies beyond a simple level of structural or economic organization. Both Rousseau and Marx hypothesize a creatively self-realizing stage at the dawn of history, or pre-history. Thereafter, for both thinkers, alienation from our "real" selves has been our general condition, and for both this came about through the development of fissures between some humans and others. Our identities for both Rousseau and Marx being essentially social, these fissures are not between one individual and another, but between one group of individuals and another. Again, both Rousseau and Marx identify these social fractures as coinciding with the rise of (private) property. Sundered—alienated—by class and the having or lack of property, we cannot become whole, cannot become ourselves, until classes and (materially significant) private property are dissolved in an organically unitary future world in which all humans will be brothers and sisters. Rousseau did not prophesize or advocate the realization of this dream through armed revolt of the oppressed many. But those who read his work and acted under his aegis—the creators of the French Revolution and the first French republic—did. So here too Rousseau is the prefiguring model for the structural blueprint of Marx's conception of history, human nature, and humanity's condition in history, and the transformative seizure of the world for the realization of our *telos*.

Claude-Henri de Saint-Simon (1760–1825) is another of the many "lesser" thinkers with an interesting and distinctive philosophy of human nature that we will be unable to do other than sketch. Although the man and his ideas were in part eccentric, and the ideas were never fully or adequately developed, Saint-Simon has an important place in the history of ideas, obscured by the greater fame that came to his one-time follower Comte. Saint-Simon analyzed history as class struggle, with the few oppressing the many and masking their control by ideological mystification. This is precisely what we find in Marx. (Features of this understanding will also be found, still earlier, in Giambattista Vico's *New Science* [three editions: 1725, 1730, 1744].) Also like Saint-Simon, Marx has a profound belief in the liberating powers of applied science. Unlike Rousseau, and quite at odds with the prevailing anti-industrialism of the creative writers and most of the philosophers of the Romantic Age, Marx held that scientific technology held the key to smashing the otherwise unendingly revolving wheel of history. The cycle of class warfare, of one group seizing power (often in the name of the many) from a previous gang of thugs can for Marx (and Saint-Simon) only be ended by the really large scale, global mastery of environmental transformation that came into the world concomitant with capitalism. Better living through chemistry: only that better living is to come about not through the actions of the Du Pont family or company, or their like, but through the appropriation and direction of technological ingenuity by the majority for the majority. The seeds, and quite a lot of the flower, of these ideas are to be found in Saint-Simon, who had his cairn of recognition as a founder of socialism in the Kremlin.

There are other important prefigurings of Marx's ideas in Rousseau, Hegel, Saint-Simon, and other thinkers than those mentioned. Always, though, there are also differences. Marx is without Rousseau's romanticizing of the simple, natural, rustic life. However impaired his version of it be, Marx's materialism is real and genuinely contrasts with Hegel's view of ideas as the determinative motor of human process. And unlike Saint-Simon, whose heroes are inventors and engineers, energetic (and individual) movers and shakers who must and will throw off the shackles of feudalism and ecclesiasticism—Saint-Simon is essentially a leftward extension of Condorcet—Marx claims the role of Atlas for the proletarian many. To be sure, Saint-Simon believed that the heroes must move and shake for the gain of the oppressed many, but he expected little from the latter on their own. In fact many critics of Marxism hold that this is also true of Marx, notwithstanding his fine words on the proletariat as a revolutionary class and the real creators of the objects of our lives. At any rate, Marx's theory at least formally places the ordinary labouring many at the centre of history, their potential—soon to be actual—self-mobilization to be what sets in motion the chain of events that leads to the end of history.

Marxism is a complex interconnected system, providing an analysis of historical and economic process, the relationships of both to culture, a set of causal principles, and a distinctive ethical understanding of the human world. It rests on a theory of human nature. It would be difficult to accept the system as a whole without seeing people somewhat as Marx sees people, but one could accept his theory of human nature without assenting to the accompanying economic or historical theories.

The foundational idea for the theory is historical materialism. This is, however, an extremely broad umbrella conception. There are a number of materialist theories of humankind, several quite different from Marx's. Marx saw his view as hardheaded and scientific; critics, as we have said, already think Marx's view of humans partly idealist, and hence imperfectly materialist. As with a pure materialism, so also with an idealist/materialist analysis there is more variation than the dialectical materialist could feel comfortable with, at any rate without a convincing basis for dismissing the alternatives. I will argue in general that a *pure* materialism in human nature theory is an exceedingly difficult position to defend. If this is correct, it should accord Marx's theory a greater plausibility; whether it is enough to allow the Marxist view to stand as a convincing understanding of humanity remains to be seen. But it is important to register explicitly that, in spite of Marxist prose, a scientific approach to human beings, even supposing that that means a primarily materialist view, or one with approximately the same mix of the material and the ideal found in Marxism, need not closely resemble Marxism. Marxists (especially one-time Soviet bloc writers, but also some Western Marxists) often write as though being scientific about people is synonymous with being Marxist—rather like Catholic writers and thinkers who write as though being religious is synonymous with being Catholic.

Marx's materialism is, to be sure, a complex matter, involving a certain evolution, even perhaps substantive rethinking and redirection, over the course of Marx's career. Throughout a variety of formulations, some of them obscure, Marx clearly means to be a historical or cultural materialist. This is shown above all in the *Theses on Feuerbach,* but frequently elsewhere also. Feuerbach had had the idea of materialism, though quite imperfectly, and Marx is revising and modifying him. Marx and Engels convey the concrete or practical sense of the idea effectively in *The German Ideology:*

> We must begin by stating the first premise of all human existence, and therefore of all history, the premise, namely, that men must be in a position to live in order to be able to "make history." But life involves, before everything else, eating and drinking, a habitation, clothing, and many other things. The first historical act is thus the production of the means to satisfy these needs, the production of material life itself. And indeed this is a

historical act, a fundamental condition of all history which today, as thousands of years ago, must daily and hourly be fulfilled merely in order to sustain human life.[2]

When these formulations are examined closely with a view to giving them real precision—just what *exactly* are the "many other things," and what is criterial for inclusion?—matters get more complicated. Marx's relationship to naturalism is variable and differently resolved in different contexts. He is, of course, an atheist and anti-supernaturalist. But naturalism and supernaturalism are contraries, not contradictories. That is, someone can reject both, as different forms of views that may be called "cognitive dualism" have done. Some version of cognitive dualism and an ontological conception it expresses—the sort of view more explicitly associated with Descartes, Kant, Dilthey, and the twentieth-century hermeneutic tradition, and probably also Hegel himself—seems plausibly identified in Marx's work. According to this way of thinking, although the universe is physically unitary and entirely subject to natural law, the genera of its fundamental parts—and maybe, as with Descartes, there are just two such genera—are irreducibly distinct and dissimilar. It is an altogether different thing to be a conscious being than to be an inert natural object.

A view of this sort—irreducibilist ontic pluralism, we could somewhat gracelessly call it—is not compatible with naturalism. But it is quite compatible with materialism, that is, with the idea that consciousness or ideas have little causal efficacy, and that what does have causal efficacy are physical conditions of the world that determine the existence (both the fact of existence and the form it takes) of the kinds of things there are. For conscious beings this would mean the physical factors bearing on their survival and conditions of life.

Where will agency figure in this conception? For Marx, like Hegel, seems clearly to think of full humanity as involving free, creative, rational, self-conscious agency. Nonetheless this idea, though clear in Marx's early Hegelian writings and implicit in polemical passages in *The Communist Manifesto* and later work, does not seem to receive developed theoretical integration with Marx's materialism.

A particularly lucid and succinct statement of Marx's materialism appears in the preface to *The Critique of Political Economy:*

[2] *Basic Writings on Politics and Philosophy,* p. 249.

In the social production which men carry on they enter into definite relations that are indispensable and independent of their will; these relations of production correspond to a definite stage of development of their material powers of production. The sum total of these relations of production constitutes the economic structure of society—the real foundation, on which rise legal and political superstructures and to which correspond definite forms of social consciousness. The mode of production in material life determines the general character of the social, political and spiritual processes of life. It is not the consciousness of men that determines their existence, but, on the contrary, their social existence determines their consciousness. (p. 11f.)

Note that this passage formulates an unequivocally materialist view, and also that quite distinct materialist principles and positions than Marx's are formulable. The stress in Marx's position is on *social* and *production*. Other materialist stances would give a more individual focus, or would centre on other aspects of the human organism than productive activity. Moreover, theoretical attention targeted upon the social and the productive need not be materialist. Indeed, some twentieth-century renderings of Marxism give these ideas a decidedly idealist cast, adopting an organicist (or anti-atomic individualist) ontological position requiring networks of community intersection for the construction of human individuality; and seeing productive activity as a kind of spiritual need, a requirement of the (socially formed) individual soul for self-expression and self-realization. And there are an abundance of Marxian texts[3] that easily nurture these idealist or seemingly idealist construals of Marx.

The fact is, Marx's materialism appears compromised in many of its formulations, developments, or applications. Marvin Harris, among other (generally sympathetic) critics, attributes this to the accretions of Hegelianism and elements of revolutionary praxis in Marx's work.[4] As Harris sees it, these can be factored out, and a reasonably pure materialist understanding of human social development, and the causal determinants of all primary levels of human activity, can be recovered. This seems persuasive, though it will be

---

[3] Especially in the more overtly Hegelian phase (chiefly those assembled in *The Economic and Philosophic Manuscripts of 1844*) or the more polemically anti-capitalist passages in many of Marx's writings, decrying the special evil of the perversion of the human work-need under capitalism.

[4] See Harris, *The Rise of Anthropological Theory*, pp. 220–22, 229–30.

at odds with the more humanistic hermeneutical rethinkings of Marx and Marxism in the twentieth century, in thinkers like Gramsci, Lukacs, and Marcuse.[5]

It is important to try to be clear about these matters, partly because so many of the twentieth-century Marxists (following some of the Marx texts, to be sure) have not been, and because it does make a difference. If human beings cannot be *happy,* feel *fulfilled,* feel that their lives have meaning or occasions of creative joy, without having work in which they express themselves, that will be a psychological fact about human beings, a matter of a certain kind of psychic need, cognate with the Hegelian need for *recognition* from autonomous others, or needs for love, or spirituality, or God, that other theories assign to us. While any such views might be accorded material bases, they are all idealist views, in that they account for human behaviour in terms of conscious attempts to satisfy such needs, involving reasonably developed degrees of symbolic recognition of situations in which the need can be satisfied and what will count as satisfying it. Conscious agents will be the ones who know when they have found meaningful work, or love, or not (possibly at an unconscious level, to be sure; one could build a depth-psychological dimension into an idealist theory of this kind). But—it should be clear—this is not materialism. A genuinely materialist theory cannot make how I feel about my circumstances—whether I feel they accord me dignity, respect, self-respect, work that matters to me or to others—the primary motor of my behaviour, for these states of feeling are of course (valuational) states of consciousness.

In fact, in the passage quoted above, and not infrequently elsewhere, Marx makes it plain that he has expressed a genuinely materialist view. According to this view how we think and feel is a function of factors quite exterior to consciousness, namely, a causal network the principal constituents in which are the physical environment of a human community and the technological structures that community uses in supporting life in its particular context. Thought and its products, ideational culture (religion; philosophy; ethics; individual, tribal, and national ideology) are mostly epiphenomenal reflections, pale realities stemming from those economic conditions of life.

Richard W. Miller, making a case for a reconceived Marx, argues persuasively that Marx was not a technological determinist. He

---

[5] Antonio Gramsci (1891–1937) in particular produces an idealist version of Marxism, in which ideas and ethical values (Marxian ones) have significant causal power.

goes on to try to fill in and defend Marx's materialist conception of history—more fully, the mode of production theory—as empirical, falsifiable, deeply plausible, and significantly contrasting with idealist alternatives:

> The mode of production that regulates processes of change is, of course, the mode of material production: the tools and techniques with which material goods are produced, the relations of cooperation through which people produce material goods, and relations of control over tools, techniques, land, labour-power and people employed in the production of material goods. Change is due to the pattern of resources and priorities and the consequent actions that are explainable in terms of people's location in this quite material mode. Suppose, on the other hand, that a change in basic type was due to a religious movement, arising from the personal charisma of a religious leader and due to religious feelings that had no explanation in terms of the mode of production. Or suppose that a basic change was due to the military successes of a politically ambitious military genius, and that the occurrence, sooner or later, of such a socially transforming military process was not explainable in terms of people's location in the mode of production. Suppose, in short, that Weber's Calvin or Carlyle's Napoleon existed. Then there would be a counter-example to this materialist conception of history. (*Analyzing Marx,* p. 228f.)

I will comment only briefly on Miller's claims (which are developed, and illustrated, much more extensively than this passage shows). With the examples given here Miller may be said to have loaded the dice. The idealist alternatives to materialism, whether Marxian or of some other stripe, are by no means limited to "great man" hypotheses, according to which solitary individuals of genius shape the course of history. (Miller acknowledges this in his later elaboration of Weber versus Marx.) Many idealist views dismiss such ideas. Weberians and others who attribute major causal efficacy to, say, a certain *work ethic* found in a particular population group and operating independently of individual relationships to production modes, need not assign the causal force of that ethic (particularly as time goes by) to dynamic leaders. On the other hand, one of the most distinguished world historians of recent years, W. H. McNeill, has argued that a clearer example of the significance of the individual than is afforded by either Calvin or Napoleon is provided by

Mohammed.[6] It is very difficult to believe that the Arab expansion into the whole of the Middle East in the seventh century would have occurred but for the personality and religious vision of Mohammed.

At any rate, there are other idealist positions. Perhaps most notable in relation to Marx is that of his predecessor Hegel. The Hegelian conception of a need/desire for recognition—the recognition of one's status, as an equal or superior human being, from other human beings—is a core component of the Hegelian theory of human nature. It seems plausible that something like such a drive or desire might explain human dissatisfaction with life in a materially secure slavery.

Although Marx's views of the human world are imperfectly and incompletely materialist, they are nonetheless materialist. Even with many shortcomings in the theory as a whole, some of them damaging to Marxism's status as an even adequate theory of history or human nature, it is worth emphasizing that there is a quantum leap between Marx's attempt at a systemic, diachronic analysis of the human condition and almost anything that precedes it. The elements and roots of the Marxian synthesis are, as we have said, to be found in Rousseau, Saint-Simon, and Hegel, and also in Mandeville, Vico, Smith, and Turgot, but that synthesis offers something that is more than the sum of these parts. It is, as Marx claimed it was, science; flawed science to be sure, but science nonetheless. It is more impressively so in its discernment of patterns of social activity that both unite the felt motivations of individuals and operate transversally, securing outcomes that are functions of environmental forces entirely independent of any such states of motivation. Marx is impressively scientific also in combining large general theory with a great wealth of detail. He is deeply interested in both.

The difficult thing to see—the circle that Marxism must square—is, why would it be in the individual's material self-interest to advance the community interest? This seems particularly challenging when we remember that this is not supposed to be a matter of a rational calculation. Given the materialism of the theory, the idea can't be that fundamentally self-interested persons can be given arguments or evidence that will *persuade* them they will be better off if they act cooperatively and socialistically. Philosophers from Socrates on have sought to convince us that our interests coincide with those of the collective, with about that degree of success that a historical materialist could have predicted. The Marxian individual isn't someone who

[6] McNeill, *The Rise of the West* (1963), p. 421, and *The Pursuit of Power* (1982), p. 21.

reasons through to a cooperative outcome in a prisoner's-dilemma-type[7] calculation of his or her best bet. There would be little point in the Marxian revolutionary strategy, and its centrality, if anything like this were the idea. Clearly, proletarian revolt is intended to appeal to the individual self-interest of each individual man and woman—*he* and *she* will be better off than under capitalist oppression and exploitation. But this appears to be in tension with the idea that our natures are (but for alienation) solidaristic and cooperative, at least more deeply than they are individualist or egoist. It also appears to threaten the stability of the communist utopian future. It seems as though the appeal of proletarian revolution and its victorious outcome is to a certain sort of delivering of the goods. What if socialism or communism falters (as, of course, the historical East European versions did)?

There is a possibility of steering between Scylla and Charybdis here, with Scylla a materialism that is apparently also an implicit egoism in at least one part of the Marxian theory, and Charybdis an idealistically grounded altruism (whether stemming from the warmness of sympathetic hearts or Gauthier-like[8] practical rationality). We could argue that there is an enduring human nature that has survived through millennia of class society and the alienation this has caused, and which a socialist society can and will unleash. The idea is that social awareness and social altruism, manifest among us now only in some, lives dormantly in more or less everyone. Moreover, the appeal of proletarian revolution will not be purely or primarily to naked self-interest, but in quite significant part to this suppressed communal feeling, that would prevent any individual happiness that did not coincide with or further the general happiness. If it is not to constitute the surrender of Marxian materialism, however, this has got to be meant rather literally—almost, or perhaps directly, biologistically. It cannot be a matter of appeal to higher selves or the persuasion of compassionate ideas. It must be that what we *are* (or, just possibly, can become in materially caused developments from our present constitutions) is a creature whose material well-being is materially bound up with the well-being of our fellows.

---

[7] Prisoner's dilemma situations are ones where cooperative altruistic behaviour will secure a best outcome, egoist behaviour a second best, and altruistic behaviour where the others in the situation do not do likewise will result in the worst outcome for the individual.

[8] Cf. Chapter 4, note 21.

Another Marxian possibility might seem to be an anti-democratic (or extra-democratic) one along the lines of B. F. Skinner's conceptions of a behaviourist utopia in his novel *Walden Two*. According to a Marxian version of the Skinnerian paradise—and there is historical evidence that flesh-and-blood Marxist individuals and regimes have implicitly held such views—even if people do tend to egoist or individualist pursuit of self-interest, if they are constrained to live in a cooperativist social order its material benefits will be sufficient to keep them there reasonably contentedly until such time as general altruism (as a motivating factor that will generally trump socially injurious individualism) evolves to become their actual natures. As well as the ethical challenge posed by the anti-democratism of such views, and an apparent extreme elitism (almost as though different species were involved) dividing humanity into the knowing, shepherding leadership cadre and the great mass of the human sheep who will be cajoled and steered for their and everyone's benefit, there are conceptual difficulties not easy to evade. What would be the *material* cause of the leadership's taking this shepherding role? Why, other than for ethical or altruistic—that is, for *ideal* as opposed to material—motives, would they do this? (And if for ethical motives, if humans in general are the manipulable sheep this version of the theory supposes, why are they *worth* benefiting and guiding?) There is also grave empirical doubt whether people, if as self-interested as this view holds, could be conditioned to altruism by any merely political or institutional means.

Finally, there is serious ground for doubting whether there is any such thing as the supposed dormant impulse to mutualism (where, once again, this means not merely *some* altruistic motivations, but a disposition not to achieve individual material benefit that would fail to coincide with general community material benefit). This seems even more dubious than the alternative basis, of extreme plasticity, for the Marxian attempt to preserve materialism and its alleged convergence on socialism.

There is no room in Marx's picture of non-alienated humanity for *homo mercantilis*—mercantile humankind, with a deeply based disposition to trade, an eye to the trader's advantage. Equally absent must be any gambler's instinct. The Marxian utopia would not have racetracks, or dens filled with card or dice enthusiasts. Both of these types of human being are sinners in the Marxian religion. They are as drunkards (or, for that matter, moderate drinkers) to temperance colony proponents: they aren't supposed to be there. The right exorcising formula of socializing nurturance should eliminate them, make it impossible for the type or kind to reappear. It is likewise with those who would dominate their fellows, humans with a will to power. Curiously, this type seems easier to fit into a Marxist scheme than gamblers and businesspeople, since the will to dominate can be channelled into leadership roles of socially useful kinds. Risk-taking desires and impulses can presumably also be sidetracked, into sports competition, bridge tournaments, friendly regional productivity competitions, and the like. But—it isn't the same thing. The desire to outwit your fellow sojourners in a deal, in trade, cannot be viewed as a healthy human impulse by the Marxist; it can no more have a degree of acceptability than can criminality.

A major criticism of Marxism as a theory of human nature is that, like some other theories, it takes as the image of well-functioning humanity what is at best true only of some human beings, even among those who function well. The Marxian model of a human being is someone without national, ethnic, or tribal passions, comfortable in and with his or her body, finding creative satisfaction in both physical and mental work, egalitarian in spirit—which means, in part, undisposed to hero-worship—without desire for commercial competition or advantage, and having a measure of fellow-feeling with the rest of humanity. (Marxian humanity may also be thought to be without hankerings for realities beyond the material world, but this need not be insisted on, whereas the preceding really do seem crucial and ineliminable.) Marx is, of course, aware that some people don't correspond to this model, but they are viewed, in some cases compassionately and in others not, as pathological or else as accidental consequences of a humanly defective but corrigible social system. More purely historicist readings of Marx would insist that all deviant cases fall under the second of these two grounds of exception. At any rate, Marx's conception of human nature will not allow that a human being could be genuinely well with himself or herself, yet fail to correspond to the above characterization. They would, necessarily, be at least somewhat alienated, adrift, anomic, victims (or guilty) of false consciousness, or deluded, and certainly less than a fulfilled, truly thriving human being can be.

There is an element of moralism in Marx's portrait of humanity that seems inescapable, and that sits ill alongside his materialism and his historicism. This is given most direct and revealing expression in the concept of the *Lumpenproletariat*. The people to whom this concept applies are, as Marx sees them, scum and riff-raff, idlers, parasites, whose class interest favours the survival of the existing socioeconomic system because they profit from it. They are pimps, criminals, gamblers, and assorted low-life people living off the labours of others, themselves having no genuine materially supportive assets. (Property in Marx's developed sense, recall, is conceived as possessions affording a living, of one degree of comfort or other.)

The problem is that there seem to be people who are not pathological in a plausible psychiatric or medical sense, who may give every indication of being *happy*—at least as happy as people fitting the Marxian model seem to be—and of having some reasonable understanding of themselves and the world they live in, but who don't measure up to the model. Some people seem less gregarious than others, less fond of their fellows; some really don't care to do much with their bodies or with their minds; some appear obviously and joyously competitive from as early in their lives as any character traits seemed discernible; some appear to be "made for commerce," simply natural horsetraders; some have strong feelings of family and kindred, extending to pride of ancestry or of nation. Even after proletarian revolution these last might find themselves with apparently inexpungible dispositions to root for their home team in soccer matches, and to *care* who wins. Doubtless these, like other human traits, are explainable, and much of the explanation will in most cases be social or cultural, not biological. But it seems unconvincing that a single socioeconomic order could be devised that would, even given conditions of material abundance, produce only humans fitting the Marxian model, and all of them happy and thriving in doing so.

Bibliography

Blackburn, Richard James. *The Vampire of Reason*. London: Verso, 1990.

Cohen, G. A. *Karl Marx's Theory of History: A Defence*. Oxford: Oxford University Press, 1979.

Fukuyama, Francis. *The End of History and the Last Man*. New York: Free Press, 1992.

Gellner, Ernest. "The Last Marxists: Pretensions, Illusions and Achievements of the Frankfurt School." *Times Literary Supplement* 4773 (Sept. 23, 1994).

Harris, Marvin. *The Rise of Anthropological Theory*. New York: Harper Collins, 1968.

Ionescu, Ghita, ed. *The Political Thought of Saint-Simon*. Oxford: Oxford University Press, 1976.

Marx, Karl. *Capital*. 3 vols. New York: Vintage, 1977.

—————. *The Critique of Political Economy*. Chicago: International Library, 1904. [1859]

—————. *The Economic and Philosphic Manuscripts of 1844*. New York: International Publishers, 1964.

—————. *The Poverty of Philosophy*. New York: International Publishers, 1963. [1847]

Marx, Karl, and Friedrich Engels. *Basic Writings on Politics and Philosophy*. Edited by L. S. Feuer. New York: Anchor Books, 1959.

—————. *The Communist Manifesto*. New York: Washington Square Press, 1964. [1848]

McNeill, W. H. *The Pursuit of Power*. Chicago: University of Chicago Press, 1982.

—————. *The Rise of the West*. Chicago: University of Chicago Press, 1963.

Miller, Richard W. *Analyzing Marx*. Princeton: Princeton University Press, 1984.

Singer, Peter. *Marx*. Oxford: Oxford University Press, 1980.

Vico, Giambattista. *The New Science of Giambattista Vico*. Translated by T. G. Bergin & M. H. Fisch. Ithaca, NY: Cornell University Press, 1968. [1744]

Weber, Max. *The Protestant Ethic and the Spirit of Capitalism*. New York: Scribner's, 1950.

CHAPTER 9 /

Darwin and Some
Biological Successors ——

THIS CHAPTER DISCUSSES THEORIES OF HUMAN
nature that focus on the fact that we are members of the animal
kingdom: on our biological identity. Although the currently best
known and most controversial such theory is sociobiology, it is just
one of the views that see our most fundamental character as biological, and highlighting it in our discussion may fail to do justice to
the power of the broad underlying idea of which it is just one representative. Similarly, effective criticisms of sociobiology may altogether fail to touch this broader understanding.

The perspective we now explore notes that there is no evidence
of the slightest species-modifying change in at least the past 35,000
years, and possibly more than twice that period. Fully modern humans emerged from a continuous ancestral hominid and pre-hominid
set of stages that stretch millions of years into a primate past, and
our nearest living relatives, chimpanzees, are hematologically almost
indistinguishable from us (genetically, about ninety-eight per cent
similar to us), and in countless features of both physiology and
behaviour strikingly similar. Thus, the biological point of view holds,
it simply beggars belief that any human developments of the last
mere thousands of years could have appreciably altered what we are,
and the ground-level bases of our actions. From this perspective, to
ignore our animality and what can be learned of us by studying our
relatives is to adopt a stance that is wilfully blind, or at any rate
hopelessly incomplete.

The biological perspective also finds much to fault in its cultural
and idealist alternatives. Since humans have evolved so effectively to
suit a range of environments, with gradually formulated resources
adequate to meet all manner of hazards, internal as well as external,
can it seriously be supposed that the delicate puffs of cultural or
interpersonal current could markedly redirect individual or group
development? Not, of course, that any organism is impervious to the
shifting constraints of habitat. But the cultural/idealist theories—
perhaps most problematically some postmodernist and feminist ones—
seem to suppose that a few ill-chosen parental words or insufficient
examples of "role-modelling" can turn what would have been a the-

oretical physicist into a gas station attendant, or a major musical innovator into a backup singer. Surely we are tougher than that, protests the voice of biological theory, and perhaps the voice of other materialist views; surely we are more resilient, less easily blown about and fashioned by such accidental and symbol-encrusted winds. The fibres of our being run deeper and more forcefully than such ephemera—the allegedly empowering and disempowering, privileging and disadvantaging—could modify. For better and for worse—and, the biological view affirms, it will be both—we have a set of strategies articulated over the many dozens of hundreds of thousands of years of human evolution, capacities, and active, reactive, and interactive dispositions that constitute a highly successful nature. This nature, or range of human natures (because of its varieties), is more enduring (and arguably more interesting) than the little shifts of current of a decade, a generation, or a century or two. This may seem particularly persuasive when we note that the shifts that advocates of anti-biological views are drawn to are, like those advocates, mostly confined to white, middle-class western Europeans and their relatives.

Charles Darwin (1809–1882) is the founder of modern evolutionary theory, and the discoverer (with Wallace)[1] of the principle of natural selection, which is (with random genetic mutation) the primary determinant of the trajectory of evolutionary change. His *The Descent of Man* (1871) is the first attempt to give a more or less comprehensive account of human beings as animals, as members of a natural world related to other kinds of animals and natural terrestrial beings. It is preceded by an extensive literature in human anatomy and physiology, and a number of attempts at a physiological psychology, but there is nothing earlier that portrays biological humanity and attempts thereby to delineate what we are. This simply could not have been undertaken in a serious way before the case had been made for our descent from non-human ancestors and our evolutionary links with other primates. And, of course, it was Darwin who made that case, largely in *The Descent of Man* itself, though it is implicit, and the reader seems plainly intended to reach these conclusions in the earlier classic *The Origin of Species* (1859).

It is correct to point out that the idea of evolution did not originate with Darwin: the half-century and more preceding *The*

---

[1] Alfred Russell Wallace (1823–1913) independently arrived at most of the basic ideas of evolution via natural selection.

Origin of Species saw a veritable flood of evolutionary conceptions, philosophies, and undertakings in the sciences. The idea of evolution almost typifies early and middle nineteenth century theoretical thinking in western Europe.[2] The specific idea of species evolving— one becoming transformed over time into another, no longer capable of reproduction with the earlier form—is also not original with Darwin. What is original (or co-original with Wallace) is the idea of the *mechanism* of species transformation, namely, natural selection.

The idea of natural selection is extremely simple. (It was not, of course, so simple to formulate and develop a systematic body of evidence for it.) That idea has also often been misunderstood, so we do well to give it explicit formulation. Darwin says, in the opening chapter of *The Origin of Species,* that he got the idea from agriculturalists' and horticulturalists' practices of carefully planned interferences with livestock and domesticated plants, to develop desired traits or eliminate or minimize unwanted ones. Darwin also mentions the ideas of Thomas Malthus (1776–1834)[3] as an important influence on his views. Malthus formed the notion of what he took to be laws of nature governing food supplies and population levels. Populations always tend to increase at higher rates than resources can support, thereby ensuring, Malthus supposed, a fairly permanent condition of misery for most of humanity. Any increase in food productivity or efficient delivery would, by an iron law of fertility dynamics, tend over time to be more than offset by increases in human numbers, which would again ensure deprivation or famine for most of those numbers. Although Darwin did not wholly share Malthus's pessimism, his thinking was stimulated by the idea of the terrestrial environment as a system of pressures that would in most habitats dictate a competition between species, and between individuals within species, for generally scarce resources.

The principles of natural selection—and hence of Darwinian evolutionary theory—may be reduced to just three: (1) no characteristic acquired in the course of an individual organism's lifespan is hereditarily transmissible to that organism's offspring;[4] (2) individuals

[2] This theme is usefully explored and lavishly illustrated in Milton Millhauser, *Just before Darwin* (1959), especially Chapter 3.

[3] Expressed in *An Essay on the Principle of Population* (1803–1826).

[4] The view that acquired characteristics are sometimes transmitted to progeny was advocated by the pre-Darwinian evolutionary theorist the Chevalier de Lamarck (1744–1829). This view, called Lamarckism, seems

within a biological population will tend to manifest a diversity of heritable characteristics; (3) a biological population will tend to produce greater numbers of offspring than an environment can support. From the diversity of heritable characteristics alone, it is clear, some of these characteristics will tend to promote an individual's living long enough to reproduce, others will be damaging for that end, and others will be neutral, neither advantaging nor disadvantaging the individual. The joint operation of the second and third principles generates a greater likelihood of transmitting advantaging heritable traits. Over time some population groups will survive and others will not; the greater success of surviving populations will tend to be a function of the increasing presence of advantage-conferring heritable traits in successive generations of the population group. Over sufficient time these will stabilize as traits of entire species, and eventually in the formation of new species in some cases, as new advantage-conferring random mutations appear (since the second principle never ceases to operate). What needs explaining, and what natural selection does appear to explain, is why new species arise in some circumstances, why in other circumstances they do not (a species stays unchanged), why some species either survive or adapt (change into a new species), and why other species become extinct, which is, as biological history discloses, the most frequent case.

What is striking is that natural selection operates—and Darwin explicitly saw it as operating—in a wholly mechanistic, non-teleological way. This implies in turn that, contrary to some semi-popular accounts of the theory, there is no universal "urge to survive" in species of living things, not even in those that do survive. Nor is the competition for survival—in virtue of the third, Malthus-derived principle—necessarily won by those that are, in a muscular or similar sense, the strongest or most fit. Ferociously powerful dinosaurs and sabre-toothed tigers went extinct. In the trivially analytic sense the

---

suggested or implied in Darwin's work for quite exceptional cases of traits, though it is formally and explicitly repudiated. Certainly many nineteenth- and some twentieth-century advocates of evolutionary views, often supposing they were representing Darwinian positions, have been Lamarckian. Some of the confusion at least appears to stem from imprecision or ignorance about the term "acquisition." An adult male, for example, may be described as having "acquired" a beard, and the capacity for doing so will generally be transmitted to his male descendants. But this "acquisition" was of course the maturative realization of an innate—genetically programmed—capacity.

fittest survive (being fit can just *mean* having whatever traits are required to survive), but what makes for fitness is wholly a function of the demands and other features of the individual's and the species' environment,[5] which itself changes over time (the same territory changing, or the species moving to another one). In the Darwinian picture there is a great deal more "luck" than skill in species adaptation and success, much of that luck having more to do with features of habitat, predators, and competing species than with the traits of the individual plant or animal concerned.

Darwin also came to believe that animal species that reproduce sexually change subject to principles of what he called sexual selection. Sexual selection, he thought, operates autonomously of natural selection. That is, some characteristics (always only heritable, and hence for Darwin innate, not acquired characteristics) are selected for reasons that do not confer habitat advantage. An individual with these traits is no likelier to live to reproductive age than not. The traits are "chosen," Darwin held, because the males and females of the species happen to find them appealing in the other sex, and so tend more frequently to mate with individuals who have them. Although Darwin himself, especially in *The Descent of Man,* argued for the autonomy of sexual selection, the Darwinians of the present century have sought to show that so-called sexually selected traits actually do tend to confer competitive advantage. Some of these traits will increase, for example, the likelihood of healthy offspring, or of comfortable life beyond reproduction, enabling parents rather than just the characteristics of individual and habitat to play a role in the individual's survival.

The full content of Darwinian evolutionary theory, both in Darwin's original versions and in subsequent elaborations and refinements, is a great deal more complicated than just indicated, and than it is possible to explain here; so too is the wealth of evidence Darwin provided for it. The chief element of modern evolutionary biology missing in Darwin's account was genetics—the science of the gene, the cellular unit that carries the biological identity of the individual. (Most bodily cells contain clusters of genes that constitute the genotype of the animal—a conjunction of material and "information" that is unique to each individual animal. A gene itself is a segment of chromosomes.) For modern evolutionary theory the gene, not the

---

[5] Including individuals' internal environment—the presence and properties of invasive organisms and non-living entities.

individual plant or animal, is the primary unit upon which natural selection operates. The traits of the individual that are naturally selected (or fail to be) are genetic traits, and it is in virtue of properties of genes that individuals and populations of individuals survive to reproduce. Some advocates of sociobiology, including the theory's founder, E. O. Wilson,[6] have extended this fact to a sometimes lyrically expressed metaphysics of genes as quasi-atoms seeking (note the psychologism) immortality and using living bodies as temporary vehicles in this quest.

The Victorian novelist (and amateur biologist) Samuel Butler famously reversed the view of "folk biology" that the purpose of a chicken's egg is to produce another chicken, with the quip that the chicken is only an egg's way of producing another egg. The insight implied in the aphorism is not what evokes the smile, but rather the realization that teleology is mostly a function of the perspective or purposes of some conscious observer. Because it is as empirically well supported to suppose that eggs produce chickens in order to produce more eggs as it is to think that chickens make eggs so as to make more chickens, supposing that either reveals the "real" purpose at work is entirely misguided. There is no real purpose at work. E. O. Wilson cites Butler's quip but doesn't seem to get the point. He writes as though he thinks there is a real teleology going on evolutionarily, and it is nature's design or purpose of perpetuating DNA. Richard Dawkins—discussed later in this chapter—writes similarly. Both scientists, of course, know Darwinian biology extremely well; nonetheless, something of the spirit of Darwin's outlook seems lost in such thinking.

Many sins are committed in Darwin's name, some of these against Darwin himself, by over-zealous enthusiasts. The first such sin was the creation in the nineteenth century of the view labelled "social Darwinism," according to which battle-to-the-death competition, economic or military or both, between social groups, is necessary for the preservation of the health of the human species, and the key to its future progress. Regarding such struggles as tonic, social Darwinists oppose efforts to diminish a struggle-fostering socioeconomic climate or to mitigate its hazards or miseries, particularly when such efforts stem from government. Social Darwinism, which continues in one form or other in twentieth-century political life, is a political and economic philosophy, not a science (not even a mistaken science).

[6] Edward O. Wilson, *Sociobiology: The New Synthesis* (1975), p. 3.

Currently, sociobiologists claim Darwin as the first sociobiologist. Marvin Harris, for the most part a reasonable and accurate (if definitely non-neutral) intellectual historian, accuses Darwin of also being a Lamarckian, a racist, and a social Darwinist.[7] (He complains with regard to the latter that the label is wrong, since the set of ideas constituting social Darwinism appear, notably in Herbert Spencer, well before Darwin's publications. But he doesn't doubt that Darwin shared these views.) Possibly excepting a Lamarckian treatment of physical systems atrophied through disuse, none of these four identifications is in fact justified by anything in *The Descent of Man,* or elsewhere in Darwin's writings. Darwin explicitly affirms the causal autonomy of culture and the lessened applicability of natural selection to modern societies. He is a Victorian Englishman, and certainly views the world as consisting of more and less civilized peoples and superior and inferior human individuals. He also makes plain some of his values: Darwin believes in progress, in the high normative significance of science, technology, and the arts, and cares about what he thinks may foster and inhibit the advance of the species intellectually and economically. But an age, like ours, that insists that science is rarely if ever normatively neutral can hardly complain if one of its leading practitioners occasionally allows himself explicit valuational comment. Darwin himself would never confuse such comment with science itself.

Again, unless one adopts an exceedingly narrow conception of racism—and there is indication that Harris himself does—there is no good cause to regard Darwin as a racist. Harris takes the view that human groups—ethnic, genetic, or racial communities of humans—are so similar in all but the most trivial and insignificant respects that in a single generation any one group could switch cultural settings with any other with the resulting next generation exactly as if no such interchange had occurred, fully and indistinguishably manifesting the culture new to the group (*The Rise of Anthropological Theory,* p. 132). Clearly, this conception, an extreme version of nurturism or environmentalism, involves thought experiments that would be quite impossible to put to the test. It may be true; but even if it is, it does not seem quite reasonable to regard everyone who does not share it as a racist. There might be interpenetrations of culture and genetics

[7] Marvin Harris, *The Rise of Anthropological Theory,* pp. 118–123. I noted above that Darwin's formulations do sometimes suggest Lamarckism. Even this is arguable; at any rate, Darwin makes it quite clear that his evolutionary theory is conceived for innate traits of organisms.

that make for differences not so easily erased or cancelled, at any rate not in a single generation; some might be considerably more deeply placed than that. This need not involve or imply judgments of "superiority" or "inferiority" of any kind, but only kinds of difference that correlate culture and ethnicity at some level of depth. If such a view were confirmation or even evidence of racism, a great many thinkers not usually considered racist at all would fall under the taint of that charge.

Certainly Darwin supposed that human groupings are sufficiently genetically differentiated that there are traits, or degrees of them, that promote or impede environmental and reproductive rates of success in some groups. He also thought that such traits could well include adaptive intelligence. Darwin supposed, as most evolutionary biologists before and since have, that high intelligence was naturally selected in humans as a trait conferring strong degrees of habitat advantage. However, some recent theories have argued against this extremely widely held view. One of them—a theory Harris is in sympathy with—holds that intelligence developed non-adaptively in humans, as a byproduct of brain cell replication, itself naturally selected as part of a body cooling system for the early protohuman African primate ancestor (Harris, *Our Kind,* pp. 50–56.) Whatever the origins of human intelligence may be, no one disputes its survival value in fully modern humans once it was there, if not earlier. Darwin supposes some humans have or have had (most of these groups are now extinct) repertoires of differentially selected skills and propensities that confer greater or lesser competitive advantage vis-à-vis other groups. Otherwise put, he does not suppose all competitive outcomes are functions of environmental depletions or other contingencies, or in general solely the workings of extra-human nature, perhaps in conjunction with chance facts of culture. Even so, Darwin makes it abundantly clear that he regards all humans as comprising a single species, and discusses human nature in generic ways that only on a secondary (and relatively infrequently met) plane involve fundamental or racial subgroupings. In contrast with a great many of his ethnological contemporaries, Darwin never contrasts allegedly globally "superior" white or civilized humans with supposed "inferior" non-whites or uncivilized humans.

In common with his contemporaries he does, however, distinguish "savages" from civilized populations, and he plainly thinks the former at competitive risk from the latter. Moreover, Darwin clearly indicates that he thinks some measure of struggle or competition is "good for" people, gives them stimulus for achievement and prevents their falling into idleness, lethargy, or a placid self-satisfaction that might threaten the prospects of the species. But that is about as forcefully as Darwin puts the matter. Nowhere in his writings will there be found a shrill advocacy, of Spencerian, Nietzschean, Randian, or any other stripe, of the tonic value of jugular social combat or the bracing good of capitalism.[8] Just as Darwin was not a racist, he was not a social Darwinist. (The latter, by the way, in both the nineteenth and twentieth centuries took divergently racialist and cultural forms, with frequently marked contrast and even opposition between the two. Racialist social Darwinism—German National Socialist (Nazi) ideology was an extreme representative of this view—holds that racial groups are strongly differentiated by their qualities, with some inherently much more amply endowed with intelligence, energy, courage, creativity, and propensities to high culture, science, military skill, and other esteemed qualities; and that the level a racial group attains is only achieved and sustained by competitive struggle, typically a bloody competitive one. Cultural social Darwinism shares the emphasis on the need for competitive struggle, but does not particularly identify winners and losers with genetically linked population groupings. Rather, national societies, cultures, social classes, or distinct individuals are seen as the competitors, and some mix of war and commerce—with sometimes only a very little of one or the other of these in the mix—is viewed as the field of competitive struggle.)

The following passage from *The Descent of Man* shows Darwin as Victorian, moralist, and as having the balanced perspective of the scientist. It will also, I think, refute the charge of social "Darwinism."

> With savages, the weak in body or mind are soon eliminated; and those that survive commonly exhibit a vigorous state of health. We civilised men, on the other hand, do our utmost to check the process of elimination; we build asylums for the imbecile, the maimed, and the sick; we institute poor-laws; and our medical men exert their utmost skill to save the life of every one to the last moment. There is reason to believe that vaccination has preserved thousands, who from a weak constitution would formerly

[8] Herbert Spencer, Friedrich Nietzsche, and Ayn Rand were all—though in quite different ways—advocates of or deeply influenced by social Darwinist ideas. (In Rand's case this might be disputed, since the case she makes for the high ethical value of capitalism formally rests on moral axioms about private property and autonomous rationality.)

have succumbed to small-pox. Thus the weak members of civilised societies propagate their kind. No one who has attended to the breeding of domestic animals will doubt that this must be highly injurious to the race of man ...

The aid which we feel impelled to give to the helpless is mainly an incidental result of the instinct of sympathy, which was originally acquired as part of the social instincts, but subsequently rendered, in the manner previously indicated, more tender and more widely diffused. Nor could we check our sympathy, if so urged by hard reason, without deterioration in the noblest part of our nature. The surgeon may harden himself whilst performing an operation, for he knows that he is acting for the good of his patient; but if we were intentionally to neglect the weak and helpless, it could only be for a contingent benefit, with a certain and great present evil. Hence we must bear without complaining the undoubtedly bad effects of the weak surviving and propagating their kind ... (I.168f.)

Interestingly, Darwin groups human beings with ants and bees as a gregarious and social species, whose competitive success vis à vis other species has been significantly due to cooperation and altruism. The anarchist theorist Kropotkin, forceful and eloquent critic of social Darwinism, saw this clearly,[9] as have all who read Darwin with care. We have been, as Darwin sees us, naturally selected for a significant measure of fellow feeling and mutual aid. It is in our nature, it must be viewed as coinciding with the development of language. Lines of hominids more individualist than our mutualist selves, we may plausibly suppose, fell by the competitive wayside.

That there is such a thing as being naturally good at some activity—and correlatively, *not* being good at it—where the aptitude coincides with a genetically identifiable human community, seems strongly indicated by more than one cultural practice or phenomenon. Social and economic factors, and the cultural experiences of the previous several generations of the community in question, or of its neighbours, can be difficult or, some argue, impossible to factor out. Still, some cases seem persuasive. Take skill at playing basketball. Young males in most cultures tend to prize and aspire to athletic prowess, especially prowess in popular sports. This seems to fit the young white male American population, and basketball, rather well: basketball is a highly favoured sport, and by general consent young

[9] See Peter Kropotkin, *Mutual Aid* (1902), Introduction and Chapters 1 and 2.

white American males are among the most favoured of privileged populations on earth. They could be expected to succeed, or at least to be present in numbers reflecting their percentage of the population, in more or less any area they attached enormous value to. But this is not what one finds in the highest reaches of skilled basketball playing. In the highest professional and amateur levels one finds, from a demographic point of view, white males markedly under-represented and black males very strongly overrepresented. It is difficult not to believe that white males would be there in greater numbers if they could. It is therefore difficult to believe that they have as great an aptitude for playing basketball, generally speaking, as black males do. The latter seem *naturally better* at playing basket-ball than whites, generally and overall, even though very many indi-vidual whites are extremely good at playing basketball.

It also seems right to call the relevant aptitudes *natural* ones—biologically based, genetic, not primarily a matter of socialization or cultural experience. It seems reasonable to think that two or three generations of remedial state-sponsored action to try to bring white youths up to par with black youths (where the latter's experiences were not modified to adversely affect basketball skill) would not appreciably diminish the greater skill of blacks at basketball.

Of course, there are no genes for playing basketball. Rather, there are genes for skills needed in playing basketball, and blacks seem to be more abundantly supplied with those genes. Blacks did not invent basketball, and there was a developed basketball sports culture before blacks began to play the game. But when they did, it seems clear, they took to the game in a manner that seems to reflect non-social, non-cultural aptitudes. Of course, it would probably be mistaken to discount sociocultural factors altogether. There are now probably sociocultural pressures on young black males to develop basketball skills. And there may be within non-blacks socioculturally grounded tendencies to resign themselves to the likelihood of at best secondary success in basketball.

Nonetheless, the overall case seems persuasive. In a manner we can describe as reasonably straightforward and more or less fitting folk intuitions and experience-based judgements, there is at least one case—and therefore surely others—of "natural," primarily biological-ly based skills and aptitudes that correlate with genetically constituted human groupings. To affirm that blacks tend to be better basketball players than non-blacks, and that this is not primarily a matter of socialization or culture, is not racist. It is not racist in part because it is *true*. (Presumably racist views are views that are necessarily untrue or unjustified.)

Now, even if the general point is granted here and is acknowledged to be important, and we note that part of its importance is the degree of support and fit it provides between serious science and "folk" science, it will by no means follow that any very wide range of social skills can be correlated with ethnic or genetic grouping. Unlike basketball, most social skills involve factors that are too centrally socioeconomic and ideational to offer much prospect for distinguishing biological and non-biological components. Indeed, in typical cases the idea of factoring out such components is conceptually problematic.

The nature-versus-nurture debates have been going on since the eighteenth century, and show no signs of abating. These are charged topics, regarded as having significant implications for issues of public policy, resource allocation, cultural and other forms of dominance, and the self-esteem of huge numbers of individuals. It is perhaps not surprising, therefore, that a high degree of polemic characterizes much of this debate. Nurturists insist that their position is the more sophisticated and modernist (or postmodernist), naturists that theirs is the more scientific. Nurturists, on the other hand, often claim that theirs is the better science. Both parties view the other as actuated more by a political agenda than by disinterested love of truth: nurturists are supposed to want to use their account of the "data" to further social egalitarian programs and naturists theirs to preserve a social status quo, or even to return to a status quo ante, where general social equality is given up as an unrealizable dream. There seems to be much truth to imputations of sociopolitical motivations on *both* sides. Competing paradigms of human nature are at issue, but also competing ethics linked to those paradigms. On the other hand, surely it is plausible to believe that if there is such a thing as more or less disinterested Aristotelian *curiosity* about *anything,* there can be and is disinterested curiosity about human beings and what we are like. Unless all inquiry is committed in advance to normatively preferred outcomes—and though some contemporary views hold that this is the case, unless itself assumed in advance to be necessarily true there seems no good reason to believe that it is—some people genuinely want to learn what is true and significant about human beings, and are willing to live with what they think investigation shows. Moreover, there are people who honestly, honourably, intelligently, and apolitically come to differing views about human beings.

The trait, or alleged trait, of intelligence is the one that is most bitterly contested in these debates. What intelligence is, whether it is a more or less unitary sort of thing, whether it is alterable, and whether it is measurable with any precision are the issues. Some want to deny that there is even such a thing as intelligence. This seems not a reasonable view: that there is *just nothing at all,* or nothing with any clear content, that is being said about someone if they are described as very intelligent—or the reverse—seems unconvincing. Other views insist that intelligence is no one thing, no single characteristic that is identifiable (still less measurable) in someone. Of course things *are* complicated, about all manner of phenomena. Many folk concepts are too unsubtle to capture a human reality. But something other than pure devotion to conceptual precision may be operative where a politically and emotively charged issue is concerned. And if we say that there is not one but four, or seven, or an indefinite plurality of kinds of intelligence, we won't be able to say that one person is more intelligent than another, and that might be a reassuring thing to be able to say.

In fact it is easy to argue that there is no single such thing as good looks or athletic talent. Some people manifest one kind or aspect of beauty or talent for sport, others another. And the idea of actually calibrating beauty, at least, seems quite absurd. Yet there does seem to be something we can discern as general impressiveness in personal aesthetics and athletic skill; and also in the brains department. We might not *want* to bring attention to intelligence (or some other matter of talent or skill) because it would be socially divisive, or make some people feel bad, or not deserve to matter as much as it does; but that is quite a different matter from whether it exists.

Finally, if there is such a thing as general intelligence, a certain kind of commodity that people have in differing degree—an ability or range of abilities to conceptualize and figure complex things out, reasonably quickly—it is hard to see why this should defy the possibility of measurement in some more or less universal way. Unlike good looks, it seems at least feasible to try for an objective measure of braininess. Whether standard IQ tests are effective or accurate measures of general intelligence will be, of course, another matter. But if they can be convincingly argued to be less useful for capturing general intelligence than some other proposed instrument, possibly a more adequate technique could be identified. Whether intelligence is alterable over the course of life, and if so how, is still another topic, as is its degree of heritability—which is of course the heart and core of the nature/nurture issue all over again.

There are, then, many facets of this matter both to affirm and to keep distinct. That there is such a thing as (general) intelligence does not indicate where it comes from. The respective contributions of early-life environment—including adequate protein and other brain nutrients at key early-life stages—cultural factors, education, general health, and genetics might be highly complex, and difficult or impossible to disentangle or measure with precision. On the other hand, it is hard to see why intelligence wouldn't be inherited to a significant degree, since so many other general aptitudes and abilities seem clearly to be. Coming to conclusions about the mean intelligence, or intelligence range, of particular population *groups*—men and women; genetic, ethnic, or racial communities; or other non-socially defined classifications of people—is a considerably more complicated as well as more politically charged matter. Almost all such groupings correlate with significant sociocultural differentiations, which diminishes the already uncertain prospects of isolating a peculiarly genetic group component. There seems in any case good reason to believe that whatever group genetic commonalities there may be, these are dwarfed by differences (both genetic and non-genetic) between individuals within any single genetic group.[10]

Darwin's view of humans may now be outlined. Most of the characteristics we think distinctive of ourselves Darwin sees as occurring in a simpler form in other species, and not necessarily just in other primates: "there is no fundamental difference between man and the higher mammals in their mental faculties" (I.35). He argues for, and illustrates, a shared and variegated emotional register that includes pleasure, pain, happiness, misery, and capacities for terror, suspicion, courage, timidity, ill and good temper, rage, revenge, love and the desire to be loved, grief, kindness, jealousy, pride, self-satisfaction, shame, sulkiness, enjoyment, excitement, boredom,

---

[10] This discussion of nature, nurture, intelligence, and human subgroups will seem to many too vague, meandering, and inconclusive to have been worth stating or reading. Some will think there is some unstated subtext, perhaps a biologistic one (or, on the other hand, a liberal one). Its main intent is in fact to affirm the importance of intellectual courage, and honesty, even with uncomfortable subjects. (I say *even with,* not *especially with;* for there is also importance in tact, sensitivity, and an awareness that political topics don't become apolitical just because someone says that *they* at least are ignoring their political dimensions.)

wonder, curiosity, watchful attention, imagination, a disposition to imitation, and powers of memory and even reasoning. In his meticulous way Darwin gives examples, from his or other naturalists' experiences, of each of these traits exhibited in other primates or higher mammals. He goes on to argue for still closer affinities between humans and other animals. "It has been asserted that man alone is capable of progressive improvement; that he alone makes use of tools or fire, domesticates other animals, possesses property, or employs language; that no other animal is self-conscious, comprehends itself, has the power of abstraction, or possesses general ideas; that man alone has a clear sense of beauty, is liable to caprice, has the feeling of gratitude, mystery, & c.; believes in God, or is endowed with a conscience" (I.49). Darwin proceeds to argue that non-human animals exhibit at least versions of each of these characteristics. His case—presented in Part 2, Chapter 2 of *The Descent of Man*—is a fascinating and largely persuasive exercise in ethnological advocacy, arguing firmly for a human location within a wider mammalian framework, with most of what we see as both special and valued in ourselves also identifiable within that framework.

More similar to the other animals than we might have supposed, or welcomed, we also possess a set of instincts. (The *concept* of an instinct is not very usefully explored by Darwin. Like Freud after him, he takes for granted that this is a clear, well-understood idea. Elucidating the instinctual was to be a primary contribution of modern genetics.) We have fewer instincts than any other species, but we do have some: "Man has also some few instincts in common, as that of self-preservation, sexual love, the love of the mother for her newborn offspring, the power possessed by the latter of sucking, and so forth" (I.36). The additions turn out to include the capacities for the states or dispositions listed above, together with our fundamental gregariousness, our social instincts. For Darwin, in this respect we importantly resemble ants, bees, and other social animals.

Remarkably, the characteristic that Darwin believes most markedly distinguishes humans from other animals is morality: "I fully subscribe to the judgment of those writers who maintain that of all the differences between man and the lower animals, the moral sense or conscience is by far the most important" (I.70). Darwin's view is that a moral sense is a more or less inevitable consequence of high intelligence united with social instincts. These developments, in humans, take a form and a direction only partly assignable to natural selection or instinct. "In many cases it is impossible to decide whether certain social instincts have been acquired through natural selection, or are the indirect result of other instincts and faculties, such as sympathy, reason, experience, and a tendency to imitation; or again, whether they are simply the result of long-continued habit" (I.82). These habits and dispositions, learned or instinctive, include large measures of self-interest and sympathy—imaginative awareness of the feelings of others—some conjunction of which, manifested also in strong and probably instinctually grounded (i.e., formed through natural selection) identification with members of one's own group and suspicion of others and their groups, creates the basis from which advanced morality and culture arises.

Darwin is silent about many facets of this portrait. He clearly accords a great deal in the human repertoire (as also in that of higher mammals) to learning. There is no presumption at all of total biological determination of human behaviour. Yet the portrait is of a bio-based creature who continues, even in civilized version, to manifest traits that have definite analogues in non-human nature.

Darwinian biological science, from its early base, continued to extend and consolidate its place in the sciences in the twentieth century. The importance of the addition of Mendelian genetics to the enterprise would be difficult to exaggerate. Genetic understanding discloses the mechanisms of natural selection and removes a considerable number of mysteries left essentially as bald facts in *The Origin of Species* or Darwin's other works. At the same time, the fundamental Darwinian picture has survived remarkably well, mostly augmented rather than revised or reversed. (Darwin himself was the first to acknowledge the uncertain character of some of his guesses and the probability of future reconsideration and new advance.) The evolutionary history of humans has of course been filled in, and continues to be, in ways and to a degree that would have astonished and delighted Darwin. This has included the discovery of the closeness of our kinship with the anthropoid apes, above all to the chimpanzee (and especially the pygmy chimpanzee, or bonobo, our closest living relative).

A dramatic attempt at an overall or integrated "revisioning" of humanity going beyond the Darwinian and Mendelian backdrop was, however, not attempted until the appearance of sociobiology, in the work of E. O. Wilson. In four major books—*Sociobiology: The New Synthesis* (1975), *On Human Nature* (1978), *Genes, Mind, and Culture* (1981), and *Promethean Fire* (1983) (the latter two with Charles Lumsden)—Wilson developed a set of theses, some of them modified in the later volumes, that purport to provide a genuine science of human behaviour along Darwinian biological lines. The project is conceived as ambitious, and comprehensive: to show that fundamentally all human behaviour is actuated by genetic imperatives, or else has goals and aetiologies that tend towards fulfilling genetic imperatives—that is, commands or instructions, encoded in our genes, that strongly predispose us in directions naturally selected for the perpetuation of our genes. Sociobiology affirms as well that these genetic imperatives will inevitably and indefinitely constrain the horizons of possibility for distinct kinds of human beings.

As mentioned earlier, even if a Darwinian account of human evolutionary history does not imply marked human differentials affecting abilities, correlated with lineage or sex, it also does not imply that there are no such differentials. A Harris-like conception of the human range—of the kind implied above for "races," together with the fundamental natural sexual equality Harris and many others also affirm—is wholly compatible with the Darwinian perspective. (Harris's own theory of human nature rests firmly on the shoulders of the Darwinian account.) Similarly, views implying extremely different clusters of abilities and propensities for the sexes or ethnic groups, or both, are not ruled out. Darwin himself seems to have thought there are considerable sex differentials, and that genetic isolation had already produced significant bio-based aptitudes and profiles in human populations. Other Darwinians, independently of E. O. Wilson, have come to even more pronounced versions of such contrasts.

The ethnicity case, at least, is linked to the still unresolved paleontological dispute between proponents of the "Eve hypothesis"—the view that all living humans descend from an East African female living about one hundred thousand years ago, the sole surviving hominid population having partly come out of Africa into Asia at approximately the same date—and the more complex early diffusionist view, which envisages much earlier hominid departures from Africa and much lengthier periods of separate development for human groups (with possibly some minor looping conjunctions) in disparate parts of the old world. If the latter were the correct view, the five (or so) distinct human races would have longer separate histories, and a proportionately greater chance of having acquired genetic repertories with bio-based sociocultural implications. It is clear in any case, and important to recall, that other hominid species than our own could perfectly well have survived into modern times. There once were, but long ago wholly disappeared, hominids who would have been viewed, had they come into contact with us only in this century, as of dramatically lower intelligence and lesser aptitude than ourselves. It is an understandably sensitive matter whether any existing human group is, in any way that bears on sociocultural performance, importantly biologically distinct from any other. There are real conceptual complexities contained in the very question. The fact that there could still have been Australopithecine hominids on earth establishes that these complexities must, in principle, be solvable; but translations to effectively transhistorical transcultural realities of differences that in *all* versions of the data will be rather slight are sufficiently challenging that suspicion of non-scientific motives for the attempt seems justified. Claims of important bio-based differences between the sexes—again, it must be stressed, differences that have sociocultural implications, that impose boundaries on human possibilities—are yet another matter, involving a different kind of complexity.

At any rate there was, independently of Wilson, plenty of room for what we can call (anticipating the terminology of feminism) "equality" Darwinism and "difference" Darwinism; and lots of Darwinians have grouped themselves under each of these banners. There is nothing new, in other words, in the idea that natural selection has differentially advantaged or disadvantaged particular kinds of humans in respect of particular parts of the broad sociocultural range.

The innovation that sociobiology brings to the table is the idea that human behaviour is fundamentally guided (if not quite altogether determined) by a drive to maximize inclusive fitness, that is, a drive to maximize the proliferation of the genes the individual is carrying. Sociobiologists are "difference" Darwinians who suppose we are, at the deepest level of all that we do, servants of our genes.[11]

Of course, Wilson and his colleagues and disciples do not just "suppose" this: they make a case, a highly technical case, that we will not be able to examine here. (For a very thorough, accessible,

---

[11] Most sociobiology takes a "difference" stance with respect to both race and gender. For the position that there are no significant ethnic or racial differences among human populations but *are* significant biological differences between the sexes—translating into substantial unmodifiable psychological and sociocultural differences—see Robert Wright, *The Moral Animal* (1994).

Not all sociobiology is in fact of "difference" perspective with respect to either sex or race. There is even feminist sociobiology, notably in the work of Sarah Hrdy. See her book *The Woman That Never Evolved* (1981). Hrdy is a primatologist who has given special attention to the evolution of female primates, including human ones. It seems reasonable to hold that her stance subtracts features of more familiar or mainstream varieties both of feminism and of sociobiology.

non-neutral but, I think, persuasive discussion of that case, the reader is referred to Philip Kitcher's *Vaulting Ambition*.[12]) There are methodological difficulties in sociobiology's claims to be genuine biological science; and problems of providing a literal rendering of talk of sperm and egg "strategies"—assigned to genes, not merely to individual humans—that will not imply there are something like homunculi in the genes or whip-wielding incubi in the mind. There is also a very severe problem of *evidence*.

The obvious and most powerful argument against sociobiology—as mentioned above, this will not touch other biologistic stances in human nature theory—is that human behaviour seems patently not always actuated by considerations of genetic success. Indeed, this puts the point too weakly. Although many of us, possibly most, have some sort of impulses to produce offspring, and others of us may satisfy *possibly* related impulses when our siblings have offspring, there are plainly large numbers of human beings whose behaviour manifests no such urges. This appears obvious. Of course, many things seem obvious that aren't even true; but it is clear that sociobiology confronts an uphill battle, which it shows little sign of seriously acknowledging, much less dealing with. There are large numbers of humans who don't have children and give every indication of not wanting them, and this doesn't appear to correlate in any significant way with whether their lives are otherwise satisfying to them or whether they are amply endowed with fertile siblings or first cousins. Moreover, it certainly appears that much engendering of children has occurred for psychological, social, or cultural reasons quite independent of genetic or dynastic impulses. Still more fundamentally, an immense amount of human behaviour does not seem motivated by desires to survive or to be sexually attractive to potential partners. What sociobiological account could be given, for example, of stamp collecting, alpinism, or casino gambling? All

---

[12] R. C. Lewontin, Steven Rose, and Leon J. Kamin's *Not in Our Genes* (1984) also provides a useful, if still more polemical, critique of major sociobiological theses. Mary Midgley is another critic of sociobiology with a significant arsenal of objections; see *Beast and Man* (1978), "Gene-juggling" (1979), and "Selfish Genes and Social Darwinism" (1983), and the articles she discusses or that reply to her critiques: J. L. Mackie, "The Law of the Jungle" (1978) and "Genes and Egoism" (1981), and Richard Dawkins, "In Defence of Selfish Genes" (1981). Midgley's primary concerns are with the ethical implications of sociobiology, for altruism and egoism.

competitive activity can of course be viewed as training for, or as miming, genetically significant competitive activity; but this will put sociobiology's claims to falsifiability—that is, to being genuine science—at risk.

It is important that we not "idealize" sociobiology. It is supposed to be a materialist theory, for which surface-level or everyday, consciously felt desires may be very insecure guides to systemic aetiology. Our genes are supposed to be dictating our behaviour, and they are supposed to operate with a cunning of reason,[13] putatively more thorough than Hegel's. At the same time, there seem to be "idealist" components of sociobiology that the theory does not discern. I seem to need to *know* about my kindred, in a presumably verbal and culturally displayed way, for actions regarding them to be motivated—altruistic deeds I perform on their behalf, or feelings I have when I discover that they have reproduced, nudging a little more of my genetic makeup in the direction of immortality. Or am I supposed to have a kind of radar that tells me who is related to me and how closely, and that operates automatically, whether or not I recognize or care about it? Biological mechanisms of this kind doubtless operate. Our several cuings, scentings, sniffings of each other—all of the stuff of body language, and subliminal levels of biochemical priming and response—might well include components of kinship recognition. It is difficult to believe that this could extend with any subtlety beyond parent-child interrelations, but possibly some sort of kin-identifying mechanisms do exist. If so, they appear gross, inefficient, and frequently wholly non-operational. People murder their close blood kin, and often are utterly indifferent to their welfare, needing, it seems, all the pressures of law and culture to display concern for them. Civil war also poses a problem for sociobiologists. In any case, knowing that particular people are your relatives, and how closely they are related, requires *learning*. We seem, again, to have a crucial *idealism* in the theory: what the individual consciously has learned, involving detailed and culturally specific data, activates a repertoire of biological behaviours that would have been quite otherwise given other content in the head. This appears, as we said above, to compromise the materialism and indeed the scientific cre-

---

[13] The cunning of reason is Hegel's variant of the Mandeville/Smith idea of an "invisible hand" (cf. Chapter 6, note 1)—an underlying pattern that operates as though purposefully to achieve results that the conscious agents involved have not seen or intended.

dentials of the theory. It also, of course, appears deeply implausible and at odds with the experiences we have.

Sociobiological ideas, and permutations and combinations of them, appear in a number of semi-popular scientific (or semi-scientific) publications of recent years. Perhaps most influential of these are the writings of the Oxford zoologist Richard Dawkins, especially his *The Selfish Gene* (1976), *The Extended Phenotype* (1982), and *The Blind Watchmaker* (1986). The core idea in Dawkins' work is that of "the selfish gene." This corresponds to earlier sociobiological proposals that the gene, not the individual animal or other living organism, should be regarded as the primary or essential unit of natural selection, with the individual functioning as a vehicle for its maximal proliferation. Dawkins developed this conception in innovative and imaginative ways. His writings also personalize the gene—as though assigning it a miniature mind—in ways clearly not intended literally,[14] yet not easily replaced with a literal, mechanistic account that still says something interesting or plausible about the causes of human behaviour. The matter is further complicated by Dawkins' stepping back, in *The Selfish Gene,* from a pure mechanistic approach. He assigns us a structure—a so-called non-genetic replicator called a meme, essentially symbolic contents (beliefs and ideas)—that competes with our genes for determination and control of our behaviour and that differentiates us from other living systems. The result is a more philosophical, and a less original, view than had first appeared. Memes notwithstanding, the behaviour of the sexes is conceived in fairly orthodox sociobiological terms, and confronts the same objections the sociobiological account of human sexuality does.

Between Darwin and sociobiology, both chronologically and in some theoretical respects, we find another biological theorist of human nature of originality and importance, Konrad Lorenz (1903–1989). His scientific work was chiefly in ethology, the study of animal behaviour in the wild, and the theory of instincts (Lorenz received the Nobel Prize for his work, jointly with two other scientists, in 1973), and he wrote a number of semi-popular books on animal and human behaviour that cumulatively and collectively give expression to a Darwinian theory of some interest.

Lorenz is common-sensical, non-technical, eclectic; also good-humoured, synoptic, sage-like. He is not *deeply* original. He follows very much in Darwin's footsteps, with expanded interests in special

[14] Dawkins says this quite explicitly, more than once.

facets of our behaviour, like our capacity for aggression. Lorenz also respects and makes some accommodation to Freud.

As the latter fact might intimate, Lorenz is not a clear or unqualified materialist. The proof of this, and a good central indicator of his theoretical style (of what admirers might specially admire and detractors deplore) is found in the key role he assigns human *curiosity*. Like Aristotle, Lorenz regards humans as by nature deeply curious creatures, with this trait necessary in accounting for our evolutionary development and our behaviour from before what Marvin Harris calls "cultural takeoff" on to the present. Clearly Lorenz, like Darwin, regards human intelligence, and curiosity as one of its multiple facets, as naturally selected for its adaptive success, and as causally fundamental in our ongoing saga. This is in direct conflict with the Harris variety of materialism, at least: for Harris the two scientific sins that thwarted the otherwise extraordinarily impressive Enlightenment initiatives towards a science of culture were the belief in progress and the view that ideas, prompted by such things as intelligent curiosity, had anything importantly to do with human prehistory or history. In this latter respect at least, Lorenz is a throwback to the Enlightenment approach and its assumptions.

He shares with Freud a belief in the fundamental role of instinct in human as in other animal life. For Lorenz this takes the more distinctively biological form of focusing on instinctual constituents in same-species, not internal and highly symbolic, behaviour. Like the subsequent sociobiological school, Lorenz thinks that our naturally selected prehistory continues to operate in and has important explanatory significance for life within urban, technological modern social conditions. But unlike sociobiology, Lorenz assigns an independent aetiological role to culture, taking features of culture and technology as functionally equivalent to acquired but transmissible traits.[15]

Lorenz's account of aggression in humans (expressed above all in his widely read book *On Aggression* [1963 in German, 1966 in English]) sees the range of behaviour collected under this label as having evolved as a highly functional cluster of traits in the conditions of human life before the development of agricultural societies—that is to say, for the many hundreds of thousands of years of natural selection operating on our ancestors in their east African homeland. Patterns of aggressive behaviour, and responses to it (equal or greater

---

[15] Others—among them Harris and Midgley—argue for essentially the same idea.

displays of aggression or submission, again taking a variety of forms) were key to individual, interpersonal, and group adaptive success, with well-developed elements of bluff and degree of posture and risk, and dominant and subordinate strategies effectively serving the players of all roles. These modes of behaviour, only rarely lethal or seriously disabling on the African savannah or during the tens of thousands of years of nomadism prior to the beginnings of settled agricultural life, became increasingly dysfunctional in civilized conditions of human life. The technology of weaponry, in particular, has at an exponentially accelerated pace over the past five centuries led us, individually and often collectively, to circumstances in which our reach, as it were, exceeds our grasp. Lorenz expresses no Rousseau-like call to a restored simplicity; doing so would be implausible, since humans have long been able—and usually eager—with spear and arrow to kill each other impersonally, long distance. He is instead guardedly optimistic that our fundamental curiosity, and other facets of intelligence, including the morality he thinks it has created, will steer us beyond the destructively aggressive predicament in which nature—our human nature—has currently lodged us.

Lorenz's understanding of evolutionary possibilities, and occasional realities, is more elastic than, say, Marvin Harris's. The latter envisages a fully articulated, closely similar species, its members by kind or genetic variety easily interchangeable with each other, and no more than a generation or two needed for any one human population group comfortably to occupy the sociocultural place of any other. Lorenz, by contrast, takes the extra-human and some human evidence to show the possibility of quite substantial genetic variation in a relatively short time. The two views are not deeply at odds over the somewhat longer term, since a relatively rapid departure from a genotype could in principle be followed by as quick a return. Yet Harris's picture is clearly more uniformitarian; Lorenz's will allow that a particular population may have gone out on a genetic limb, that might well translate into distinctive behavioural or cultural patterns not readily matched elsewhere in the human community. Lorenz's view, then, is closer to Darwin's on "difference."

Presumably this is an empirical matter, and in principle experiment should be able to determine whether Harris or Lorenz is right. In practice it is not at all easy to envisage tests that would be ethically acceptable, require less than a century to perform, and be genuinely decisive, that is, be able to control sociocultural variables. Of course, these are also delicate, potentially volatile matters.

Harris's stance is a particularly extreme instance of uniformitarianism, a common shared humanity strongly affirmed.

Social constructionist views notwithstanding, it is surely folly to claim that primatology—the study of primate species and their behaviour—is *irrelevant* to learning about human beings. Any understanding of human nature must at least include a biological perspective; and that perspective must involve human evolution. Indeed, all of the theories in this book, with the possible exceptions of Christianity, liberalism, and feminism, make at least some explicit acknowledgement of our *literal* species-being. And none of our theories is incapable of accommodation to biology and our animality. Some versions of feminism, for example, lay special stress on the body, negatively in claiming it is ignored in much reason-focused masculinist theory, and positively in proposing reproductive and nurturant bodily realities as the core of human reality.

The question of dispute, then, is the extent to which biology reveals who and what we are. The role of our biological origins in understanding contemporary human beings is also open to some question. Interestingly, there are non-biological, indeed non-materialist analogues of the latter: cultural idealist theories differ about the weight and status to accord the past in understanding present realities. Some think "tradition" lives on and on in our circumstances and is ignored at our peril, others that traditionalism is itself a primarily ideological stance without much serious empirical warrant, chiefly used to block change, especially egalitarian change.[16]

Thinking of ourselves as a certain kind of ape isn't just a matter of being literally Linnaean.[17] It is to give weight and significance to some of our features and withhold them from others. It affords escape from some present challenges. We can imaginatively see ourselves as Tarzan and Jane (or something comparable) and take flight to a simpler, more elemental thought-world. Or we can persuade ourselves that some social or historical problems don't matter—what importance does this petty contemporary concern have under the eye of biological, still less of geological time?—or are insoluble, the possibility of meaningfully dealing with them whisked out of our

---

[16] The metaphorical California/New England contrast of the first chapter may be viewed as also a division of perspectives over the weight different kinds of past still have (or perhaps should be allowed to have).

[17] Carl von Linné (Linnaeus) (1707–1778) was the originator of the modern scientific system of classifying plants and animals.

hands by genetic predestinarianism. Yet even so, we are a certain kind of ape. We also have particular family histories, health patterns, profiles of luxury-good consumption and voting behaviour. To some degree, it seems, we *choose* to accord these and others of our characteristics greater or lesser significance, and we thereby live our lives differently.

I do not mean to imply—here or elsewhere—that there is no effective reply to these queries. The extreme sociobiological claim that essentially all of our behaviour is driven, directly or indirectly, by naturally selected reproductive strategy does seem difficult to defend. But lesser biologistic claims and stances might fare better. Few positions have been more frequently urged in our time than different forms of *contextualism,* the view that phenomena cannot adequately be grasped independently of a context in which they are found. What context is wider and deeper, it may be claimed, than our biological one? And on this decidedly inconclusive note we leave the biological approach to human nature.

Bibliography

Appleman, Philip, ed. *Darwin*. Norton Critical Edition. 2nd ed. New York: W. W. Norton, 1979.

Darwin, Charles. *The Descent of Man*. Princeton: Princeton University Press, 1981. [1871]

—————. *The Origin of Species*. Harmondsworth: Penguin, 1978. [1859]

Dawkins, Richard. *The Blind Watchmaker*. Oxford: Oxford University Press, 1986.

—————. *The Extended Phenotype*. Oxford: Oxford University Press, 1982.

—————. "In Defence of Selfish Genes." *Philosophy* 218 (October 1981).

—————. *The Selfish Gene*. Oxford: Oxford University Press, 1976.

Harris, Marvin. *Cultural Materialism*. New York: Random House, 1979.

—————. *Our Kind*. New York: Harper & Row, 1989.

—————. *The Rise of Anthropological Theory*. New York: Harper Collins, 1968.

Hrdy, Sarah Blaffer. *The Woman That Never Evolved*. Cambridge, MA: Harvard University Press, 1981.

Kitcher, Philip. *Vaulting Ambition*. Cambridge, MA: MIT Press, 1985.

Kropotkin, Peter, Prince. *Mutual Aid*. Harmondsworth: Penguin, 1939. [1902]

Lewontin, R. C., Steven Rose, & Leon J. Kamin. *Not in Our Genes*. New York: Random House, 1984.

Lorenz, Konrad. *On Aggression*. New York: Harcourt Brace Jovanovich, 1966.

Lumsden, C., & E. O. Wilson. *Genes, Mind, and Culture*. Cambridge, MA: Harvard University Press, 1981.

—————. *Promethean Fire*. Cambridge, MA: Harvard University Press, 1983.

Mackie, J. L. "Genes and Egoism." *Philosophy* 218 (October 1981).

—————. "The Law of the Jungle." *Philosophy* 206 (October 1978).

Malthus, T. R. *An Essay on the Principle of Population*. Edited by D. Winch. Cambridge: Cambridge University Press, 1992. [originally published in successive editions 1803–1826]

Mayr, Ernst. *One Long Argument*. Cambridge, MA: Harvard University Press, 1991.

Midgley, Mary. *Beast and Man*. Ithaca, NY: Cornell University Press, 1978.

————. "Gene Juggling." *Philosophy* 210 (October 1979).

————. "Selfish Genes and Social Darwinism." *Philosophy* 225 (July 1983).

Millhauser, Milton. *Just before Darwin*. Middletown, CT: Wesleyan University Press, 1959.

Weiner, Jonathan. *The Beak of the Finch*. New York: Knopf, 1994.

Wilson, E. O. *On Human Nature*. Cambridge, MA: Harvard University Press, 1975.

————. *Sociobiology: The New Synthesis*. Cambridge, MA: Harvard University Press, 1975.

Wright, Robert. *The Moral Animal*. New York: Pantheon, 1994.

CHAPTER 10

Freud ─────────────────

THE INFLUENCE OF SIGMUND FREUD (1856–1939) on modern culture is so great that it is difficult or impossible to conceive of a twentieth-century western outlook with the ideas that he contributed to it factored out. At the same time, Freud's ambition to create a science of mind whose extension from a Darwinian base would be psychoanalysis has not been realized. The result is a somewhat bewildering cultural magic or illusion where Freud is both everywhere and nowhere in the late twentieth century world-view.

Freud's ideas have been very much discussed, and they have been quite controversial. Early controversy attached to his "sexualizing" of all of life—most infamously, its preadolescent portion—and to his apparent sabotaging of morality with the idea that love and cruelty are two facets of a single reality. Psychoanalytic dethronement of a rational self that is in knowing command of its agency and destiny, while also ill received, had forerunners in the views of Spinoza, Hume, Schopenhauer, and others; and the also unsettling conviction that our freedom is precluded by a scientific understanding of the world continued traditions frequently affirmed since the Greeks. Later controversy has stemmed from claims of Freud's androcentrism, misogyny, political insensitivity or opacity, and (alleged) suppression of uncomfortable data. Early and late, Freudian psychoanalysis has met with severe criticism from scientists and philosophers of science. Freud's theories have been assailed as unempirical and not genuine science, or at best completely unsupported by serious evidence.

While developmental stages in the evolution of Freud's views are acknowledged, there is a tendency to see psychoanalysis as a single completed theoretical edifice.[1] This has much plausibility, but I want to argue that one should distinguish core components of Freud's views from views that were—either for Freud himself, or by virtue of their logic or evidentiary link to what is core—less settled. (The term "peripheral" would be misleading. Some of what is non-core

---

[1] The full theory is usually regarded as completed in all essentials by 1926.

consists, I think, of bold conjectures on Freud's part, but which psychoanalytic evidence may not justify, and whose detachment and rejection leaves the core unimpaired.)

The aim, then, will be to locate and describe this Freudian centre of theory and depict in general terms the distinctively Freudian vision of humanity. I will also say something, but not much, about the scientific status or credentials of psychoanalysis. My view is that most or all of the core Freudian theory is empirical. Some of it might never admit of full confirmation or disconfirmation, but largely because of logistical and ethical limitations on psychological testing of human subjects. Some of the unsettled accretions or non-core theory is a little "wild," empirically,[2] and *some* of it possibly not falsifiable.

I want also to give space to and respect for positions that view Freud's theories with complete contempt. As will become evident, I think Freud's theories are serious, insightful, and often plausible: I think quite a good case can be made for Freud. But the constituency that views him as a quack or charlatan,[3] or simply a philosopher masquerading as a scientist, deserves representation.[4]

A particularly sober, straightforward, and brief summary of the major components and claimed results of psychoanalysis may be found in an article Freud wrote in 1922 intended for inclusion in a

[2] I mean by this, a little more precisely, that some of the theory constitutes speculative extensions of what were already, from Freud's own point of view, speculations. Other parts rest on bad science—most notoriously, the theory Freud developed in *Totem and Taboo* (1912–1913) and subsequently elaborated, of the actual prehistoric killing and eating of a patriarchal leader and father, memory of which was somehow transmitted genetically, and which was the foundation of religion. There seems no other construal of these hypotheses than as Lamarckian.

[3] A standard and much-respected text in philosophy of science, Ronald N. Giere's *Understanding Scientific Reasoning* (3rd ed., 1991), for example, relegates psychoanalysis to "marginal science," along with astrology, mental telepathy, and similar fields.

[4] Similar remarks apply, in my view, to the ideas of Hegel, Schopenhauer, Marx, and Nietzsche, all of whom are taken very seriously by their supporters yet viewed with disdain or derision by some among their many critics.

reference volume on sexology.[5] The article, called "Psycho-analysis," was first published in 1923. At the time he wrote it Freud's
views were in transition, and the reasonably settled position he came
to on the famous triad of id, ego, and superego was in the course of
formulation. So we find here a developed expression of Freudian
theory, following upon more than twenty years of clinical experience
since Freud's first articulations of psychoanalytic theory in the 1890s;
some forty years of professional practice as a physician, neurologist,
and psychiatrist; and the publication of five major books and a large
number of articles.

Freud conceives his enterprise as having begun with the treatment, and then with theorizing upon the causes, of certain nervous
or psychiatric disorders. He thinks of psychoanalysis in the first
instance as a method of treating these disorders. Out of this study and
practice Freud sees himself as expanding the range and purview of
psychoanalysis to include all psychological functioning and states,
culminating in a general theory of human psychology, itself in turn
claiming to offer a general theory of human nature with explanatory
significance for a broad spectrum of cultural, social, and historical
phenomena. To these larger ends Freud identifies psychoanalysis also
as a method of evidentiary access, a reliable technique that can provide data not otherwise readily attainable about psychic processes. A
third significance is attached to the term: "psychoanalysis" is also the
name of the overall psychological theory Freud develops.

Freud calls that theory a *depth psychology*. By this he means a
view that accepts the existence of psychological phenomena as a
distinctive kind of state or process, encountered by first-person
introspection and inferred as accompanying or underlying the verbal
and other behaviour of other people. (Hence a depth psychology may
be called a *methodologically dualist* view.) Many of these states are
regarded as having meaning, meaning that may not be consciously
felt by the person whose states they are, and that is central to
understanding the behaviour of the individual. Any such view will

[5] There are other excellent general presentations of psychoanalytic theory,
primary and secondary. Freud is so lucid and careful a writer that he is
almost invariably the best source for his views. *A General Introduction to
Psychoanalysis* (the popular edition of *Introductory Lectures on
Psychoanalysis* [1916–17]) is a very good exposition of his theories as they
had evolved by 1915–16. This work's sequel, the *New Introductory
Lectures on Psychoanalysis* (1933), written fifteen years later, is also a
valuable source.

express a depth psychology. Note that such theories need only be methodologically dualist. Freud implicitly denies any ultimate commitment to irreducible mental states in his own theory, which he formally places within a biological—indeed, a Darwinian—framework. The primary biological concept Freud actually utilizes (in fact, makes very heavy use of) is the notion of an instinct. He also views the psychic system as a system of energy flows and pressures, with tensions building and requiring release (which they are sometimes unable to obtain in normal or straightforward ways). Otherwise, Freud's biologism is largely formal, or promisory; that is, later investigations, but not his own, will seek to provide bridges between psychoanalysis and biological theory.

Freud also formally houses his enterprise within what he conceives as mainstream orthodox science. This includes assumptions we would call naturalist and determinist. The programmatic commitment to meanings and their role in explaining behaviour will suggest that the alignment of psychoanalysis is idealist, not materialist. This is fully confirmed when one discovers the central places in Freud's view of the symbol and interpretation, and their operating often independently from, even at odds with, anything identifiable as individual (material) self-interest. At the same time, the biologism and naturalism of Freud's avowed commitments, together with the etic character of much of the theory—we are acting as the theory says whether we know it or not, often even though we deny that we are—make this idealism with a difference.

I will say almost nothing about the epistemic or evidentiary character of psychoanalysis as a reliable data source. This is, of course, an aspect of the theory many critics, including many philosophers of science, find most questionable. What is involved is whether the clinical experience of analysts, and the observational claims it produces, can on its own corroborate psychoanalytic conclusions, without independent confirmation. The status of the evidence is problematic.[6] Concomitantly it seems correct to affirm that first-

[6] Two recent prominent challenges to the scientific character of psychoanalysis have argued that the empirical evidence for effectively all psychoanalytic claims is inadequate (the book *The Foundations of Psychoanalysis: A Philosophical Critique* [1984] and journal articles or interventions by the philosopher of science Adolf Grünbaum); and attacked the Freudian concept of repression (notably Frederick Crews, "The Revenge of the Repressed," *New York Review of Books,* Nov. 17 and Dec. 1, 1994, with extensive subsequent exchange in the Jan. 12, 1995 issue).

person observational and introspectionist—broadly, phenomenolo-gical—evidence can be both epistemically well grounded and valu-able. I will proceed to (some of) what Freud thinks the evidence that he has amassed shows.

Much of the Freudian view is not only quite familiar, but has also entered general discourse and understanding and become, one might say, part of our common-sense view of the world. Parts of this shared conviction, owed largely to Freud, are that there are uncon-scious thoughts, indeed that we have something like an ongoing unconscious mental life that sometimes intersects with familiar con-scious experience; and that very much of human life is deeply and inherently sexual, in ways that propel and also trouble our behaviour both directly and indirectly. Further, we commonly share with and significantly owe to Freud the idea that many things we give psychic attention to have a meaning or importance for us that is hidden from us: things we think about and that matter to us often represent, usually in disguise, something other than themselves. Along with this is the idea of dualities, or opposing tensions, in our affective relations to situations and people in our lives: love-hate, attraction-repulsion relations that don't merely indicate indecision or confusion on our part. Both the meanings we are drawn to but find opaque and the dualities in our feelings are seen as involving a kind of self-shielding from thoughts we would find (sometimes intolerably) pain-ful to think about directly and consciously. Or if common sense isn't quite prepared to *link* opacities and dualities with psychological self-defence, as Freud does, it certainly has come to agree with him that such *defence mechanisms* operate in our lives.

Freud's theories go beyond this now shared base. He thinks his data show that our unconscious lives are particularly fully revealed in our dreams, and that we can see there that we want things we would be consciously unwilling to admit we want. Almost every dream is for Freud a wish; and the particular wishes of dreams are part of a network, a typically fragmented idea-structure of fantasy

Repression figures prominently in the large number of cases of allegedly repressed experiences of childhood sexual abuse, restored to consciousness in adult life by the endeavours of a particular persuasion of psycho-therapists. There is a double load of calumny for Freud in this, since earlier quarrels, notably in the 1980s, had taken him to task precisely for failing to acknowledge the reality and extent of childhood sexual abuse, chiefly by fathers of their daughters. Freud is accused of choosing instead to view these daughters' later clinical reports as expressions of fantasy.

mingling components of love, fear, hate, lust, and guilt, often in the kinds of duality indicated above, and going far back into our pasts. Sequences in early life, almost all of them concluded before we were eight years old and most considerably earlier, constitute a set of passageways we had to navigate, as symbolist pilots, with our success or lack of it supplying the symbols that the rest of our lives would juxtapose and steer by, symbols invested above all with pleasure and pain.

In the most general sense, Freud's is a theory that says our private or inner selves, our individual mental lives, are the primary ingredient in what we are. Freud's theory of human nature, then, is psychological—rather than sociological or biological or historico-cultural—and essentially individualist.[7] Each of us builds up inwardly a (more or less stable) self, founded in impulses towards pleasurable bodily states (the relief of various bodily tensions) and away from painful ones. The pleasure originally sought and most acutely felt is, we might say, of a genus for which we have no name, but whose pre-eminent species is erotic sensation. The drive or energy fuelling this quest is the primordial duality, alternatively or simultaneously what may be called love and aggression. Consciousness emerges by gradual degrees. Awareness of non-self (or non-bodily) exterior objects is accompanied by coming to distinguish self from sources of the conferring or withholding of libidinal sensation. Typically, the major object so differentiated from one's self-body is one's mother. Differentiation creates complication: Mother provides, and withdraws, erotic satisfaction. She is loved/hated. Loving union—life's prototypical romance—becomes complicated in turn by the differentiation of another exterior object, also implicated in one's sensations and their possibilities of satisfaction. This is normally or typically one's father. (Freud virtually always assumes a conventional nuclear family, but the theory doesn't strictly require this.) Other objects may also be discerned, and provide additional sources of threat and, more rarely, of pleasure—siblings, or others. The raging, importunate, lustful egotist that all of us were modifies itself in the face of threat, competition, and first glimmerings of the objective realities of our case. We negotiate with ourselves, internalized

[7] Compare Freud's comments on the sciences: "Sociology too, dealing as it does with the behaviour of people in society, cannot be anything but applied psychology. Strictly speaking there are only two sciences: psychology, pure and applied, and natural science" (*New Introductory Lectures on Psychoanalysis,* p. 179).

Mother and Father, and reality, with varying degrees of success, and for none of us is the degree that high. After all, we are only little children; only a little reality (and hardly any of it involving accurate causal apprehensions) has entered our minds. The burden of our frantic lusts, the now-threatened tranquillity of our union with Mother, and the challenges and threats from Father and the world cannot be borne. Their weight compels us to hide them;[8] and we find that we can, we are not killed or dismembered, and reality as it grows for us begins to offer pleasures as well as pains. Or, if we are female, we effect a transference of the psychosexual roles, with Father coming to occupy the place Mother had held and vice versa. For both males and females these structured patterns are just what normally happens, with many individual variations leading to alternative pathways, though all other alternatives are for Freud dysfunctional or inadequate for achieving such adult psychic maturity as is possible. Some kind of package of a self is then assembled out of the parts that have been taken inward—introjected—and concealed; and a growing, expanding, conscious human being takes its place in the world, with a conscience, a reality navigator, a continuing pleasure-pain operator, and a hidden part that never goes away. Displacement, transference, something serving as something else (something more desired or feared) will propel and dominate the subsequent voyage, along with the ample rewards and pains of living in the world.

We should note that, as well as imputing to us a richly symbolic mental life at both conscious and unconscious levels, Freud's picture of the mind is of a strikingly *cognitive* entity. That is, we are regarded as functioning to a remarkable degree in a web of epistemic relations to facts of the world as we experience them—things we know, or think we

---

[8] This is the central and paradigmatic instance of what Freud means by repression (one of the psyche's principal defence mechanisms). The idea is misunderstood if taken as implying the complete hermetic sealing of large chunks of a past—as in some current "recovered memory" claims. Repression is the simultaneous preservation and concealment of painful experiences that have been significant to the individual. Repression admits of degree—something may be more or less deeply repressed, and more or less enduring. An appointment expected to be unpleasant can be repressed, the individual both knowing and "forgetting" that it is to occur. Such cases evidently disappear once the occasions they involved have passed. Others have a lifelong duration. A central Freudian view is that the repressed always "returns," manifests itself in disguised form in some facet of our behaviour.

do, and retain as knowledge-items as our lives go forward. These are above all things we think we know about ourselves and people important to us, and pleasure and pain that significant experiences have had for us. Most of this knowledge is unconscious, and has been repressed if there was pain associated with it, as there typically has been. Accordingly, we *resist* conscious confrontation with these painful truths. In general we develop habits, indeed strategies, of resistance to what we unconsciously or semi-consciously recognize as realities, including realities conscious acceptance of which might free us from patterns that make us unhappy or less than functional. The phenomenon of resistance is indeed one of the central components of psychoanalytic therapy. The therapeutic system is also a remarkably epistemic matter. For Freud it is the truth, and acknowledging it, that alone can set us free, not some matter of feeling good about ourselves or about life. The Freudian human is, then, not just a subject of fantasy and image and a centre of libidinous pleasure and pain, but also a knower.

This is just an outline of Freud's theory, and omits many details as well as the claimed mechanisms for the elements sketched. The particular cases of male and female children are said to be originally the same but soon distinctly different; and Freud's focus is unquestionably primarily on the male. The male, his loves and fears, and his sexual organ are the centres around which Freud's theory, as well as the male's own infantile fantasy life, revolve. This androcentrism is heavily censured in current evaluations; so also is much in Freud's positive account of female psychological development, and destiny. There may or may not be something to be said in Freud's defence. The ultimate basis for the individualism and psyche-centrism of the theory can at least be identified and given its due: human beings have by far the most prolonged and helplessly dependent infancy of any creature in the animal kingdom; years of it, a felt eternity of inner life, then life with one other, then with one more.

Prolonged helpless infancy, (usually) involving dependency on a Mother and some kind of complicated connection to a Father, constitutes a very powerful case for *some* variety of depth psychology; and the usual proximities to a mother (with significant focus in that relationship, over a protracted period of time, upon pleasure-inducing bodily orifices) at least nudges the dialectic in Freud's direction. The advocates of our alleged primordial social being, our holistic species-being, our never absent culturo-historical location, our rationally self-interested foundation—and these four are the major rival bases in understanding human nature—do not seem to offer anything to match this Freudian anchor. It doesn't seem seriously *possible* that our identities could be bound up with a wide social web of others for the long months, stretching into years, of the first stage of our lives. This *is* an individualist time, at least as experienced inwardly; we seem plainly totally impervious to our cultural or historical setting at its universally similar beginning, and only very gradually to move into it as those long months becoming years go by. And our helplessness, united with the urgency of the urges biology has conferred and the motility of our emotions, leaves us fragile, lovestruck, soft as down, frenzied—surely a radical antithesis to the cunning, self-serving calculator that we are alleged by rational self-interest theories to become. We have been for *so long* at the mercy of That Woman's pattern of attentions, and then That Man's worrisome, possibly also welcome interventions or presence. Can *that* deep and prolonged a sequence of experience, at the very beginning of life and continued well past a stage when we have become richly, symbolically conscious, really just fade away, superseded by *altogether* new and different bases and structures? When we have loved that much, that long—and feared and hated; but above all, loved?

I will try to bring out further individual features, and also more of the "flavour" of Freud's view of humanity by comparing that view with those of three thinkers all of whom differ strongly from each other but bear interesting similarities to Freud: Hume, Hegel, and Marx.[9]

The eighteenth-century theory of human nature developed by David Hume might at first seem utterly different from Freud's. The differences between Hume and Freud are in fact considerable, and the commonalities, while impressive, cannot be allowed to detain us long. But they are striking. Freud, like Hume, draws a sharp contrast between the safe, comfortable, rational, unitary, organized selves we take ourselves to be and the largely irrational or nonrational congeries of psychological subsystems existing in fuzzy, incompletely realized connection with each other. The latter is for both the reality, of course, and the former a constructed illusion. Both espouse naturalist and determinist theories, which are cold-eyed, analytical, and deflating of human dignity as rational cognizers of self or world. For both we don't do things for the reasons we think we do, but for other reasons or causes that operate compellingly or coercively on us.

---

[9] The discussion that follows makes no comment on matters of direct intellectual influence. Freud will certainly have had some degree of acquaintance with all three thinkers. He gives a brief but perceptive critique of Marxism in the *New Introductory Lectures on Psychoanalysis* (pp. 176–181).

Moreover, both are associationist psychological theories, and in each case the associationism is central to explaining and understanding our behaviour. In Hume's case this is quite obvious, since he explicitly identifies all changes of mental state as having been actuated by principles of association, namely, resemblance, contiguity, and causation. It is only a little less obvious that the Freudian system involves the same principles, equally centrally (though not so exclusively). The process of being led from one thought to a symbolically charged other requires unconscious recognition (in some cases it seems more like imposition) of resemblance. Reacting to a shape that isn't a sexual organ, for example, as though it were one, requires discerning a resemblance between that shape and the shape of the sexual organ. Our moving into and out of overt, manifest, and hidden or repressed symbolic transferences crucially depends on and daily, hourly, involves just the sorts of mental operations Hume's theory centres on.

The grand synoptic philosophy of culture and of humanity's place in the world developed by the nineteenth-century philosopher Hegel also bears instructive connection to Freud.[10] The central visions of each may be seen as exhibiting a fundamental complementarity. Freud's is the dark face of a single coin, Hegel's its sunny, radiant, optimistic side. For both the all-significant units of attention and understanding are three: the individual, the family, and the state (or civilization). The satisfactory, functional, and also potentially satisfying construction of all three is similar. It requires balance, compromise; it is artificial—requiring artifice—even as it gives form and substance to deeply natural human reality. The three are symbiotically linked. Obvious enough in Hegel, this is also Freud's conception. The processes involved mirror and echo each other, micro-cosmically and macro-cosmically. The economic construction of the self, intersecting union with specific biological others, and an order of social reality where one is participatory agent as well as recipient of irresistible others' agencies, all require long, sustained juggling acts, which most (not all) of us tend to get rather good at, with occasional lapses. Hegel's conception is sanguine, and philosophically pleasing on a grand scale, with the promise of feeding and nurturing an ever-expanding stream of Beauty and Knowledge, above all Self-Knowledge.

Freud is perhaps too often seen through child-focused lenses. This is not surprising, since he sees childhood as so magisterially

[10] The primary text for the Hegelian themes explored here is G. W. F. Hegel, *The Philosophy of Right* (1821).

determinative of adult life. But it is the adult, complex human being that is the real theoretical centre of Freud's concern and vision. In the real world Oedipus does not kill Laius and marry Jocasta, and our fate is to be and carry the burdens of those adults, not the lusting homicidal child within. The complex, multifaceted reality of being solitary voyager, sexual partner, husband/wife, parent, producer, consumer, citizen, nest-builder combines to offer us pains and joys of a qualitatively different order than those of childhood, even if they are only somewhat pallid displacements of the latter.

There are for Freud, as for Hegel, a cluster of foci on which the perambulations of history—individual, interpersonal, and societal—come to rest, often with wild perturbations and fluctuations, sometimes arrested before (always only temporary) equilibrium has been achieved or renewed. Thus there are civil wars, lesser forms of social unrest and sundering disquiet, family violence and fissure, sometimes collapse, and individual evasion of adulthood, the estate of agency and cognition and touching. But Freud knows, as Hegel does not (or not as fully), the cost such equilibrium as is possible exacts of those who sustain it. The burden on those shoulders is great; it kills all of us eventually. Yet for Freud—as for Hegel—it is the fullest expression of what we are. It is our *telos,* our end and satisfaction, even though we die trying to sustain it. We could not be children again; and when we have attained such wholeness as is possible (through psychoanalytic understanding), we quite truly would not want to be.

There is, however, no "solution" here to the problem of being a human being. There is a kind of systemic prescription, which will fit most but definitely not all individual lives, more or less adequately (sometimes *much* more, sometimes *much* less): live through the journey and its stages—the stations of the cross—whether they are mostly inner or a mix of inner and outer (real-life actions and reactions); then "fall in love," marry, have children, create the conditions for their own developmental journey; as a part of your doing so, and as a part of your own self-expression, participate in institutions of societal or community life; and alongside these functions find such peace and such excitement, but above all such understanding as seems possible to you. There will be no full or final peace; you will fall to debilitating illness or death in mid-step, with some personal war or project still unresolved.

This systemic prescription provides also Freud's account of the sexes and their prospects. We are Laius and Jocasta (sometimes Agamemnon and Clytemnestra) much more than we are Oedipus or

Electra. There is a possibility of adult conjugal love, and partnership, though mirror's reflections are probably illusions. Men and women want in a nearly literal sense to devour or eat each other, and in the Freudian compromise a large net benefit is achievable, immense pleasures to be had, if they refrain from cannibalism. Restraint can be worth it (and sometimes also definitely not), but there is cost; and the possibility of Aristotelian friendship between the sexes probably is inversely proportional to degree of sexual attraction (so long, perhaps, as the gendered Other is not *less* pleasing than the internally preserved Imago of Mother, or Father).

Some comments noting contemporary perspectives relevant to Freud should be added. According to many feminists, all, most, or too many men want to "eat" women, but it is not true that women in general want to eat men. Women just want to have a chance to realize their potential, or to be alone (with themselves and the children), or to live in peace and harmony with all being; or else no one, including women, *knows* what they want since they have been so controlled, confined, harassed, and victimized by men that it has been impossible to discover what their true desires are, independent of social conditioning or coercion. There is little doubt that Freud would not have shared any of these views.[11] All humans, for him, are aboriginally motile masses of object-directed cravings, localized in pleasurable, nerve-sensitive body parts. We all have inward drives to consume, possess, engulf what is sensed as feeling good. This is part of how natural selection has worked, for us, to get us to eat, drink, and reproduce. In the earlier version of psychoanalytic theory erotic and aggressive drives are conceived as compacted together; in the later Freud thinks of aggression as part of a distinctive instinct

---

[11] Freud was not unmindful of sociocultural pressures on women. Indeed, some of his remarks in this direction are of almost feminist coloration. Thus, in *New Introductory Lectures on Psychoanalysis* (p. 116): "We must beware ... of underestimating the influence of social customs, which ... force women into passive situations"; and (ibid.) "the suppression of women's aggressiveness which is prescribed for them constitutionally and imposed on them socially favours the development of powerful masochistic impulses." Women's aggressiveness is just human aggressiveness, what, for Freud, all infants share in abundance. The passage show too that Freud is willing to assign some female behavioural patterns in current western societies to systemic or sociocultural features of these societies. But for him these cannot seriously modify fundamental psychic structures and developmental patterns.

cluster, *thanatos,* the death wish. But in any case, all humans have aggressive as well as pleasuring orientations to objects (and subjects) of sensory interest to them. This *need* not preclude greater degrees of one instinct or other in individual humans or kinds of humans (men and women, for example); but there will be no particular Freudian reason to expect women to have strongly diminished libidinal-aggressive impulses towards men.

The kind of understanding that Freud brings to our awareness of ourselves and our fellow humans is one that makes sense of affinities that do not have obvious (or possibly even non-obvious) rational connection. These range from correlations between political or even metaphysical outlook and matters of temperament and lifestyle to degrees of success in realizing one's claimed goals and food and clothing preferences. As there is a sociology of knowledge, with Marxian and non-Marxian variants, that subsumes cognitive states under class or cultural realities, so Freud offers a "psychology of knowledge" that undertakes to explain that one's political allegiances have to do with how one dealt with nuclear-family psychodramas in early life; and similarly with at least many matters of career choice, and profile, and fundamental view of the world.

For Freud as for Marx, these matters are an ideational superstructure that rests upon some fully knowable objective realities. Both thinkers assume objectivity, and the broad project of science. Freud is readier to psychoanalyze psychoanalysts and scientists broadly than is Marx to "Marx-analyze" Marxists—they tend to be seen as scientists or heroes prompted by ideals—but for both the formal theory includes a slot into which its own practitioners can fit.

Freud and Marx contrast, however, in the degree of agency or causal efficacy they accord human beings. Both theorists are, formally, determinists, and both assign relatively minor degrees of conscious rational control and direction to the individual. Both also have a teleological vision of a condition of some greater genuine freedom, achievable through the operation of the praxis component of the theory. But for Marx that praxis—proletarian revolution and the condition of humanity to which it leads—will in due course produce a lavish measure of freedom, in an integrated, creative life-mode made possible by technology working for the common good. For Freud, on the other hand, praxis—psychoanalytic therapy or psychoanalytically informed insight—will achieve at best a limited and incomplete freedom. Like Spinoza's philosophy, Freud's view chiefly involves a conception of freedom as consisting of knowledge of causal networks we are part of, acceptance of which allows us to partly modify them. Ironically, for Marx we move to the full and generous measure of agency indicated from a condition of extreme unfreedom. Marx's view, like many perspectives in social science, sees us as largely helpless, passive recipients of the operation of forces, classes, and individuals we do not control or much influence. Marxian understanding is supposed to show us that and how we are being done to, and to offer keys for the acquisition of our own agency. For Freud we were all along participant in the shaping of our destinies, and we deceive ourselves if we think we had no hand in our fate. Even though our full consciousness of this agency is incomplete or missing, it is nonetheless there. We know, we are responsible, we are guilty. For that agency discloses, among other things, our participatory aggression, our malevolence. Thus Freud writes, in 1916:

> Look away from individuals to the great war still devastating Europe: think of the colossal brutality, cruelty and mendacity which is now allowed to spread itself over the civilized world. Do you really believe that a handful of unprincipled place-hunters and corrupters of men would have succeeded in letting loose all this latent evil, if the millions of their followers were not also guilty? Will you venture, even in these circumstances, to break a lance for the exclusion of evil from the mental constitution of humanity? (*A General Introduction to Psychoanalysis,* p. 153)

I write here not primarily to show how difficult it is to combine Marx and Freud—something that does seem of importance to show,[12] since a number of thinkers, most notably Marcuse, have attempted to do so—but especially to bring out some of the contrastive components of Freud's view of human nature.

There is still another important dimension to Freud's ideas and their influence: their special significance in and for art, particularly literature and painting. Of our eleven theories, Freudian psychoanalysis, humanist liberalism, Christianity, and Marxism may all be said to have had some impress on the creative imaginations of artists and to have informed works of art that have shaped or resonated with

---

[12] Compare Mary Midgley, *Beast and Man* (1978), p. 3: "Every age has its pet contradictions. Thirty years ago, we used to accept Marx and Freud together, and then wonder, like the chameleon on the turkey carpet, why life was so confusing." The attempt at repeating this conjunction continued into the 1950s and 1960s, and has not been altogether abandoned even now.

readers and viewers. None of the other theories have. (There is a promise of deep cultural enrichment from feminism. It is early days yet for feminism as a cultural movement, and it is unclear whether or how that promise will be fulfilled.) Of these four, the greatest importance and influence has been, I think, Freud's.

Individual creative artists, including people of exceptional gifts, of course continue to be Christian; but their Christianity is usually individual, indeed solitary, quirkish, privately lyrical or tortuous. It does not evoke or create affirming Christian response in those their art reaches. (Christian art *once* achieved this effect. Many a non-Christian modern has privately agreed that Christianity's finest, highest, most enduring contribution to world civilization has been its achievements in the fine arts—supremely in architecture and music, although also in painting. The great bulk of that cultural gift was provided before the end of the eighteenth century.) They admire, possibly even are changed, by the art, but it doesn't lead them to understand the universe they live in in Christian ways.

As for liberal humanism and Marxism: ideas of the potentially self-perfecting individual are arguably at the centre of most American movies. The Hollywood central character is (in what are supposed to be deep, subtle, realistic films as well as less substantial efforts) almost always the embodiment of what might be, or in tragic cases might have been, achieved given a level playing field and a few breaks. This is the liberal art form *sans pareil,* manifested also in many novels. And while a considerable contingent of creative artists have been Marxists, and their Marxism, unlike the Christianity of Christian artists, does become an enveloping, energizing faith for audiences, the mechanisms of effect and the ideological meaning achieved in the art are chiefly just a more "radical" version of liberalism. That is, Marxist heroes and victims are individuals, denied self-realization by capitalism or triumphantly achieving it through capitalism's vanquishing. There does not seem to be a distinctively *Marxist* contribution to art, except perhaps for the illumination of mass-scale social injustice.[13] Satire possibly has been the most effective and successful of artistic forms for a Marxian view of the world, but it is better at showing what is amiss than in depicting a positive image of integrated humanity.

[13] The paintings and murals of Diego Rivera might be argued to comprise a significant counterexample to this claim. Some early Soviet art may also be. Painting would seem to be, apart from satirical literature, the most promising vehicle for the expression of a Marxian outlook.

In any case, both liberal and Marxist contributions to art are relatively low-level: popular, and populist, iconographic feedings of individual dreams or fears. The contribution of Freud has been of a different order—or so it may be reasonable to claim.

One view held by many is that one reads great literature above all to learn about life, that is, about the realities of human nature. This view is regarded as distinctly old-fashioned by many or most members of university literature departments, but it perseveres nonetheless among other people who read and think about literature. Those with this view sometimes think that social-scientific theory about people has had limited success in expressing the knowledge about human beings that personal experience can afford. Some think this points to an ineffability in this knowledge, an intrinsic impossibility of rendering in a systematic or theoretical way what we are capable of knowing experientially about ourselves. Others are agnostic about this matter, holding that in any case a first-rate novel or play of psychological depth can convey insight into humans that we, as audience, can recognize to be sound, and more rapidly and integrally comprehensible than a theoretical account. Sometimes there are notions of texture and layers of depth in human life, from outward appearances to one or more levels of reality or of content, matters of subtlety and nuance that seem to resist a systematic or theoretical rendering.

It is from this perspective, and this level of awareness, that the special degree of Freudian infusion in art and thinking about art should be seen. Freud offers the idea, and some tools for its application, of exhibiting and scanning human emotional life without rose-tinted, sentimental glasses, accepting and depicting human personality in a layered ambiguity that can combine love and hate, desire and aversion, and can discern unblinkingly the mind's hidden recesses and night-time places.[14] Not all subtle or psychologically honest art

[14] Shakespeare's works—especially *Hamlet,* but other plays as well, and many of the Sonnets—seem particularly to lend themselves to Freudian interpretation, or to have psychoanalytically layered texture. Freud himself attempted psychoanalytic explorations of a number of literary works, among them Shakespeare's *Richard III* and *Macbeth* and Ibsen's *Rosmersholm.* (See "Some Character-Types Met with in Psychoanalytic Work" (1916), in *Character and Culture.*) And sometimes the central theme of many twentieth-century novels, plays, and films is the idea that individual liberation or self-understanding lies in some kind of resolution of the relationship to or feelings about one's father or mother or both. The

is, of course, inspired by or expressive of psychoanalytic insights; but a Freudian perspective can give a particular depth and a psychosexually nuanced quality to such art. The high symbolism of the Freudian perspective also makes it natural that psychoanalysis would have interest and appeal for artists of all types.

Of course, none of this makes the Freudian picture true, or even of indefinitely continuing artistic significance. For nearly a century following its rediscovery in the 1850s, Schopenhauer's gloomy understanding of the human condition—importantly anticipating Freud's—had immense and widespread influence on a lay and extra-academic readership. Probably no philosophers were as widely read and assimilated outside the setting of a university during this near-century as Schopenhauer and Herbert Spencer. Schopenhauer had special meaning for writers, artists, and musicians, doubtless augmented by the high status the great pessimist philosopher assigned to art, as capable of relieving, briefly, our otherwise futile and self-frustrating estate. But though he endures as an interesting and serious thinker, and has been to some degree rediscovered by professional philosophers, Schopenhauer is little read now by artists or novelists, few of whom base their understanding of human life on *The World as Will and Representation,* or on an indirectly apprehended Schopenhauerian outlook. A similar fate may overtake psychoanalysis. At any rate, there is no question that artists and writers accord a psychoanalytic perspective, even when they do not share it, a respect and an attention that speaks forcibly for its impress in our culture.

Trying to summarize, and to meet the queries of reasonable critics and skeptics, we might say that Freud's most important and plausible contributions to human understanding of humans are these. First, sex—in the specific but wide sense of genitals, feelings about them, biochemical and psychic connections to gender identity, and relations and reactions of psychosexual kinds to others—matters *a lot* throughout human life, even when it doesn't seem to or is denied to. Indeed, sex forms, or deeply contributes to, our identities and our fundamental desires and fears. Second, how we felt and, derivatively, feel about our parents and early-life connections and disconnections with them also matters a great deal, and has much to do with the character of our relations with other people. Third, the previous two

individual is represented as unable to be whole otherwise, or to love. This idea is entirely due to Freud's influence in twentieth-century culture; nothing like it can be found in earlier literature, at least not as an explicit conception for a life's odyssey.

ideas are related to each other yet, as we consciously experience our lives, *disguised* for us or, sometimes, from us. Fourth, the ideal of a full, autonomous, rational, mature adulthood is an unattainable illusion, something that will always be over a hill ahead of us or behind us (even if a satisfying simulacrum may some of the time be achieved). Fifth, many of the things we genuinely feel or want are not consciously registered, but are manifested in our behaviour in diverse and somewhat disguised symbolic form: slips of tongue, pen, or other indirect expression on our part that it is possible, with psychoanalytically informed awareness, to come to recognize. Sixth, because we ourselves are what withholds from conscious awareness many things we know to be true about ourselves but find too painful to acknowledge, we tend to resist the recognition of many things we know, or fear, are true. These results constitute an essential core of psychoanalytic theory, and have survived remarkably well as Freud's primary contribution to the study of human nature.[15]

In criticizing Freud, it is not sufficient simply to claim that his views diminish or demean particular categories of humanity, especially, of course, women. Freud's views diminish or demean *all* of humanity, and if the degree of negativity is not uniform, still his views and his arguments for them must be met on their own ground. That ground, as Freud sees it, is empirical, observational, and contingent. It is not (as some critics of the whole edifice of psychoanalysis claim) an interlinked structure that is non-falsifiable, unassailable because all evidence will confirm it.

Take Freud's conviction that all dreams express wishes of the dreamer. Few of Freud's views would be as summarily dismissed by contemporary psychologists, even some with broadly psychoanalytic sympathies. Without entering into the specifics and merits of the Freudian stance on dreams, it is instructive to see how Freud poses and responds to objection to the universalism of that stance. He imagines a critic who asks:

> Admitting that every dream means something and that this meaning may be discovered by employing the technique of psychoanalysis, why must it always, in face of all the evidence to the

---

[15] Compare Freud's own capsule summation of his theory: "The theories of resistance and of repression, of the unconscious, of the aetiological significance of sexual life and of the importance of infantile experiences—these form the principal constituents of the theoretical structure of psychoanalysis" (*An Autobiographical Study* [1935], p. 74).

contrary, be forced into the formula of wish-fulfilment? Why must our thoughts at night be any less many-sided than our thoughts by day; so that at one time a dream might be a fulfilment of some wish, at another time ... the opposite, the actualization of a dread; or, again, the expression of a resolution, a warning, a weighing of some problem with its pros and cons, or a reproof, some prick of conscience, or an attempt to prepare oneself for something which has to be done—and so forth? (*A General Introduction to Psychoanalysis*, p. 232f.)

The beginning of Freud's response to this honest questioner is as follows:

My first answer to the question why dreams should not be many-sided in their meaning is the usual one in such a case: I do not know why they should not be so, and should have no objection if they were. As far as I am concerned, they can be so! But there is just one trifling obstacle in the way of this wider and more convenient conception of dreams—that as a matter of fact they are not so. (Ibid.)

This is too quick, and may seem unjustifiably confident of what the evidence is or shows. But it indicates Freud's claim that his clinical data just does happen to evince what he holds it does, and that this is a matter of fact, possibly surprising, certainly with its contrary easily conceivable, and needing (and Freud, of course, supposes obtaining) confirming empirical evidence.

Now, there are real problems with how valid psychoanalytic evidence is—especially for universalist claims—and with whether the desire for a universalist result may not produce ways to exclude apparently contrary evidence. But either every dream is wish-fulfilment or it is not. And a *lot* of acceptable clinical data that a *lot* of dreams are wish-fulfilments, including many apparently otherwise, reasonably engenders the hypothesis that all dreams are so, and all seeming contrary cases explainable as not really exceptions. This is not, of course, to say that Freud's dream theory is correct; there seems to be very powerful evidence that it's not true of all or even most dreams. But it does show that the theory is supposed to be empirical, and empirically refuted or confirmed.

Similarly: there is no question that *many* boys from ages three to five experience castration anxieties, or concern about penis deprivation, and there is similarly no question that many young girls in the same age range express the wish that they had penises. Such phenomena are quite explicit, overt, and widespread. One simply cannot be around children in fairly close quarters, one's own or others, without becoming aware of these facts. It is possible to attribute such penis envy as one discovers in this way to early manifestations of male-dominant acculturation, to view these young females as reacting to male power, and expressing desires not for a penis but for its symbolic power. But these children are too young to be aware of power imbalances in the wider society. They might, of course, sense some within their own families, or receive coded female-disvaluing messages from parents or others. But even if they did it is not obvious why this would translate, often, to envy of the male organ, rather than other male attributes, or to resentment, rather than envy. And in fact lots of cases of penis envy among young girls seem to show up in contemporary families that at least appear to be gender egalitarian. Young children are not skilled scientists, and quite often their lives are filled with fears. Freud's idea was that typically females come to think—in some cases it might be that boys had told them this—that they did have penises, but were dismembered. Without a fully Freudian account, one could see some penis envy as aris-ing from morbid fear of this kind. In any case, it is plausible to see much early-life female penis envy as real but not deeply troubling to the child in question. Envy can be brief, and it can be "positive," whether it is of persons perceived as having more talent, wealth, glamour, strength, or anything else that is prized. Only sometimes is a condition of *resentment* or a feeling of inadequacy or inferiority induced. None of this is intended to imply that most, still less all females do experience even ephemeral versions of penis envy. I take it that one does find that lots of young children have the anxieties and envies referred to, and that they are what they seem to be. However, there is quite a gap between *lots* and *all,* and a better case has to be made that of the very many anxieties and envies that young children have, these ones (even if they were universal by sex) stand out as particularly deep or enduring, as determining a *very great deal* about later life.

Freud's argument for the strong universalist claims he makes stems from the fact that these anxieties and envies are connected to bodily parts that are especially sources of infantile pleasure (and risk of pleasure loss). Seeing an amputee—even a child amputee—does not engender such deep and long-term results because arms and legs aren't major pleasure zones. Still, there are widely differing kinds of early-life exposure to other-sex nudity, that vary significantly by culture, social class, and chance individual experience. At the extremes, some lead quite isolated early lives as single children raised by same-sex parents in physically isolated contexts, and others are surrounded by adult and child nudity of both sexes from birth. It is hard to believe that universal facts about adult life can be a function of such variable early facts.

We find here a case, I think, where a broadly Freudian understanding can be preserved though Freud's actual claims are modified. Let "all" become "some." Some adults of both sexes have "natures," fundamental features of their self-understandings and approaches to the world, that are deeply a function of early-life anxieties about genital loss or non-possession, and chains of events those anxieties happened to lead to. Still others can be held (by the Freudian) to have anxieties and inadequacy feelings that stem from parallel early-life apprehensions, that are in many ways *as though* they had had troubling experiences of the kinds that the first group actually did.

One more summary stance of objection to Freud may acknowledge considerable and even unqualified validity in what we have called core psychoanalysis—expressed as the six theses above, for example—but see little or nothing to be said for the many particular causal analyses of human behavioural patterns and personality types that Freud, and colleague analysts, went on to provide. The particular aetiological theories—for example, of homosexuality, stuttering, criminality, or ambitious, aggressive, passive, and other personality types—do not follow from the core, nor seem particularly to develop in a way any more natural than incompatible alternative core-respecting theories. (In this respect, Freudian theoretical methodology is like Hegelian dialectic.) The theories seem a grab-bag of hunches or speculations, supportable doubtless by some experiential data but without obvious (or perhaps any serious) empirical control. Perhaps the most troublesome, even embarrassing, case of these theories is Freud's foundational theory of dreams, which was above all what launched psychoanalysis into the scientific world,[16] which Freud took to be particularly well supported of all his detailed hypotheses, and yet which seems among the least accepted of all Freudian views.

It is not possible in this limited investigation of psychoanalysis to pursue this matter further, to see whether some particular aetiological Freudian hypotheses seem much better grounded than others. There is certainly a valid concern here, which an expanded account or defence of Freud would need to address.

[16] In *The Interpretation of Dreams* (1900).

One of the most telling indicators of the power and substance of a view of human nature is its being rediscovered in subsequent generations and in new cultural or intellectual contexts. This feature is true of most and possibly all of the theories explored in this book. It is certainly true of Freud. Freudian psychology has been declared dead by one or another category of critic since psychoanalysis first appeared on the international stage in the Edwardian period.[17] And it continues, almost uninterruptedly, to be discovered anew by readers and thinkers many of whom would formerly have doubted that they would find any validity or utility there.

Somewhat surprisingly given Freud's views on gender and women, among those most drawn to Freud in recent years have been a number of feminist thinkers. I don't mean to imply that Freud's views are essentialist and sexist or misogynist, at least in the ways or to the degree that feminist critics have held. But they are views that see gender identity and role as differentiated early, deeply, and in more or less universalistic fashion. They do imply a somewhat tragic destiny for women; but so do they also for men. Some critics say that for Freud women's destiny is *more* tragic than men's. Whatever we say here, there is nothing in Freud's vision to imply that any category of humanity has a pre-eminent claim to, or is excluded from, that state of insightful, humanistic, scientific rationality which is our highest and most genuine human possibility. Men and women can equally know the truth, and can equally find some release and some nurturance in it.

At any rate, it is by no such direct reappropriation of Freud that feminists have found value in his work. The route has been more indirect, via a number of "revisionist" psychoanalytic views and programs with varying degrees of departure from Freudian orthodoxy. Chief of these has been what is called object relations theory.[18] The guiding idea here is that the ego as self is chiefly constituted of internalized images of significant childhood "objects"

[17] Perhaps, given its original setting—argued by some to be by no means unimportant for understanding the system—we should more properly designate the cultural provenance of Freudian theory's beginnings as late Hapsburg.

[18] Object relations theory was originally formulated by Karl Abraham, one of Freud's closest associates in psychoanalysis, in 1924. It was subsequently taken up and developed in what became somewhat "deviationist" directions by another of the early analysts, Melanie Klein (1882–1960).

(chiefly persons, notably parents) and preserved internal symbolic relations to them. The chief advocates of this theory of interest to feminists have been Dorothy Dinnerstein and Nancy Chodorow, perhaps especially the latter.[19] This has led some recent feminist writers to a revised respect for Freud himself. It is almost always qualified by strictures and reservations; but who would insist that any important thinker of the past must be accepted in totality? Freud now meets with respect and, more importantly, is *read* by some (definitely not all) feminists with wide sympathies with depth psychology and its broad perspective on human nature.

A number of criticisms of Freud's theories seem to be well founded or to demand qualification and revision of the theory; others seem to be wide of the mark, often through failing to realize the *kind* of theory Freud's is. Freud's is above all a theory of *significance,* of what matters to individuals, or would if they could know it and face it. Freud's theory takes the high ground; it is about our whole life, our individual destinies. Accordingly, it is as plausible to fault Freud for taking insufficient account of everyday rhythms, and successes and failures, as it would be to fault a universal historian (Hegel, or Toynbee, say) for inattention to individual, provincial battles or road-building. Accordingly, there can be something wrong in spirit even in claiming that Freud is incomplete or partial—that there is little or no place in his account for behavioral strategy (conscious or unconscious), for example body language or other structures of cuing and learning.

Let us take an example. There is evidence that characteristic patterns of personality profile are correlated with where one falls in an order of siblings. There are Freudian possibilities here—the character of the nuclear romance might be thought to shift in various conjecturable ways as more offspring appear, and gender alters—but these seem rather dim. And in any case there is something extra-Freudian if not actually anti-Freudian in these sorts of patterned results, because to the degree there is validity in claims of significance for sibling order, it will reflect some dynamic among and between the siblings (possibly also with lodestar reference to the anchored mother

[19] See, principally, Dinnerstein, *The Mermaid and the Minotaur: Sexual Arrangements and Human Malaise* (1977), and Chodorow, *The Reproduction of Mothering* (1978). Like other revisionist psychoanalytic views, these are hopelessly optimistic from a strictly orthodox Freudian perspective, holding as they do that different parenting patterns would change gender patterns—would, in effect, change human nature.

and father), and this appears to *socialize* destiny, where the Freudian conception is individual.[20]

Some hold Freud to a very strict accounting, according to which his published work offers a body of claimed results, with a descriptive apparatus of parts of the mind and stages of psychic development and a set of causal hypotheses that Freudian clinical experience is supposed to have confirmed or rendered highly probable. These hypotheses are supposed to be transcultural and exceptionless; if they are not, or if Freudian (or reasonably resembling) experimental methodology has not been adequate for their corroboration, Freudian theory is disconfirmed: shown to be, if not quite altogether worthless, certainly eliminated from serious consideration as an account of human reality.

Others are a great deal more generous and flexible in their treatment of Freud's theoretical work. They see a body of claims only some of which are given substantive support in any way independent of psychoanalytic methodologies that themselves need validation, and many of which are, even in Freud's own terms, speculative guesses or insights, resting on clinical experience (something like hunches of a seasoned practitioner) and "fit" with other parts of a body of theories held to be well-grounded empirically. From the perspective of the more generous assessment, the theories are held to be statistical/probabilistic generalizations of tendency (some with much higher probability than others), that extend common-sense or "folk" psychological theories and claims to areas where they do not usually receive application.[21]

Critics or outside observers of debates for and against Freud may well reasonably ask: Why treat Freud in a kid-gloved or specially favoured way? Why be more generous than with other theorists?

---

[20] We see here some of the lines of demarcation between Freud's view and the psychological theories of his one-time junior colleague Alfred Adler (1870–1937), one of the early psychoanalytic "revisionists." Adler's views stress sibling order, and social interactions with others than parents, as constituting a more conscious and public, and a less sexual, self than Freud sees. Probably more than any other individual psychological theorist of the modern period, Adler shapes the general contours of popular public psychology as found in western (especially North American) educational systems.

[21] An interesting, eloquently argued account and defence of Freud, in something like these terms, is to be found in Thomas Nagel's "Freud's Permanent Revolution" (1994).

Why *not* hold him to the standards of the sciences, especially considering that he himself offered psychoanalysis as science, and avowed a deep, even severe and classic commitment to scientific method and rigour? Is there not a kind of reverse condescension in seeking to protect Freud from strict controls and testing, as though one really knew that, weak kid that he is, he wouldn't be able to withstand the pummelling that serious contenders for scientific credibility are subjected to? The upshot of these queries may be that a Freudian core might remain plausible—highly plausible—but much even of that core yet wants proof.

One tack currently taken by many who admire Freud is to dismiss all psychoanalytic pretensions to science and to view Freud as essentially a literary artist—with literature regarded as unsystematic (putative) insight into human life. A particularly pronounced version of this approach is taken by the literary scholar and critic Harold Bloom, who ranks Freud among the twenty-six magisterial figures of the western canon: "Freud called himself a scientist, but he will survive as a great essayist like Montaigne or Emerson, not as the founder of a therapy already discredited (or elevated) as another episode in the long history of shamanism."[22]

A cousin perspective to the preceding is that of Thomas Nagel (and others), on which we have beliefs about human behaviour that collectively constitute a "folk psychology" that is in principle empirical, falsifiable, confirmable, and revisable—all the things good science should be—but which is both anterior to and not readily or perhaps at all (even in principle) amenable to scientific test, at least if taken as a whole. This becomes, curiously, a view somewhat like the Aristotelian account discussed in Chapter 3, according to which the boundaries of what humans can know about the world do not coincide with even possible science. The non-science part is, for the Aristotelian position, in principle unsystematic and unable to be integrated (except to a very limited degree) with science. That part is chiefly knowledge of human life and human nature. It has its own "canons" of access and of adequacy. Such a position need not, but may, formulate itself as a full so-called cognitive dualist stance. At

[22] Bloom, *The Western Canon* (1994), p. 2f. He goes on to say, *inter alia,* that "all of Freud that matters most is there in Shakespeare already, with a persuasive critique of Freud besides. The Freudian map of the mind is Shakespeare's; Freud seems only to have prosified it" (ibid., p. 25). It ought to be noted that Bloom's high assessment of the genius of Shakespeare would be difficult to rival, and impossible to surpass.

any rate, for Nagel and some others[23] Freud is best assessed as making significant, penetrating, original, and largely persuasive contributions to this Aristotelian folk psychology, that extend and to some degree revise common-sense knowledge of people.

It seems clear that Freud himself would not have been happy with the admiring perspectives of either Bloom or Nagel. Though flattering, they withhold from psychoanalysis the palm of science. *Tant pis* (too bad), one may say. Marx and others had sought that palm also, and our assessment, like many others, concluded that what was claimed as science was really normative philosophical anthropology—possibly not a bad thing at all, even if non-science. Let the same judgment be made of Freud.

In fact, I would argue against Freud's being relegated, at least quite so readily, to the (mere) philosophy heap. There are also, it seems to me, things to resist in the Nagel perspective, attractive as it in many ways is (and noting Nagel's efforts to cite experiential data supportive of Freud's views). One can, in fact, incorporate most of both Bloom's and Nagel's views—agree that literature can importantly disclose life and daily experience (with some reservations) does yield knowledge, and acknowledge that Freud makes major contributions to both—but refrain from Nagelian "Aristotelianism." It isn't obvious that common-sense knowledge and folk psychology are not amenable to systematicity, or merger with a larger, unitary scientific view of the world. Moreover, many phenomena, not just ones involving human mental states (conscious or unconscious), are in principle falsifiable or confirmable but not so in any way that a foreseeable experimental design technology can access. This doesn't establish autonomous kinds of knowledge; it may just mean that, as elsewhere, there is much we would like to know and fit into a total understanding of the world that, for now or possibly forever, must remain tentative or ungrounded. So it may be with many Freudian insights.

[23] Definitely not all—for many Aristotelians Freud is anathema.

Bibliography

Bloom, Harold. *The Western Canon*. New York: Harcourt Brace, 1994.

Chodorow, Nancy. *The Reproduction of Mothering*. Berkeley: University of California Press, 1978.

Crews, Frederick. "The Revenge of the Repressed." *New York Review of Books,* Nov. 17 and Dec. 1, 1994 (with subsequent discussion Jan. 12, 1995).

Dinnerstein, Dorothy. *The Mermaid and the Minotaur: Sexual Arrangements and Human Malaise*. New York: Harper Colophon, 1977.

Freud, Sigmund. *An Autobiographical Study*. New York: W. W. Norton, 1935.

——————. *Character and Culture*, published as one of the (unnumbered) volumes of *The Collected Papers of Sigmund Freud*, edited by P. Rieff. New York: Collier Books, 1963.

——————. *Civilization and Its Discontents*. New York: Jonathan Cape & Harrison Smith, 1930.

——————. *A General Introduction to Psychanalysis*. New York: Washington Square Press, 1952. (This is the popular edition of the *Introductory Lectures on Psycho-Analysis*.)

——————. *General Psychological Theory*. In *The Collected Papers of Sigmund Freud,* edited by P. Rieff. New York: Collier Books, 1963.

——————. *The Interpretation of Dreams*. London: Hogarth Press, 1953. [1900]

——————. *New Introductory Lectures on Psychoanalysis*. New York: W. W. Norton, 1965. [1933]

——————. "Psychoanalysis" [1922]. In *Character and Culture* (one of the [unnumbered] volumes of *The Collected Papers of Sigmund Freud*), edited by P. Rieff. New York: Collier Books, 1963.

——————. *Totem and Taboo*. London: Hogarth Press, 1950. [1912–1913]

Giere, Ronald N. *Understanding Scientific Reasoning*. 3rd ed. Fort Worth, TX: Holt, Rinehart & Winston, 1991.

Grünbaum, Adolf. *The Foundations of Psychoanalysis: A Philosophical Critique*. Berkeley: University of California Press, 1984.

Hegel, G. W. F. *The Philosophy of Right*. Oxford: Oxford University Press, 1967. [1821]

Hume, David. *A Treatise of Human Nature*. Oxford: Clarendon Press, 1978. [1739-1740]

Lasch, Christopher. *The Culture of Narcissism*. Rev. ed. New York: W. W. Norton, 1991.

Midgley, Mary. *Beast and Man*. Ithaca, NY: Cornell University Press, 1978.

Nagel, Thomas. "Freud's Permanent Revolution." *The New York Review of Books,* May 12, 1994 (with subsequent discussion Aug. 11, 1994).

Rieff, Philip, ed. *The Collected Papers of Sigmund Freud*. 10 vols. New York: Collier Books, 1963.

Schopenhauer, Arthur. *The World as Will and Representation*. 2 vols. New York: Dover, 1966.

Tong, Rosemarie. *Feminist Thought*. Boulder, CO: Westview, 1989.

Wollheim, Richard. *Sigmund Freud*. 2nd ed. Cambridge: Cambridge University Press, 1990.

CHAPTER 11

Non-self Theories ───────

ALL OTHER THEORIES DISCUSSED IN THIS BOOK
share a feature absent from the views now to be engaged: the
assumption that, whether or not with invariant content or materially
constituted, there are such things as human selves to be thought about
and explored. Some theories deny that this is true. This is not the
position that there is no such thing as human nature, taken by
existentialists and some feminists and social constructionists. The
position we now turn to is, in a way, more radical: it denies that
there are selves at all. Whether stable or otherwise, there is no such
a thing as being me or being you, there are no human or personal
identities in anything other than a nominal or fictional sense.

A theory about human beings will be a non-self view by virtue
of denying that human beings are conscious subjects or selves or
persons for at least extended periods of their existence. Accordingly,
a theory that denied that there is any such thing as consciousness at
all would be a non-self theory, even if it held that there was some
other kind of unity that human beings have. And a theory that
affirmed the reality of consciousness but denied that there is a stable,
unitary, continuing item that has it, normally just one for each human
body (or each human being), would also thereby be a non-self theory, even if it also held that there was some other sort of unity to
human beings.

Put like that, this view will sound highly metaphysical. Throughout this exploration of theories of human nature, we have tried to
steer a course that keeps the metaphysical commitments of theories
in sight without, usually, directly engaging them. That course will be
honoured here also. I will call the theories—there are more than one
of them, with considerable differences among them—non-self theories
of human beings and their natures. But on the ground level of
research and argument for their programmatic claims these theories
are empirical and concrete. They mean to be science; and if they
have the metaphysical implications I claim they have, in what follows
this is kept largely out of view.

These non-self theories are, like sociobiology, cultural materialism, and Freudian psychoanalysis, naturalistic in character, but they

are also mechanistic and reductionist in ways that none of those theories are.[1] Moreover, these theories have had considerable importance in the project of developing and anchoring a science of humanity, and some have immense influence at the present day. Our survey of human nature views would be seriously incomplete if these theories were not discussed.

The non-self theories—the theories that hold that for us, at least, the lights may be on but no one is home—include three distinct varieties, not necessarily at odds with each other or unable to be united in a single, comprehensive non-self theory. First is behaviourism; second is what may be called physiological mechanism; and third is a cluster of views in what is called cognitive science, perhaps the most straightforwardly anti-self view in the cluster being a position called connectionism. These cognitive science theories hold that human beings are fundamentally a certain kind of aggregate of information-processing systems, that might but probably does not have a master control system. I do not intend to provide more than the briefest outline of these theories; I am more concerned to uncover the central idea they share, and what would be implied—for example, for other theories discussed in this book—if a theory of this kind was true.

The *idea* of a non-self theory is that ongoing, unitary, conscious selves are fictional or illusory in the way in which various natural phenomena may create an appearance of unity where there really is none, apart from a grouping that may be artificially devised by external observers in particular conditions of observation, for practical or other purposes. Thus, from the ground there might seem to be a single large fluffy cloud in a distinct region of the sky that, were one nearby in an airplane, would be seen to be several clumps of cloud, some quite vaporous and disconnected and all at considerable distance from each other. Similarly, there are objective states of the world that give rise to the illusion of the (unitary) self, but there is nothing that corresponds to the unitary appearance. Non-self theories differ on what the objective items are that create the appearance of a self. All believe in human bodies, and a unity of individual human organisms. These might seem rather obvious concessions, that would at best impress a very skeptically inclined and somewhat old-fashioned philosopher. But in fact they do indicate something about these theories: that they are individualized, or individualist theories. They are

---

[1] Though possibly one or more of them *could* be if the right additional assumptions were made.

theories of psychology, or of biology, or of machine-science. There could be theories holding that selves are fictional appearances arising among *sets* of organisms or machines, only created out of some sort of interaction among the individual organisms or machines; these would be *holistic* non-self theories. But in fact the historical non-self theories that have appeared so far have been atomic individualist.

The first non-self theory was suggested by David Hume in the eighteenth century. In a famous passage of the *Treatise of Human Nature*, he denies that he has experience of any such thing as his self. "For my part, when I enter most intimately into what I call *myself,* I always stumble on some particular perception or other, of heat or cold, light or shade, love or hatred, pain or pleasure. I never can catch *myself* at any time without a perception, and never can observe any thing but the perception" (p. 252). Hume goes on to argue that a self is (we might say, at best) what he calls a "bundle of perceptions"—a grouped aggregate of experiencings, or thinkings (these are what Hume's term "perceptions" applies to). We *call* these perceptions cases of a me-thinking-(or sensing)-such-and-such; and someone might ask who the *me* is. (Just *who,* for example, is the one who, Hume says, has entered most intimately into what he calls himself?) But, Hume will hold, this is just how we speak, *as though* there were a stable, continuing object we refer to by the first-person singular pronoun, when really there is not. All there really are are thinkings, not persons carrying out thinkings. These thinkings resemble each other or are temporally adjacent to each other, or form chains whose members have overlapping resemblance and temporal connectedness to each other. He could have added (but doesn't seem to have) that these "bundles" are contained within or somehow associated with individual living human bodies.

Hume's non-self theory involves an ontology of inner, introspectible psychological states (the primary cases of them states of sense perception, that we suppose typically also involve and perhaps even *are* bodily states, as well as exterior objects or events that cause these states). It is a genuine non-self theory, though, because the earliest members of the sequence constituting a "bundle" will have nothing significantly in common with the latest members save joint membership in the sequence and, perhaps, causal connection to the same human body.

The classical behaviourism of J. B. Watson (1878–1958) is also a non-self theory.[2] This theory emerged by degrees in Watson's work, appearing first in *Behavior* (1914), then more fully and explicitly in two subsequent books, *Psychology from the Standpoint of a Behaviorist* (1919) and *Behaviourism* (1924). In these writings, Watson developed a psychological theory denying the existence of introspection or internal mental states for introspection to be aware of. The explicit character of these claims, and Watsonian progression from methodological to fully ontological behaviourism, may be seen in the following quotations.

> Introspection forms no essential part of [scientific psychology's] methods, nor is the scientific value of its data dependent on the readiness with which they lend themselves to interpretation in terms of consciousness. (*Behavior*, p. 1)

> The time seems to have come when psychology must discard all reference to consciousness; when it need no longer delude itself into thinking that it is making mental states the object of observation. (Ibid., p. 7)

> It is possible to write a psychology, to define it as ... the "science of behavior" ..., and never go back upon the definition: never to use the terms consciousness, mental states, mind, content, will, imagery, and the like. (Ibid., p. 9)

> Due to a mistaken notion that its fields of facts are conscious phenomena and that introspection is the only direct method of ascertaining these facts, it has enmeshed itself in a series of

---

[2] Classical or ontological behaviourism is not to be confused with *methodological behaviourism*. The latter holds that whether consciousness is real or not, it is unavailable as a postulate of empirical science because it is (the theory supposes) not publically or intersubjectively observable; and that empirical psychology can and should proceed with no assumption of its reality (or of anything else that would in turn presuppose consciousness). Hence methodological behaviourism takes no position one way or the other as to the reality of consciousness, but does suppose that a significant, contentful science of humanity is possible without reference to conscious awareness. All classical or ontological behaviourists are also methodological behaviourists, but the converse is not invariably true. There are probably no living ontological behaviourists, but certainly many living, working methological behaviourists. Often this stance is piecemeal, and only implicit or half-articulated in the psychologists who practice it.

speculative questions which ... are not open to experimental treatment. (Ibid., p. 26f.)

Psychology ... needs introspection as little as do the sciences of chemistry and physics. (Ibid., p. 27)

"States of consciousness," like the so-called phenomena of spiritualism, are not objectively verifiable and for that reason can never become data for science. (*Psychology from the Standpoint of a Behaviorist*, p. 1)

The behaviorist finds no evidence for "mental existences" or "mental processes" of any kind. (Ibid., p. 2)

Consciousness, with its structural units, the irreducible sensations (and their ghosts, the images) and their affective tones, and its processes, attention, perception, conception, is but an indefinable phrase. (Ibid., p. 3)

Since Watson denies the reality of consciousness, the items that create the appearance of a self obviously cannot be conscious states of an organism. Rather, they are a select set of bodily movements—some of them very subtle and not easily perceived ones—evoked by the effects on the body of a select set of exterior objects and events in accordance with a set of laws that govern or summarize these interactions. Some of these bodily movements are also caused by other bodily movements, including internal ones, not readily detectable from an external vantage point; but the theory gives primary focus to movements involving exterior stimuli.

The history of Watsonian behaviourism did not prove favourable. The desired laws were not readily forthcoming, and although the long-term goal of the project was to build from simple cases of "behaviour" to more complex ones, and ultimately to everything that human beings do, this endeavour never really got off the ground along the lines Watson had envisaged. Again, it is not my purpose here to fill in the details of this scientific enterprise, and such (modest) successes as it had, failures, and subsequent redirection. The result was *de facto* abandonment of the project, with the apparent return of consciousness and a stable self in neo-behaviourist and subsequent behaviourist-inspired undertakings in experimental psychology. Watson at least had a theory about human beings; it is not so clear that the behaviourist epigones of recent decades have.

Watson's theory, like Hume's, was that we are essentially *reactive* creatures: our bodies move because they are prodded.[3] Some proddings produce sounds, which when sufficiently complex we call speech and language. "The self" is a fictional abbreviation for a structure of highly complicated bodily movements involving just such movements of our vocal chords or our bodily responses to movements of the vocal chords of other bodies, together with bodily movements to which we assign the label "memory behaviour."[4]

The second non-self theory I want to identify does not seem to have a fully explicit or theoretically developed advocate in the twentieth century, though it seems implied in the work of some physiological psychologists. The original historical impetus for the theory, in the history of philosophy and science, is perhaps the view Descartes formulated on non-human animals, conceived also as natural machines without mental lives. A mechanistic physiological view of human beings, along these Cartesian lines but seeking to incorporate mental states (as physiological states) in the system, was most prominently and comprehensively developed in the eighteenth century by Julien Offray de La Mettrie (1709–1751), partially in his book *L'histoire naturelle de l'âme* (*The Natural History of the Soul*) (1745), but above all in his essay *L'Homme machine* (*Man a Machine*) (1747).[5] La Mettrie's theory appears to differ from most twentieth-century materialist philosophies of mind—and hence, unlike at least some of them, to qualify as a non-self theory—by analyzing thought as physiological states that, like Humean impressions, have

---

[3] For Hume, we also have the successive thoughts we do primarily because our bodies are prodded. As a philosophically adroit psychologist, Hume "brackets" the supposed contributions of the external world to our impressions. That is, he doesn't assume that those contributions are being made, or take any particular account of them. But the idea is that either the external world is producing our impressions, or it is as though it is.

[4] No actual remembering occurs, since this would imply both consciousness and a self that exists at the times remembered, those at which the remembering happens, and presumably those between. But the illusion of a self, as behaviourism sees it, arises in part from mistaken constructions placed upon behaviour (mis)called remembering behaviour.

[5] Other eighteenth-century French materialist theories, notably those of Condillac, Cabanis, Holbach, and Destutt de Tracy, exhibit similarities to the "medical" analysis La Mettrie developed, but his seems the most clearly self-repudiating.

only causal and same-body relations, and nothing that makes them states of a continuing, unitary, conscious self. The contemporary materialist position called eliminative materialism—which, strictly speaking, denies the reality of consciousness and of thoughts—resembles La Mettrie's theory in this respect. La Mettrie's theory, or a more sophisticated physiological mechanist view, might be seen as in principle converging on Watson's theory. However, it need not involve attempts at discovering laws of conditioned reflex (as Watson had sought). The idea, rather, is that our bodies are aggregates of highly complex physical systems, elements of some of which interact causally with elements of others, and that this is all we are.

It would be unreasonable to hold that belief in selves requires (metaphysical) dualism, the belief that there are immaterial substances, we ourselves or some organ of thought within us being such a substance. Certainly some contemporary metaphysical materialists would insist that their views involve commitment both to the reality of consciousness and to a stable object whose consciousness it is. (They typically hold that a self or person is a human being, and that human being is a human body. And consciousness is, for these so-called reductive or central-state materialists, a brain state, or cluster of brain states.)

La Mettrie is unquestionably a materialist. This might have seemed in doubt from the early stages of his essay *Man a Machine,* which more easily suggest a strict one-one psychophysical correspondence theory (for every mental state there is a physiological—typically, brain—state it is causally correlated with) or epiphenomenalism (every mental state is a causally ineffacious byproduct of purely physiological states). But La Mettrie's method is to argue to his full views by progressive stages, with the claims of one stage replaced by a more refined version as his argument advances. By the end we learn the full truth. "Let us, therefore conclude boldly that man is a machine, and that *the entire universe contains only one single diversely modified substance.*"[6] This can only be a fully materialist position, incompatible both with one-one psycho-physical correspondence theory and with epiphenomenalism.

But is it incompatible with selves? Le Mettrie talks in different passages of souls, of mental states, sensation, imagination, and emotional conditions. But he says also that all animals, and indeed plants, have souls. Moreover, his essay is short, bombastic,

[6] *Man a Machine,* p. 76, my emphasis.

rhetorical, inexact, moving from one flourish to another. The materialist non-self view is the view that relevant *parts*—states of consciousness—do not make up the relevant *whole*—the somebody whose states they are (where the somebody is not simply defined as a human body). It is the view that a human being is a purely physiological mechanism, with no other identity or unity than bodily identity or unity, and that there is no single state (certainly no mental state) that obtains over significant intervals of that body's existence sufficient to constitute the state of a person.

The flavour or spirit of La Mettrie's position is, I think, non-self. All our mental states are analyzed by him as metabolic or physiological ones, by no means confined to the brain. We are viewed not just as animals, as the Aristotelian tradition also always held, but as of like nature and type with all other living things, our psychologicality not manifesting anything diverse in principle from any other life form. (*Versions* of most of these claims will, it is true, be endorsed by self-affirming materialists.)

> Grant me only that organized matter is endowed with a motive principle, which alone differentiates it from what is not so organized ..., and that everything in animals depends on the diversity of this organization, as I have sufficiently proved, and this is enough to solve the riddle of substances and that of man. It is obvious that there is only one substance in the universe and that man is the most perfect animal ... [N]ature had necessarily to employ more art and install more organs to make and maintain a machine that might mark all the throbbings of the heart and mind over an entire century. Because if the pulse does not show the hours, the body is at least the barometer of heat and vivacity by which one can judge the nature of the soul. I am not mistaken. The human body is an immense clock, constructed with so much artifice and skill that if the wheel that marks the seconds stops because of rust or derailment, the minutes wheel continues turning, as does the quarter hour wheel, and all the rest.[7]

The third of the non-self theories of human nature is connectionism, and other views resembling it. These views have emerged in what is now generally called (critics claim misleadingly) cognitive

---

[7] *Man a Machine,* p. 69. Le Mettrie continues in similar vein, then goes on to extol Descartes as having had entirely the right view about non-human animals—viewing them as mindless automata—and erring only in not coming to the same position on humans.

science. Most prominent, and certainly most literarily engaging, of the cognitive scientists, and one who at least flirts with connectionism, is the philosopher Daniel Dennett. Fully declared connectionists include J. McClelland, D. Rumelhart, and John R. Anderson.

I have indicated that all three non-self theories are more complementary than rival. Behaviourism focuses on the exterior and the observable: a science of humanity taken as far as it can go in terms of collected, causally linked behavioural phenomena. Physiological mechanism looks inward, to the clockwork of the subsystems making up the human organism. Connectionism attempts a certain sort of amalgamation of the two, but with a new emphasis: on the human being as an information processor, a (somewhat artificial) unit comprising various physically coterminous and causally interlocking specialized information-processing subsystems.[8]

Again, I cannot here provide even an outline of the relevant theoretical details, which for connectionism in particular would be lengthy, and much of it technical. There are also conceptual challenges posed in the endeavour, since these theories borrow a great deal of their vocabulary from informal, everyday contexts, usually filled with psychological content, where the literal meaning of the term in its new home (or whether there is even supposed to be a literal meaning) is unspecified. Interestingly, this theory involves a kind of return to the views of Hume, or something close to them. The key concept for cognitive science is that of information, which is, among other things, the idea of something abstract and realizable in a variety of distinct physical (and for some, possibly non-physical) systems. Information is "software" and the brain or some other structure the "hardware" that instantiates and processes it. Information-processing states will be, functionally, close cousins of Humean impressions. The resulting tale that connectionism tells, in a great deal more detail than Hume did, is of information-processing modules only some of which interlock with others, and some of which "assert themselves" as self-scanning, or total-system-scanning;

[8] It should be noted that not all theories of mind that utilize concepts and models from information theory or computational science are non-self views. Many philosophers (and some scientists) have thought these concepts and models provide insight into our mental states and how they work. Fred Dretske is a particularly interesting philosopher of mind with views of this kind, and Dretske is not a non-self theorist.

but where the latter is not only untrue[9] but also unable to ground a metaphysical reality, a genuine conscious mind. Connectionism as such developed (in the 1980s) as an alternative to previously prevailing computer modelling for human intelligence. Difficulties with attempts to view the human brain as a "serial, digital, stored-program, symbol-processing Von Neumann–type"[10] computer—Von Neumann was the mathematician primarily responsible for the architecture of the modern computer—led to the idea of what is called parallel distributed processing. Instead of a Von Neumann–type computer, the brain, connectionism proposes, is a parallel distributed processing (PDP) computer. "PDP models, like brains, consist of very large networks of very simple processing units, which communicate through the passing of excitatory and inhibitory messages to one another. *All units work in parallel without a specific executive.*"[11]

Only a very limited critique of the non-self theories will be attempted here. The more deeply metaphysical matter of just what consciousness is, and the wider project of a satisfactory theory of the mental, may be left to other occasions. Though some philosophical views, among them classical behaviourism, have disputed whether consciousness exists, I am here content to assume that it does, or to claim that its reality is daily confirmed in conscious experience. That leaves open, of course, what the nature of consciousness is, and what its causal connections are to other parts of the world.

Excluding behaviourism—since it denies consciousness—we may raise some queries for the remaining non-self theories, among them whether these views, if true, *make any difference* for what we have thereby learned about ourselves, and if so what that difference is. Knowing what objects or processes *consist of* of course responds to fundamental questions about the nature of things. It is likewise with learning the mechanisms of characteristic doings of living or moving creatures: how does a particular thing *do* that (rather complex) thing it manages to do every week or month of its life? Science—possibly Dennett's science—provides at least a partial explanatory account of

[9] That is, even if there are modules that register states that "say" that they are self-scanning, or total-system-scanning, it is untrue that they are really doing either.

[10] David E. Rumelhart, "Towards a Microstructural Account of Human Reasoning," in Steven Davis, ed., *Connectionism: Theory and Practice* (1992), p. 70.

[11] Ibid., my emphasis.

the mechanics, and the dynamics, of our activities. And this is important information about ourselves.

Yet from some other perspectives it is arguably not. Of course we are somewhat complicated organisms; and of course there is *some* way or other that we manage to walk to a refrigerator holding a novel we are reading, looking for a beer and a sandwich, finding beer and a piece of pizza instead, and selecting them, all the while humming a favourite Verdi aria. We do these and a myriad other things, and if synchronic science (science describing and explaining phenomena within a single time interlude) or diachronic science (science traversing time frames) can explain how we do these things, that is interesting and important. But we already knew we *could* do them, and knowing *how* doesn't seem to give us new information about what we are.

Furthermore, Dennett was a student of Gilbert Ryle's and a (not uncritical) admirer of Wittgenstein's—both of whose philosophies of mind at least have a lot in common with behaviourism—and as in these philosophers' theories, Dennett's repeated claims about his own results seem to tell us that these results very much leave things as they were. A distinction is drawn between Theory and Life, where it is obstinate philosophers' confused theories (for Dennett especially *methodologies*) sometimes foisted upon Ordinary People that are the problem, and of which the Good Philosopher (Wittgenstein, Ryle, Dennett) is showing the inadequacies.[12] Life then just goes on as merrily as it was in the first place. Science, mechanistic physiological science or cybernetic science, has deprived us of what (certain) Theory had held we do or should have, but not what Ordinary People, fetching those beers and sandwiches, had ever wished or believed to be true.

If we take these metatheoretical claims at their word, and remind ourselves that the Good Philosophers too are Ordinary People, and so presumably *their* theoretical and metatheoretical moments belong with Life, not with (bad) Theory, the result may indeed be nothing worth worrying about. It may also be nothing worth wanting: not an image or understanding of who or what we are at all.

On the other hand, there *is* indication that more than just a narrow circle of intellectual specialists (and some whose thinking they

---

[12] See L. Wittgenstein, *Philosophical Investigations, passim;* G. Ryle, *The Concept of Mind,* pp. 10–17; and D. Dennett, *Elbow Room,* pp. 2–7, 12, 17–18.

have tainted with their influence) are involved, and shown in error, if any of the non-self theories is correct. No claim about "souls" need be made, nor commitments to magic or extra-naturalism. Obviously, if Watsonian behaviourism were true a large gap would open up between what we generally suppose and what human beings really are. But it appears most of us are deceived (self-deceived?) as well if any view along the lines of physiological mechanism or connectionism is correct. For most of us think the self—that is, a person who is the person one is—is a genuine item of the world, however it came to exist, whatever it consists of, and whatever possibilities (real or science fictional) there might be for its ontological complication or dissolution. Moreover, Dennett himself and others of his persuasion seem (their metatheoretical remarks notwithstanding) genuinely to suppose they are producing knowledge, and knowledge that requires the revision of very widely held beliefs people have about people. Nonetheless, it seems we can grant unequivocally that we are, among other things, a certain kind of meat machine; that our constituent parts can and sometimes do break down in ways that dissolve or fragment the unity of ongoing personhood we typically have; that, indeed, such fragmentation may occur normally, just from living too long. Still, this won't make much of a case against that personhood.

Two critical metaphysical dimensions to these themes must be aired. They both are linked and are autonomous of each other. One is the curious revival, by different thinkers in the empiricist tradition—perhaps beginning with Hume, certainly prominent in the twentieth century—of a version of the old Platonic theory of *degrees of being*. According to this line of thinking, two things might both *be*, but one has more being or reality than the other. One might have basic, four-square, ground-level *real* being, and the other attenuated, or lesser, derivative, fictional, or constructed being. Dennett in fact vacillates, I think, between a Platonic degree-of-being view and outright *fictionalism*, the view, most explicitly formulated and advocated by the German philosopher Hans Vaihinger (1852–1933), that all manner of things that appear in and are posited by discourse and theory quite literally are unreal, *sans phrase*, but can nonetheless be quite useful in developing true or adequate theories.

So, the entities posited as having causal roles in "hard science" are ground-level realia (real things), and various macro-level items are not. The latter include pains, and "haircuts and collars and opportunities and persons and centers of gravity."[13] Do they also include *stances* and *theories* and *information?* (All three of these are of central importance in Dennett's own theories.) It is difficult to see what could confer greater reality on any of the latter that would not attach also to the items Dennett lists. And if all are alike unreal, or less real, we have reason to find Dennett's theories less interesting than we might have: why believe something that isn't there to be believed? We have at least reason here to think that theories and principles of degrees of reality, or the fictionalist stance (now advocated again by Hartry Field and others), may bear a second hard look.

The second metaphysical theme important to bring into evaluation of non-self theories is what may be the most important positive contribution to metaphysics made by Kant: what he called the transcendental unity of apperception.[14] Kant himself, and certainly many who had been impressed by the view and argument that goes under this label, may have been over-sanguine, even glib, about its power and decisiveness; Kant's objections notwithstanding, it seems that non-self theories in one version or other *might* happen to be correct. But they face a formidable obstacle in Kant's argument, which invites us to take varying time slices of experience connected to a single living thing (or series of living things in a living-thing-bundle) where a state of consciousness in one of those time slices is felt as embracing or accompanying all of the others. This is, at least, a *datum*—the fact of an ongoing "I think." It does not matter if such a collecting cord (or chord) does not unite *all* of the experiences an individual, in one such state, supposes it does unite. The Kantian point is made if there is even one such unified block. In principle, eleven minutes would do it, and certainly what brings into unity today's conscious episodes with those of yesterday. For over eleven minutes, and certainly the transition from yesterday to today, a living human body will undergo significant physiological change and will "house" or contain a sequence of states of consciousness. No single such state—discriminable, enumerable, fully vivid and apprehended—will last throughout these intervals. (We will have had "*to blink,*" psychologically speaking.) And yet at the end of these intervals the conscious state *then* obtaining will include awareness, possibly only misleadingly identified as memory or recollection, of both the beginning of the interval and the course of the span between

[13] Dennett, *Consciousness Explained,* p. 460.

[14] See I. Kant, *Critique of Pure Reason,* pp. 135–161.

beginning and end. This *is* the Kantian unity of apperception, the "I think" that spans states and constitutes them as that subject's states. Of course radical illusion could, in principle, be involved in every such case. But there is no reason to believe that such illusion is occurring, and unless it is, such phenomena seem to show that a real, and not merely apparent, *me* or self existed during that span, as the subject of the sequence of experiences.

This doesn't, of course, provide an explanation or a theory. No lifelong self is shown thereby, or a simple or atomic self even in a single episode. Rather, we would as indicated have a datum, which any adequate theory of the mental and of humans must accommodate.

In fact, if this conclusion is to be much more than a debater's point, mere formal refutation of non-self theories—for whatever is involved in there being an enduring "I think" can plausibly be held to be as much as would be wanted for selves—a larger and more stable self should be argued for. But it can be. There might be something fictional in the stretch of self from middle-aged adult life to episodes of consciousness decades earlier; possibly threads of numerically self-same selfhood snap, and over a long enough time span there are only Humean-bundle similarities. But this, even if true, won't imply that the stretch is not perfectly sufficient for a genuine unity of apperception constituting a single stable self over periods of years, even many years.

Other difficulties with non-self theories grow out of these metaphysical concerns. Where can social realities, apart from those merely of gregarious animal life, be housed in such views? For example, what can be said about institutions, social and economic practices, or historical developments and patterns? The problem is worse than the implausibility of *reducing* cultural and historical facts to those of cybernetically enhanced physiology. It is hard to see how any such facts can be given even approximate *description* if such views are true.

Bibliography

Anderson, J. *The Architecture of Cognition*. Cambridge, MA: Harvard University Press, 1983.

Davis, Steven, ed. *Connectionism: Theory and Practice*. New York: Oxford University Press, 1992.

Dennett, Daniel C. *Consciousness Explained*. Boston: Little, Brown, 1991.

————. *Elbow Room*. Cambridge, MA: Bradford, 1984.

Hume, David. *A Treatise of Human Nature*. Oxford: Clarendon Press, 1978. [1739–1740]

Kant, Immanuel. *The Critique of Pure Reason*. London: Macmillan, 1963. [1781, 1787]

La Mettrie, Julien Offray de. *L'histoire naturelle de l'âme*. 1745.

————. *L'Homme machine*. 1747. (Translated as *Man a Machine*. Indianapolis: Hackett, 1993.)

McClelland, J., & Rumelhart, D., eds. *Parallel Distributed Processing: Explorations in the Microstructures of Cognition*. 2 vols. Cambridge, MA: Bradford, 1986.

Parfit, D. *Reasons and Persons*. Oxford: Clarendon Press, 1984.

Rumelhart, D. E. "Towards a Microstructural Account of Human Reasoning." In S. Davis, ed., *Connectionism: Theory and Practice*. New York: Oxford University Press, 1992.

Ryle, Gilbert. *The Concept of Mind*. London: Hutchinson, 1949.

Watson, J. B. *Behaviorism*. New York: W. W. Norton, 1924.

————. *Psychology from the Standpoint of a Behaviorist*. Philadelphia: Lippincott, 1919.

Wittgenstein, Ludwig. *Philosophical Investigations*. Oxford: Blackwell, 1953.

CHAPTER 12

Feminism ────────────

FEMINISM HAS BEEN A MOVEMENT OF GREAT significance, energy, and diversity in recent decades. Like Marxism and psychoanalysis it has had two dimensions—theory, or analysis, and praxis—both central to its concerns. Marxism and Freudian psychoanalysis have also both led to a large number of schools of thought, and action, that depart from and sometimes oppose the earlier model. Likewise, a considerable range of positions falls under the label of feminism.

And as with revolutionary socialism and psychoanalysis, there is much disagreement about what positions, and individuals, properly are called by the movement's name. Contrasted with a claimed orthodoxy are stances labelled deviationist, revisionist, heretical, or simply not "really" feminist (or socialist, or psychoanalytic).

Among the many feminisms of the past three decades some appear more ephemeral than others. Some seem peculiarly products of the academy, without much influence outside university settings. Some are distinctive, even flamboyant. Although many individual books and articles receive much praise and discussion—or focused dissent—few thinkers have emerged around whom any consensus of their stature coalesces. Some women writers regard this as cause for celebration, as an indication of gender difference (of which more below): they argue that women, unlike men, don't need to have heroes or giants, and—since all creativity is contextually based, and ultimately involves the minds and labours of many—there is to be found here a more honest and valuable indication of shared enterprise.

Even as feminist views have proliferated in the academy, undergoing changes, refinements, and realignments with sometimes bewildering rapidity, so, *ultra muros* (outside the walls), feminism in the open public forum has been cast into a single increasingly tight and unitary mold. There people think they know rather well what feminism means and is; and some are for it, and others not.

Our concerns here are not with the whole wide range of feminist theory and analysis,[1] but rather with what characteristic feminist stances say or imply about human nature, or the natures of males and females or other subgroupings of humans. Many feminist theories are modifications or extensions of independently existing theories. Thus, we find liberal feminism, Marxist feminism, socialist feminism, psychoanalytic feminism, eco-feminism, existential (or existentialist) feminism, postmodernist feminism, and so on. In most or all of these cases the independently existing theory is modified or reconstituted, preserving something integral to the original yet with some high-lighted awareness of, or focus on, the historical and contemporary significance of being female. That puts it too gingerly: all feminist views hold that women have been systematically oppressed or disad-vantaged in human societies, almost always in concrete and material ways—their bodies, economic and social options, allocations of time and liberty, dictated and controlled not by themselves or even by collectivities of women, but by males. In addition to such material control, with its resulting disadvantage and oppression, there has also typically been some measure of spiritual or psychological oppression, taking the form of being told who one is and what one wants or of a silence and omission, with the image of being human culturally constituted or defined solely as male, and in male terms, and woman conceived as Other.[2]

In the public forum feminists are charged, by men and some women, with being anti-male or man-haters. The most optimistic feminist views hold that some societies are well on the way to achiev-ing a meaningfully post-patriarchal[3] stage (even if, as all feminist

---

[1] Much feminist work is essentially *critique* of developments in modern cultural or political life, from a perspective that is often not fully defined theoretically.

[2] "One is not born, but rather becomes, a woman. No biological, psychological, or economic fate determines the figure that the human female presents in society; it is civilization as a whole that produces this creature, intermediate between male and eunuch, which is described as feminine. Only the intervention of someone else can establish an individual as Other" (Simone de Beauvoir, *The Second Sex* [1952], p. 267).

[3] The term "patriarchy," central in much or most feminist writing and theory, is itself the site of dispute and unclarity. Etymologically the word means "rule by a father." It might be defined as applying to a social system in which females (most, or all, or females in general) are under the

views hold, substantial sexist and male supremacist traces and rearguard activities remain). The others regard the alleged decline of patriarchy as tenuous, uncertain, and incomplete, mostly or wholly illusory, or as a complete joke.

Are feminists anti-male? Feminist views are that males as a class or category historically have oppressed females. This is usually meant literally, and expressed forcefully. Might surviving Jews in the 1950s plausibly be regarded as anti-German? Of course not all would be; many forgave, and many others knew of anti-Nazi Germans, resistance leaders or individuals like Oskar Schindler. Apartheid has now been dismantled in South Africa; would it be natural for black South Africans to harbour resentment or antipathy to whites, in some broad or general way, even knowing many individual whites who were kind and non-racist? I won't attempt to answer these questions. But it is well to see it with clear and open eyes: as feminism views human history, males have been the Germans and the whites in the female analogue of Jewish and black South African experience.

This introduces one of the issues I want most to bring out, one infrequently given close attention: that feminism involves analyses and an understanding of history. If offers an empirical conceptualization of the past, of what it was like, how it was lived, who did what to whom, and why; and this constitutes a Version of History, comparable to what are identified as the Whig Version of History,[4] the Marxist Version of History, and others. Like those of Marx and Whigs, the Feminist Version has strengths, coherence, and a deep level of accuracy and insight. Yet it is also selective, and to a significant degree anachronistic—sometimes truer to the times it comes from than to those it purports to understand. All history, of course, runs these risks. Some feminist historiography exhibits a penchant for "golden age" thinking: convictions of an earlier time of relative or absolute "pre-patriarchy," when gender relations were allegedly egalitarian, or more egalitarian, with a paradise lost to a darkness from which we have only recently begun to emerge. The lost golden age is sometimes a hypothetical neolithic or early Bronze

control, direction, or authority of individual males or groups of males. Feminists note that formal or legal (negative) freedom from such control does not automatically ensure genuine (or positive) freedom.

[4] This is, essentially, the liberal interpretation of the past, which sees it as a linear development of enlightenment and progress, chiefly through the expansion of liberty and democracy, especially in Great Britain.

Age time of matriarchy,[5] or a pre-Christian rural time of female Wicca power, or a pre-industrial period of rural agrarian life with a wide differentiation and honouring of essential male and female socioeconomic roles, before industrial capitalism confined women to domestic life as servants or wife-mothers. Some or all of these conceptions may, of course, have some validity; but there seems a clear element of wishful thinking in many of them. Historical realities almost always seem to be messier and more complicated than ideological lenses see them in retrospect. The past, as L. P. Hartley remarked, is a foreign country; they do things differently there. This said, I turn to a historical sketch of the emergence of feminism itself.

Feminism is yet another offspring of the Enlightenment. It first appears in the public arena as an explicit extension of the idea of "the rights of man" to include women. Feminist scholars have frequently pointed out how little the classic texts in western political theory have to say about women.[6] Women are almost invisible in these texts, or appear as a special category of humanity usually consigned to a domestic sphere with children. These works envisage the human beings their accounts describe as male. This silence about female humanity, broken only by occasional marginal and sometimes derogatory and dismissive references, continues in most of the Enlightenment texts. The chief exceptions are works of the Marquis de Condorcet[7] (1743–1794) and Mary Wollstonecraft (1759–1797), who deserve identification as the first writers advocating the full humanity of women and their right to participate in the public life and institutions of society, including education, economic life, and politics—in brief, the claim of women to be full and unqualified *citizens*.

Condorcet evidently came to his feminist views a few years before Wollstonecraft arrived at hers. They appear first in print in a pamphlet called *Letters of a Citizen of New Haven* (1787). Still, his feminism is largely submerged in a broad Enlightenment mantle of

---

[5] This idea developed in nineteenth-century British and German speculative cultural anthropology, and has been argued for in recent years by the feminist anthropologist Marija Gimbutas and others.

[6] See, among other accounts, Susan Moller Okin, *Women in Western Political Thought* (1979).

[7] In fact, a formulation of essentially feminist views appears more than a century before Condorcet, also in France, in Poulain de la Barre's *De l'egalité des deux sexes* (*On the Equality of the Two Sexes*), published in 1673.

commitment to progress through education and scientific rationality, and the transcendence of the dead weight of the past and its authorities; the idea of feminism did not become well known from this work. It did from Wollstonecraft's. She became famous—and infamous—as author of *A Vindication of the Rights of Woman* (1792).

This first stage of feminism is continued in written form in the nineteenth century in John Stuart Mill's *On the Subjection of Women* (1869). Both Wollstonecraft's and Mill's books remain classics, and should be seen as part of a wider political, moral, and social movement for emancipation and rights extension, a movement that is a fundamental part of the Enlightenment phenomenon and project. That is to say, feminism appears in the European cultural world as just one component in the dismantling of hierarchical, authoritative social structures that had conferred differential status, moral, legal, and broadly human, on different classes and categories of human being. The abolition of feudalism, serfdom, and slavery, and then the extension of the franchise to widening sectors of the population, eventually, in the twentieth century, including all adults, are part of this pattern. So too are visions and reforms in property and marital and family law. All of these developments are parts of a process of creating, out of what once were markedly hierarchically structured differentiations, a single category of adult autonomous citizenship involving a common range of rights and obligations and under a universally applicable set of legal principles and social understandings and commitments.

Within the United States, which was the first society to implement Enlightenment ideals in concrete form in the Declaration of Independence (1776), this emancipatory progression came to focus on the vote for women in a manifesto proclaimed and published in Seneca Falls, New York, in 1848—the "year of revolution" in Europe, when several chiefly liberal/nationalist revolts broke out, and the *Communist Manifesto* was published.

This first stage of feminism, which we could date 1787–1869, and call Enlightenment or liberal feminism, espoused ideals that remain very much a living constituent of feminist theory today. Many feminist accounts of recent decades tend to depict Wollstonecraft-Mill feminism as a sort of museum piece, honourable and honoured for ground-breaking enterprise, but also limited and inadequate compared to advances of more recent vintage. This, I suggest, is misleading and certainly contentious, since many contemporary people, including many who label themselves feminists, have views about women, men, sex and gender, law, politics, education, and the family that differ hardly one iota from those of Condorcet, Wollstonecraft, or Mill.

This Enlightenment conception had much to say about human nature and the natures of the sexes. It held that human, male, and female natures are all formed largely through socialization—through education, in their idiom. These gender patterns had definite bases in "nature," but their boundaries and contours were vague. As C-W-M (Condorcet-Wollstonecraft-Mill) see it, there are not many substantive differences, pre-socially or naturally, between men and women. The sexes have largely the same capacities and dispositions, and certainly such differences as may naturally be there have little bearing on abilities to function as autonomous, rational, moral agents, or as learners, teachers, voters, friends, lovers, consumers, producers, parents, or legislators. There is a measure of faith involved and candidly acknowledged in these views, or, better, a reliance on their authors' convictions about what disinterested experience and reflection will disclose; for there was little or no formal empirical research on sex and gender, equality and difference; and, of course, the living experiment of universal citizenship that would have enabled C-W-M or their opponents to see what could be accomplished had not yet been implemented.

It should be noted that the C-W-M accounts, while explicit and wide-ranging, do not cover all facets of life and experience. Recent feminist critics sometimes take these silences to reveal positive convictions or assumptions that do not seem justifiably assigned to the liberal feminist view. For example, C-W-M, living in a pre-emancipatory time, emphasize public functions of citizenship and freedom from legal bondage and have little to say about the central significance mothering has for most mothers, or about communal elements that much female experience may contribute to our understanding of being human and to the reordering of social structures. But it does not follow from this that C-W-M have a starkly atomic individualist conception of women or human beings in general, either as ideals or realities, or that they celebrate Reason to the detriment of emotion or the body. Rather, the C-W-M focus on reason has a dialectical or strategic motivation. With women depicted in both the "folk" theory of the day and the writings of most so-called intellectuals as irrational or at any rate less rational than men, flighty, emotion-driven, impractical creatures weak in head however strong in heart, it was clearly of the first moment to make the case for women's abilities in mathematics, science, economic life, and government. As Karen Offen has shown,[8] much later nineteenth and early twentieth century European feminism had considerably different emphases, indeed operated from partly opposing assumptions, from those of the earlier liberal/Enlightenment variety. These alternative emphases constitute the earliest version of what is now designated "difference" feminism. (Offen identifies liberal feminism particularly with the English-speaking world. This in fact seems inaccurate, since Condorcet, technically the first feminist, was French, and the French Enlightenment and revolutionary tradition was at least as fully imbued with conceptions of the rights of man as was the English context.) The actual term "feminism" seems to date from no earlier than 1882, when it appears—in French—in a Paris periodical advocating women's suffrage. The term occurs regularly from 1892.

Recent discussions have given special and sometimes acrimonious attention to contrasts between equality and difference feminism. While there are other important polarities in feminist theory, this one brings out in a particularly clear form salient features of feminism as a conception of human nature. Accordingly, I will devote much of the remainder of this chapter to discussing this contrast, and then consider objections to feminism in one or both these forms. As it turns out, although a few qualifications are required, virtually all feminisms espouse either equality or difference.

All liberal feminists are equality feminists. Indeed, in some lexicons the two are entirely equivalent. However, some equality feminists identify themselves as socialists, whether Marxist or otherwise. The fundamental assumption about human nature of equality feminism is that the sexes do not differ substantively, at any rate in ways with much bearing on politics or economics. In fact, as equality feminists see things, conceptions of marked *differences* between males and females (like differences between other human groups, such as races or ethnic groups) have mostly been artificially fostered for political or economic reasons, as instruments of control and social regimentation.[9] The reality, they believe, is that humans exhibit a

---

[8] Offen, "Defining Feminism: A Comparative Historical Approach," in G. Bock and S. James, eds., *Beyond Equality and Difference* (London: Routledge, 1992).

[9] Socialist equality feminists (Marxist or otherwise) see this fostering as deriving from the interests of an oligarchic ruling class; liberal equality feminists see it as deriving from the aggregation of the individual private interest of individual benefited males.

wide range of temperaments, dispositions, capacities, and energies stamped upon a template that is fundamentally profoundly similar; or else—for some equality feminists—there is nothing much any of us "naturally" are, and we can and should develop a range of qualities that will permit and encourage all of us to be free, autonomous, brave, loving, caring, socially aware, and other valuable things.[10]

Difference feminists think men and women are significantly different. Officially, practically all contemporary feminists are "antiessentialist" and oppose any view that lodges either sex in a sexspecific set of traits, dispositions, or aptitudes. Despite this official doctrine, quite a few contemporary difference feminists, like the earlier nineteenth-century advocates of this position, think being female means something that goes to the heart and the marrow, just as does being male. Many such feminists preserve consistency by holding that female so-called natures are created by processes of socialization that reflect male-dominance structures and female responses to them. This seems to have the unhappy consequence that males are the authors of what it is to be female, even if at one remove. But most difference feminists, official doctrine notwithstanding, write, and act politically, as though there are sex essences, matters of what it is to be male and what it is to be female that are or at least have been transhistorical, transcultural, and causally significantly independent of each other.

Again, nobody disputes that there are sex differences,[11] nor that there are lots of similarities and equalities. What is at issue is whether there are differences that make a difference. Equality feminists say that by and large there are not, difference feminists that

[10] A clear example of equality feminism in contemporary cultural life is provided by Katha Pollitt, whose recent book *Reasonable Creatures: Essays on Women and Feminism* (1994) collects a series of her essays on facets of current life and debate involving women and feminism. Unlike some other equality feminists in contemporary discussion, Pollitt's has impeccable feminist "credentials," acknowledged by a wide range of prominent feminist spokespersons. One particularly lucid essay in *Reasonable Creatures* gives expression to the equality/difference debate, and Pollitt's strong advocacy of the equality position: "Marooned on Gilligan's Island: Are Women Morally Superior to Men?"

[11] Interestingly, one sex difference that Mill, one of the leading liberal and equality feminists of the classic period, notes, or claims, is a special female capacity for government. See J. S. Mill, *The Subjection of Women* (1869), Ch. 3, p. 490.

there are.[12] *Accounting* for the differences that difference feminists believe are real and important varies from position to position. Almost none see much of an explanatory role for biology, except in the psychological, social, cultural, and economic consequences of women's ability to become pregnant, give birth, and have, typically, bio-based linkage to offspring after giving birth. Women's reproductive powers and experiences, then, are usually seen as going a long way towards accounting for the "differences." But some difference feminists see female nature, and contrastive male nature, as manifested long before reproductive age. This might be accounted for as a social consequence of the later fact of reproductive capacity, that is, so that young girls are socialized in ways that anticipate that capacity.

Some difference feminisms, among them the nineteenth-century versions, do not make much of an attempt at aetiological analysis one way or the other. Sex differences are seen as simple facts, the important thing being to insist and affirm that the female way of being human is just as good as (some say better than) the male way of being human. Politically, this fuels efforts to change things to give at least equal accommodation to the female way. The idea is that the male way has hitherto been the dominant one, with females forced to adjust to it. In utopia, both ways would be duly manifest and positively valued. (Some would suggest that on the way to utopia the female way ought to have a stage of priority, to achieve compensatory, redemptive, or positively affirmative balance.)

Political critics of difference feminism, most vocal among them equality feminists,[13] see difference feminism as a retreat to the position of gender conservatives, and as inevitably tending towards a kind of gender apartheid in the socioeconomic sphere. The analogy with apartheid extends quite far: former South African apartheid, while officially valorizing separate development on grounds of racial

---

[12] A view may be identified that could be thought to incorporate features of both equality and difference feminism as presented here. This view would see males and females as constituting something like (distinct) "cultures," comparable to, say, Italian or Jewish or Japanese cultures, with distinctive styles, habits, and norms. Such a view may or may not be plausible. However, from the point of view of human nature theory this model, if intended reasonably literally, would be a form of equality feminism—for Italians and Japanese have no significant differences *as human beings*.

[13] See, for example, Katha Pollitt, *op. cit.*

"difference," conferred overwhelming socioeconomic advantage on just one of the races, the whites, and viewed non-white attempts to live as the favoured racial group did as improper and inauthentic aping of the other race. Difference feminists tend to view women who "make it" in the man's world on men's terms in a similar light. Politically, critics of difference feminism fear that the latter involves surrendering a public sphere of power, competition, and gain to men, and imprisoning all women in a gridlock model of nurturing and tenderness, with those women who behave otherwise smeared and reviled as sex traitors (or condescendingly "pitied" as not having been able to learn that they "really" have female, not male or female-as-defined-by-male, natures).

Although difference feminism is, as we have said, officially anti-essentialist, it develops a very sharp contrast between ideas of women's styles of being and what is called masculinism. Equality feminist critics, and liberals broadly, see this sharp contrast as not only having political implications and consequences; they see the difference feminist portrait of female humanity as a capitulation to the traditional and conservative views of gender, especially female gender, that much effort since the eighteenth century has attempted to overturn. Difference feminists are not wholly unaware of this concern. Sometimes they affirm something like a Marxian or Nietzschean transvaluation of these old views, celebrating traits once denigrated. Formally, difference feminism can insist that it does not deny women's *capacities* for masculinist performance. Indeed, it can and does call attention to all the women who are thriving in the man's economic world, often "stepping on their sisters" to do so. Rather, it believes women, though as fully capable of logocentric, analytical, competitive, impersonal thinking and behaviour as men, were forcibly precluded from such activities historically, and as a result have fashioned a gynoculture that is more human than masculinism is.

But though this is formally a defensible line, the fact is that women are particularly under-represented in the analytical, logocentric, mechanical, competitive, and impersonal sectors of the economy. In the knowledge disciplines they are markedly and proportionately under-represented the higher the level and the more remotely the discipline is connected to people. (Thus there are more women in social sciences than in natural sciences, and more in life sciences than in physics, chemistry, mathematics, or engineering.) What do these facts point to? Equality feminists say: very little; they are facts mostly of social history, of people and their locations (and self-identifications) in an economy, which academic disciplines and similar phenomena are chiefly either preparations for or echoes of. That history, coercive and regimenting for both men and women but more so for women, created patterns for social, economic, personal, and interpersonal roles. Now these have been to some degree loosened up; and over time, perhaps accelerated by some governmental or societal orchestration, a more nearly egalitarian and demographically representative socioeconomic set of patterns can be anticipated.

Difference feminists, it would seem, are not so sanguine. Alternatively, they may have a higher and a greater optimism than their liberal colleagues: the workplace will be feminized and socialized, swords (literal and figurative) will be beaten into ploughshares. To the extent that this is not what happens, a kind of *apartness* (*apartheid,* in Afrikaans) must prevail, with gynoculture allowed to flourish and kept free of masculinist intrusion.

It is the image of women in the difference view (and to a lesser extent that of men) that is problematic. Is it the same as the gender-conservative view, only "re-valorized," or is it not? The gender-conservative view is that women aren't as good at rational thinking as men are. Does difference feminism say, "Yes, that's right, but there is a different kind of thinking that women are better at than men"? If so, and if the running of a huge, complicated world depends critically on rational thinking, and rational thinking goes with psychic needs to be in charge, then even if the world also needs the feminine variety of thought, why doesn't that end up simply reaffirming the *status quo*—or rather, the *status quo ante,* the way it used to be, socioeconomically, before some women got the idea that they wanted to compete, achieve, and do similar masculinist things, not realizing that as women theirs was "a different voice"?

Both positions face some challenge. There is evidence—which may or may not be good evidence—that proportionately more men excel in rational thinking.[14] It is extremely difficult to determine how reliable the data are, but there appears to be evidence that proportionately more males than females are at the upper end (as also at the lower end) of IQ test scores. (The idea here is that out of, say, one hundred people with IQs above 150, considerably fewer than fifty, though certainly many, would be female.) IQ testing is itself assailed as unreliable, or showing either incoherent or merely cultural results about people. Some of these issues were explored in Chapter

[14] This result is claimed, with allegedly corroborating evidence provided, in Robert C. Lehrke, "Sex Linkage: A Biological Basis for Greater Male Variability in Intelligence" (1978).

9, and I will not explore them further here. *If* the findings are as claimed, difference feminists—and gender conservatives—would be able to continue with the views they defend. Difference feminists can dismiss the results as simply reflecting the masculinist character of IQ tests.[15] If confirmed, such results pose more of a challenge for the equality view. Still, if both sexes are well represented throughout the IQ span, then even if there were, say, two or more males with IQs of 160 for every female (and this is by no means known to be fact), it is quite unclear whether any consequences would ensue for social, economic, educational, or any other kind of policy. It is perhaps what may be called heroic-positive-liberty liberalism[16] that would be most affected, or undermined, and there is good reason independently not to adopt that stance.

Turning more generally to the difference position, critics think the case for difference is not made.[17] Or, more complicatingly, they acknowledge certain behaviours or behavioural ranges that tend to be found preponderantly among females and certain others among males, but claim these tend at best to encompass no more than (say) three quarters of either sex, with many individuals of the other sex also exhibiting the relevant behavioural pattern. And the evidence from other cultures appears to weaken claims that all male and female populations exhibit even stable proportions of such traits. If there are two population groups sixty per cent of one of which has property *A,* and fifteen per cent of the other also does, while sixty-five per cent of the latter has property *B,* which twenty-five per cent of the former shares, and where only five per cent of any group has both *A* and *B,* you can perhaps see how the first group might get characterized by the *A* property and the second group by the *B* property. But you should also see how crude and approximate this is,

---

[15] On the other hand, there is certainly no question that males and females both equally occupy the 90–110 IQ range.

[16] Insisting that there must be an exact or even a nearly exact demographic match between kinds of persons in a society and occupational and other distributions is an example of what is meant by heroic-positive-liberty liberalism. This view would be affected by the hypothetical results described if successful performance in some fields of work or study correlates significantly with high IQ.

[17] See, again, Pollitt, *op. cit.,* and Christina Hoff Sommers, *Who Stole Feminism?* (1994).

and how neglectful of *large* parts of the groups in question. It is simply not an adequate conceptualization of the groups.

Let us be more specific. The pre-eminent voice of difference feminism has been Carol Gilligan, whose (1982) book *In a Different Voice* claimed empirical support for the idea that women think differently than men about morality, conflict resolution, and bases of practical rationality, relations with others, and action. Gilligan's analyses essentially reaffirm quite old ideas of women as sympathizers, nurturative, maternal, caring and sharing, and attached to others rather than autonomous. Equally old stereotypical male complaints that women lack a sense of justice are turned on their head. What's so great, Gilligan asks, about a sense of justice, and analytic, abstract, impersonal modes of thinking, with efforts to produce rigid codes of rules, that obscure or eliminate the personal, contextual, human dimension to our experiences and dilemmas?[18] Gilligan also endorses distinctive female ways of knowing, female logic, and female styles of approach to the human and non-human worlds. All of these ideas are invariably presented *contrastively,* as differing from allegedly typical male modes of thinking, acting, interacting, reasoning, problem-solving, and being in the world.[19] Gilligan's accounts, in developed form, are clearly expressions of gender stereotyping, inviting comparisons with national character stereotypes. That in itself is no objection to them, for presumably some or all of these stereotypes might be wholly or significantly true.

The main objection to difference feminism is that there seems no good reason to believe its portraits of males and females are accurate, or accurate enough. Too many women exhibit what are supposed to be masculinist traits, and too many men exhibit what is supposed to go with female "difference."[20] Large numbers of women never be-

---

[18] Thus, for example: "If aggression is tied, as women perceive, to the fracture of human connection, then the activities of care, as their fantasies suggest, are the activities that make the social world safe, by avoiding isolation and preventing aggression rather than by seeking rules to limit its extent" (Carol Gilligan, *In a Different Voice,* p. 43).

[19] For example: "While women ... try to change the rules in order to preserve relationships, men, in abiding by those rules, depict relationships as easily replaced" (ibid., p. 44).

[20] While difference feminists typically dismiss masculinist women as victims of false consciousness, they do not want to say the same thing of men who, inconveniently for those feminists, exhibit "female" traits. (False

come mothers, biological or adoptive, and there is no good evidence that almost all who don't are thereby frustrated and unfulfilled, or seek vicarious motherhood. Further, a great many mothers are miserable being so, or incompetent at the tasks involved. And many women are competitive, individualist, and seekers of power over other people; some are even cruel, or vain, or snobbish. It is not obvious that all of them have been co-opted or brainwashed by male culture or male values, or that having these traits is a pathological consequence of patriarchy. Margaret Thatcher is as good a card-carrying member of the female sex as Rosa Luxemburg, or any woman who never knew power or fame. Dorothy Parker, Joan Crawford, Ayn Rand, Barbara Cartland, Madonna: all are as female as every other woman. Individual famous people will not, of course, conclusively make the point needing to be made; what is wanted are thorough, intelligently designed empirical studies of males and females across a variety of age groups, social classes, and cultures. How relationships to social power might be factored in or out of such studies would remain problematic, as would what to make of the males and females not conforming to majority trends (assuming there are some of the latter).

I proceed to a distinct dimension of contrast between feminisms. Like the equality/difference polarity, this one too is lopsided: there are many feminisms in one group and few—arguably just one—in the other. The equality/difference contrast was in fact a special case of a wider query: whether all humans share a basically similar range of cultural/spiritual traits, or rather whether human subgroups (sexes, races, classes, age groups, etc.) constitute morally or ontologically unlike categories. The polarity I now discuss is also a special case of something met with in contexts other than those of sex and gender.

Some theories contrast an ideal human condition with what is found in particular cultural or historical circumstances. The former is the *telos* of humanity, or of some relevant subgroup, and the latter is an undesirable current condition, whose undesirability is determined by factors independent of what group members believe they find satisfying and dissatisfying. People's *expressed* desires, for instance, may be the result of social conditioning, which overrides or misshapes their *real* values. (At least, so the views advanced here hold.) In short, on such views what people think they value is not

consciousness is the Marxian idea of the condition of people who do not, or pretend not to, recognize their real class interest, because they have been hoodwinked by or colluded with a ruling-class ideology.)

decisive, perhaps not even weighty evidence of what they really value, because they may have been, in effect, brainwashed. Views that combine teleology with the idea that declared values and goals, even for majorities of large population groups, may not coincide with real values and goals, I call *Manichean*.[21] They contrast with theories that take people at their word (together with the behaviour they exhibit): if someone *says* they enjoy and like *x,* this is, other things being equal, reason to believe they really do value *x* (again, providing that their behaviour supports their avowals). Among feminisms, a clear case of a view of the second sort is liberal feminism. I now consider, then, Manichean and liberal feminism.

The Manichean set of views sees people in fundamentally black and white terms, distinguishing a bad version of humanity from a good version. A mixture of the two is in principle allowed in individual cases, but the overall vision requires the polarity. The good version of humanity, for Manichaean feminism, is cooperative, egalitarian, non-aggressive, mutualist, non-competitive, sympathetic, environmentally sensitive, nurturing, loving, and feelingly parental. It has historically been pro-socialist and anti-biologistic, and—though it is anathema to some that it be put in these terms—has advocated the classic range of liberal individual values (freedom of conscience, moral autonomy of the individual as citizen, free association with others in families or other structures, and disposal of one's own person or body and of no one else's).

Manichean feminist views differ on the relation of the good version of humanity to an underlying human nature. Some Manichean stances see the good version as what we "naturally" are, or are disposed to be, attainment of which is sometimes or often prevented by alien structures: the capitalist economic system, the "cabin fever" logistics of complex social and economic organization, or pernicious ideologies foisted on the great majority by small minorities of self-serving power-seekers. Any such view will, of course, have to explain how, if we are all naturally altruistic and "good," some can develop Luciferian impulses for control and domination. What account can be given of *their* natures that won't imply they aren't human?

Other Manichean stances see us as essentially plastic, with capacities for development in both good and bad directions depending

---

[21] After the ancient religious view that saw the world as a conflict between good and evil.

on what forces are operative. The bad version of humanity, for Manichean feminism, involves just these impulses to dominate, control, and subordinate other people, animals, and the environment. It is an individualist humanity, acquisitive, aggressive, competitive, impersonal, sexually and in other ways rapacious, alienated from softness of feeling, without sympathetic attachment to other people or non-human nature. Its historical sociopolitical expression has been capitalism, but earlier and still lingering ideologies have also included feudalism and pronounced nationalisms.

Pre-feminist Manichean views have included those of Rousseau and Marx (as well as of Bakunin and Kropotkin).[22] The deepest foundational root for all modern Manichean views is, I think, Rousseau. The distinctive addition that some feminist views have made to this fundamental perspective is the idea that the good version of humanity is pre-eminently exemplified by female humans and the bad version by male humans. (Not necessarily *all* male humans are conceived in this way.[23] Sometimes the bad version of humanity is held to be specially or paradigmatically exemplified by heterosexual males of European descent, or some subgroup thereof.) Additions and qualifications will be made to the latter claim, endeavouring to show that the *reasons* females specially exhibit the good version have to do with their experience of oppression, and not necessarily with an ahistorical or context-independent female nature. Some Manichean feminist views do, and others do not, extend this "anti-essentialism" to males. Versions of what is usually called radical feminism hold that males have natural dispositions to control, domination, aggression, individualist impersonality, and general rapacity. Sometimes this is modified by the idea that males develop such dispositions out of fear of female power, either sexual or reproductive. Others believe we have all, to some degree, been victims of a system larger and more powerful than individual wills—the capitalist system, complex material logistics (even if non-capitalist), certain western religious or sociopolitical ideologies, or "the gender system," forces of ideology that have accompanied or shaped child-rearing practices that turn humans into beings with male identities and female identities, and that necessarily make for male attempts at domination of females.

[22] Mikhail Bakunin (1814–1876) and Peter Kropotkin (1842–1921) were leading anarchist theorists and activists.

[23] Feminist writers who have characterized males in general in this way include Susan Brownmiller, Mary Daly, and Andrea Dworkin.

I want to stress that there is a strongly normative component in this variety of feminism: what are meant are versions of good and bad. This may or may not be problematic. Some Manichean feminists (and many other thinkers) reject so-called normative/descriptive distinctions; as they see it, there is nothing wrong with a normative component in their view. We should perhaps pause to say a few things about what is involved in this issue.

Traditionally, philosophers have identified what they call the fact/value distinction. The idea here is that what the facts of some situation are is one thing, and some evaluation that is made of those facts is entirely another. Facts are supposed to be objective, in the world; they include facts about what is in the minds of individuals or groups of people. Valuations placed upon something are supposed to be subjective, or to express attitudes that someone has and that others may or may not share. The matter is complicated by the view of some that matters of value can themselves also be matters of fact— for example, that it is as much a fact that torturing children is morally wrong, or that studying for exams is important, as that arsenic is toxic or snow plentiful in Canada in January. We can and, for our purposes, should avoid this complication. Unless all valuations are matters of fact—and they can't be, since some conflict with others, which no fact can do—we can put the valuations that are matters of fact (if there are any) to one side, and consider just what are supposed to be non-valuational matters of fact and non-matter-of-fact valuations.

For many years various thinkers have also attacked or disputed the fact/value distinction. Such attacks have taken different forms and had different grounds. Some have argued that certain putative matters of fact involve values, or that large classes of putative matters of fact do, and have then inferred that all putative matters of fact involve values. Others have rested their case on the idea that it is impossible to *explain* in a clear and plausible way what the boundary between or the criteria for facts and values are supposed to be. Still others have thought that all description or conception of supposed facts is actually saturated with value. (Somewhat similarly, some philosphers attack foundationalism—the so-called myth of the given—in epistemology, arguing that all description or conception of supposed facts is saturated with *theory*. Indeed, some of the people arguing against a fact/value distinction are also anti-foundationalists in epistemology, and on similar grounds.)

The last stance (or cluster of stances) referred to can, however, be misleading for our purposes. Social critics' and theorists' qualms about a fact/value contrast have not typically rested on metaphysical analyses of experience and the world. (They often involve *opinions* or *assumptions* about metaphysics, and the possibility of knowledge of reality apart from our perspectives; but usually without any detailed investigation of whether those opinions or assumptions are justified.) Quite often social critics seem to be chiefly expressing the (frequently well-justified) suspicion that something claimed to be an objective matter of fact is really anything but that, is instead the value-laden assumption or prejudice of someone who is trying to control some person or situation.

As a philosophical issue, the fact/value question gets rather complicated. It may in the end be most reasonable to say that there is not one fact/value distinction to draw but several, or that there is a fuzzy boundary with reasonably clear factual things on one side, reasonably clear valuational things on the other, and lots of cases with varying degrees of the one or the other in between. In any case, the reader should be aware that this is yet another of the big, complex issues, with a large literature devoted to it and strongly divided positions taken and defended.

Whatever the truth about fact and value may be, there do seem to be problems confronting Manichean views of human beings. Voltaire may not have been right that to understand all is to forgive all, but the endeavour of understanding—understanding people, what they are like, and why they do what they do—does seem obstructed by the strongly marked bipolar normativity of many feminists, and others of the children of Rousseau. Manichaean understanding also confronts a number of related and difficult questions. If good is as good as it is cracked up to be, why would anyone be bad? Whence evil? How is bad male essentialism to be avoided, if it is going to be?

The specifics of feminist Manichean ethics are also open to query. Is it so clear that competitive impulses are evil and ought if possible to be eliminated? May there not be a case to be made for what I will call the Ecclesiastes version of our moral estate—to everything there is a season[24]—with some idea of a balance or harmony of human qualities, including desires for power, occasions of deep impersonality, a place in the scheme of things for lust as well as love, and a role for different sorts of human efficiency?

I now turn to liberal feminism, which, like liberalism in general, is much maligned. Liberal positions have been frequently distorted

[24] Eccles. 3.1.

to the point of caricature, and this difficulty certainly extends to liberal feminism. Much of what is to be said about liberal feminism has appeared already in Chapter 5; I will try here chiefly to identify distinctively feminist or female-focused dimensions that liberal feminism adds to liberalism, and to compare and contrast the liberal with other varieties of feminism. Still, a certain amount of re-covered ground will be inevitable.

Liberals are optimists, and they identify individuals and their possibilities and actualities as the chief locations of social and human ontology. One of the distortions of some critics is to suppose that liberals always think individuals are the *only* locus of human reality. This is quite untrue. Many liberal views have stressed the individual's rootedness in networks of "significant others," familial or otherwise, in both the formation and the maintenance of the full adult person. But liberal ontology does see each individual as a unit of personhood, a fresh start in the universe for a new and distinctive personal realization. This does not need to be sentimentalized. But it does help explain the intensity of liberal conviction about a human life diminished mentally or physically, especially when owing to free and hence preventable human agency, whether active abuse or neglect.

We want as far as possible to distinguish liberal *values* from liberal views of human beings. The one will at least partly reflect and disclose the other: someone will think something important, or a right, because they think its realization is genuinely possible and also at some kind of risk. Liberals believe that, by and large, human beings are capable of happiness, via a condition of reaching, understanding, and implementing conceptions of private, individual good.

Feminist liberalism wholly shares this view; indeed, it sees itself, quite reasonably, as more fully articulating it by virtue of its greater awareness of the diminished prospects of self-realization open to disproportionately many women. The generally astute critic Jean Bethke Elshtain sees this as stemming from or producing a desire to turn women into men.[25] (This was a classic objection to giving women the franchise.) Her claim is unfair: the liberal goal is to secure for all the possibility of realizing the self each individual can become, partly through his or her own choices and actions.

It is true that for liberals, who see in each life the possibility of a fresh assault on Parnassus, it will be extremely important (if not an

---

[25] See Jean Bethke Elshtain, *Public Man, Private Woman* (1993), pp. 228–255. The subtitle Elshtain gives her discussion of liberal feminism is "Why Can't a Woman Be More Like a Man?"

inherent right) that each life be accorded, if it can be, the genuine chance of such an assault. Hence claims on others that might jeopardize their prospects of self-realization will be, for liberals, muted or given low weight. Moving from moral to factual mode, this will translate into (sympathy for) views that minimize human needs for specific human others. The state, a daycare centre, babysitter, successor lover or spouse, hospital, therapist, or geriatric institution can provide anything that I may provide to any specific other person. I should be in another's life only if I have chosen to be (the choice always subject to periodic reconsideration), and only so long as I see myself as enriched and developed by being there: my relationships with others are a part of a process of producing a better, more realized me.

This may make the liberal conception seem narcissist, indeed, encouraging of a fatuous self-absorption. There is, I think, some risk of that in the liberal view; but it seems doubtful that it is a risk that must be succumbed to.

Liberals think that all people, and therefore also women, can be free and happy. The positive point of politics—the negative one being to impede others' undesired incursions—is to further real (positive) liberty and the chance to strive for one's own good. This is why consumer protection legislation, affirmative action programs and policies, and attempts to enlarge the sphere of rights are fundamentally liberal ideas. They come into some measure of collision with *other* liberal ideas, notably the valuing of negative as well as positive liberty. The liberal ideal is not, however, inconsistent. It is an ideal cross-product of the two vectors of freedom and security. This is Mill's formulation of what human happiness consists in: some blend or mix, varying with the individual and the circumstances, of excitement and tranquillity.[26] An over-finely calibrated set of notions of what would be required for the liberal ideal to be realized may be a problem for heroic-positive-liberty liberalism; but this may just make a case for a more *relaxed* liberalism, able to live with a certain amount of contingency and disorder in social arrangements, and content that utopia, while always a goal to strive for, may never be reached.

Feminism has generated an interesting phenomenon that is sometimes (journalistically) styled "anti-feminist feminism." The advocates of the positions meant are (usually) women scholars or social critics who identify themselves explicitly as feminists but who are

[26] John Stuart Mill, *Utilitarianism* (1861), Ch. 2, p. 13.

critical, even severely critical, of currently prevailing feminist philosophies or public practices. Three important cases will be briefly discussed; their importance derives from both the range and depth of their criticisms of prevailing positions and the creativity of their own feminist work. One is a liberal equality feminist, another a difference feminist, and the third not easily classified.

Christina Hoff Sommers is a philosophical critic of what she calls gender feminism. This is the view that there is a comprehensive gender system, largely invented and sustained by men, which subjugates women by constructing social and personal roles for them and seeks control over women's bodies and minds, incapacitating them for authentic self-direction. The central, ground-level institution of control is the historical nuclear family. There is little doubt that belief in such a system characterizes large numbers of feminist positions, especially so-called radical feminist views, and hence that Sommers' target is real. Both difference and equality feminists can be gender feminists. At the same time, we should note that many feminists would only partially embrace a gender-feminist view. Alongside vigorous, spirited, and often highly effective argument against gender feminism, and in favour of respecting the actual views and lifestyle preferences of female majorities, Sommers identifies herself as a liberal feminist. Of course, in the way of these orthodoxy disputes, her gender-feminist opponents deny that she is a "real" feminist. But there seems no reason not to accept her at her own self-description as an equality liberal feminist with less commitment to guaranteeing positive liberty for women than some other equality liberal feminists.[27]

Jean Bethke Elshtain is an eloquent and prolific political philosopher and social critic who is also an "anti-feminist feminist." She has authored some of the most thorough and effective arguments against some feminist and liberal positions ever produced. Elshtain is often identified as a leading "communitarian" thinker, a champion and advocate of extra-governmental institutions—neighbourhood associations, churches, charities, trade unions, but above all the historic nuclear family. So she is attacked as a conservative, or a neoconservative. Yet neither of these labels fits well. Elshtain is also a (certain kind of) strong feminist, firmly advocating women's parti-

[27] Sommers' book *Who Stole Feminism?* (1994) is a critique of gender-feminist activities in the American educational system and media, showing patterns of distorted statistics and practices respectful of neither alternative views nor majority female preferences in the general population.

cipation in all public fora and denying the inevitability or desirability of rigid gender roles. Like Sommers, Elshtain calls herself a feminist; and similarly, the self-ascription is claimed spurious by more orthodox feminists. Nonetheless she seems, perhaps even more clearly than Sommers, to qualify. Elshtain has Freudian and feminist psychoanalytic sympathies and leanings, and may be classified as a mild or moderate difference feminist, and—despite her trenchant criticisms of liberalism—as a clear advocate of liberalism in the wide sense.[28]

Camille Paglia is the third case of an impressive and original critic of feminism who is herself a kind of feminist. Paglia is louder, more emphatic, than the other two, indeed as fierce and arguably as disposed to hyperbole as any radical feminist. But her work, in *Sexual Personae* (1990), *Sex, Art, and American Culture* (1992), and *Vamps and Tramps* (1994), presents new, energized thinking on issues of gender, culture, and individuality. Paglia is a Freudian and a Nietzschean—she believes in giants, heroes, and heroines, and in human wildness, Bacchic creative energies that operate in the night, when children should not be present. She is an unqualified opponent of Rousseau, believing in almost every case in the inversions of his analyses and his values, above all believing in the value and importance of law, and civilization, as frameworks within which human creative achievement, Apollonian and Dionysian, female and male, can occur. Paglia is also a complete opponent of victimism, of "whining," of *ressentiment* that the world comports itself as it did or does. She speaks for a regained and reasserted sexuality, for courage and autonomy. Paglia does not easily fit feminist classification. Like Sommers and Elshtain, Paglia calls herself a feminist. She shares liberal values without liberal optimism, and may be viewed as an equality feminist as qualified by Freud. Paglia is a celebrant and prophet of female possibilities in the face of the world's challenges to those possibilities. Her actual feminist affinities are closest, I think, to an earlier giant, whose feminist credentials are unchallenged though her specific version of feminism is given rough treatment: Simone de Beauvoir (1909–1986).

A feminist of enduring stature, de Beauvoir is often identified as the initiator of the current long wave of feminism. Her *The Second Sex,* published in France in 1949 and in English translation in 1953,

---

[28] Elshtain's *Public Man, Private Woman* (1993) is primarily a work of political philosophy surveying major positions of past and present bearing on gender and society. Her book is a particularly thorough critique of liberal, socialist, and radical feminisms.

had a wide impact on women. This response, more than any other single event, may be said to have launched modern feminism.

De Beauvoir tends often to share the sort of "founding mother" view accorded Wollstonecraft and Mill: thought of as historically important, insightful for the times and circumstances in which the ideas appeared, but severely limited and long superseded. Her variety of feminism is frequently dismissed as individualist, and as lacking insight into the importance of reproduction and the bodily in general for female identity. Gender and difference feminists see her as uncritically assuming androcentric models and valuations of being human. Thus, her feminism is regarded as the wistful complaint that women aren't allowed to be, or to at least aspire to be, like men. At the same time de Beauvoir receives no warm welcome from liberal feminists, for she wants people—women above all—changed in ways formal/legal reforms (even substantial affirmative action) could not achieve.

In my view de Beauvoir is often misunderstood and misinterpreted. Most of the criticisms fail to understand the kind of approach she brings to the conditions of being human, female, and male. She is, I think, first of all a philosopher, of the general type of Spinoza or Hegel. That is to say, she has a teleological conception of the best or highest human estate, and this is the condition of maximal freedom, maximal distance from mere inert nature, and necessarily therefore a highly cerebral, self-reflective, and consciously self-determining condition. Of course, not all humans have high philosophical values or aspirations. So her project is, as well as teleological, elitist—that is, aimed at a human best that, owing to historical or socioeconomic logistics, might be achievable by only a few. De Beauvoir sees no reason in the nature of the human clay itself that that few would not include a due share of females.

These matters may be put less formally: One of the features that stands out in almost all feminist theory is a global or comprehensive account of the female condition. Views are faulted for being insufficiently universal—and certainly when judged applicable only to white, middle-class, educated western women (the chief authors of actual feminist theories).

Doubtless important and salutary concerns are registered with those identified canons of universality. But there is also a rather distinct base for thinking out the contours of some variety of human reality, which is lost in this universalism. We none of us *know* how the world is felt and sensed for more than a small number of its communities, even in the case of sex/gender communities. Yet it is possible to think and write about being human, or being female and human, where one is indifferent to whether what one says is universally applicable, and yet one speaks as though it were because one is speaking for those who know the world in the same broad ways as oneself, and have the same concerns and possibilities. The vantage point or perspective is *not* me-and-my-friends, or me-and-my-cultural-group-or-class, but rather the assumed mantle of representative of anyone, regardless of class or culture, whose fundamental values and priorities I would *recognize* as shared with me.

De Beauvoir is addressing kindred souls: people who want to have touched a little bit of eternity, to have known and cared about reality, and to have acted in it as much without illusions as humans can. As the sociocultural conditions have been set up, or at least still were in 1949, they conspired to limit the possibilities of Knowledge and Agency—of genuine Ontological Seriousness—to men. Nonetheless, as Plato knew, women are as capable as men of philosophy, and of using freedom as a serious human. This is the tragedy of the second sex, the Other, defined, if at all, negatively and by relegation. And as de Beauvoir sees it—for she takes women seriously and accords them autonomy and respect—women are themselves at least partly to blame for this relegation. They were partly forced into and partly allowed their definition, and self-definition, as Other, as merely bodily, as filling interstices that would permit and encourage male freedom. This is why it is particularly important that, to achieve a breakthrough into the full sphere of highest humanity, women must—if they care, if they value that highest humanity—lessen, even scorn, their relegation to the bodily, the small, the domestic, the local, the interstitial. Even if only dialectically, to effect existential escape they must eschew servitudes, including the servitude and bondage of giving birth and nurturing children. Of course this is individualist, but in a way all philosophy necessarily is: in asking you to take your life, and the universe, seriously, to try to understand, and to do something that may matter. Jean Bethke Elshtain, one of de Beauvoir's sternest critics, is in fact a superb embodiment of the de Beauvoir hope and injunction; and if she has been able to combine a philosophic career of the highest distinction with extensive public activism (and, as she indicates in her writings, with a full family life), that may be in part due to Simone de Beauvoir and her work.[29]

[29] Writers on political topics, including political philosophers, seem sometimes to have remarkably short memories. They appear to forget astonishingly rapidly the way a social reality *felt* while lived through and

As remarked upon earlier, feminism, like Marxism, involves a certain broad analysis of the human past and the weight, hazards, and possibilities it brings to the present and the future. Also like Marxism, feminism involves a tension—not necessarily irresolvable, but also not readily seen from within the theory—between what is supposed to be historical and what appears impossible not to view as moral analysis. Still again like Marxism, all of this is rendered yet more complicated by features of the theory (and this seems true of a wide range of feminist stances, as of Marxism) that renounce or transform both moral and other kinds of putative objectivity. (*What* objectivity becomes if transformed is somewhat problematic.)

These complications may be given a stark directness by observing that according to (much) feminism little or nothing is objectively the case, and yet women (and other groups) have really, presumably objectively, been oppressed. That oppression is real, not a construction or the expression of mere contextually situated perspectives, that will shift and alter as the world shifts and alters. Moreover, the primary causal agent in the construction of gender and other roles, indeed the construction of entire social orders and the ideologies that shape and are shaped by them, is power. Power—the dual of oppression—is real, and objective. That this person or group has it and that one lacks it, these too are as objectively factual, for feminism, as anyone ever claimed any fact about the chemical elements to be.

There does not appear to be exaggeration or distortion in these claims. For feminism *power,* individual and social, needs to be fairly clear and straightforward, and to consist of objective (and objectively determinable) facts of the matter. I think part of a serious critique of feminism would probe and possibly challenge the alleged transparency and simplicity of power. The very idea of power, of what it is for some people to have more power than others or to have power over others, may be more *textured,* and historically and culturally

contended with, once times and issues have changed. One should not dwell in the past. And one should not judge the past wholly by the lights of the present, or without mindfulness of what is possible in the present *because* of what happened (including what was said or written) in the past. These comments are not directed only or even primarily at Elshtain, although it seems to me that they have some validity in her direction. In the background of these comments are also value judgments about what the past for women was like, which Elshtain and others who may seem overharsh about past advocates of liberation may not share.

nuanced, than feminism has standardly supposed.[30] Whether a reconceptualized, historically and contextually sensitive notion of power could continue to serve central feminist purposes remains to be seen.

It is similar with Marxism. Both feminism and Marxism are philosophies ineliminable from which is the possibility of laying blame. You don't have either of them, not genuinely, unless some blaming is going on: some things are happening that are both bad and avoidable, and it is someone's *fault* that they are going on, and action must be taken to make those offenders stop.[31]

This is not to discredit either Marxism or feminism. It may show that there is some problem with *consistency* in both theories; but consistency may be an overrated virtue for social or human nature theories. It can be easy enough, if we think it worth taking the trouble, to add or subtract an assumption or two to render the entirety of a scheme coherent.

Let me say also that there seems quite good reason to regard humans as having significant degrees of meaningful freedom, enough that lots of things *are* reasonably lain at the door of individuals or groups, as things they could have and often *should* have done differ-

---

[30] To give a quick idea of what this might mean: perhaps different *kinds* of power are only in complex ways correlated. Social power may be quite a different thing from personal power, the sort of power someone can exert interpersonally by force of will, of personality, charm, or beauty; and cultural, socioeconomic, or historical conditions may make power quite a different thing in different circumstances. Attila the Hun, for instance, had the power openly to order anyone in his society killed, but didn't have the power to determine the value of commodities outside the sphere of operations of himself and his cohort; a modern billionaire has the latter power but not the former. The power of a group or class is problematic to the degree to which that class is not cohesive. (This seems to be part of the problem in thinking of males as constituting a ruling "class" in any large society.) The power of fashion, of aesthetics, of superstition, or ideas is only unreal or secondary on historical materialist assumptions that are not very persuasive. Finally, some person or group might wield power over large numbers of people without having much power to initiate social or other changes, just as the converse also occurs. The role of *acquiescence* in another's power also seems a necessary complicating factor in what that power is, or means, or even sometimes whether it exists.

[31] This point is sometimes put, perhaps more and perhaps less tendentiously, by saying that feminism and Marxism are *victim-centred* philosophies.

ently. The concepts of oppression, domination, and subordination, like imperialism, sexism, racism, and many other like sins, can be given plausible content. But it will take work to do it, that work has not very extensively been attempted, and its performance might produce a feminism (or a Marxism) rather different from anything currently on offer.

The rejection of the so-called fact/value distinction, from which many feminists dissent, may be held to refute or weaken the foregoing. Proponents will say that feminism is indeed a blaming theory, but in fact all theories are praising or blaming in character, all subtly or unsubtly support or challenge the ways things are going. So feminism deserves commendation for being honest and open about what other theories are also doing in sly or hypocritical disguise. And anyway, there is no getting round the inextricable mix of information, misinformation, and disinformation, and valuation placed upon it, in whatever we undertake to say or do.

I suggested earlier that some kind of fact/value distinction, even if a revised one, seems plausible. Some notion of objectivity seems even more reasonable. I think it can be shown (though this book is not the place to try to show it) that a meaningful degree of objectivity will require some kind of fact/value distinction. Actually, if people thought more deeply about the matter they might agree that no one really *wants* the complete interdissolution of fact and value, for it would sabotage the possibility of success for one's own agenda. Of course, even a universal wanting does not guarantee that that want can be satisfied. Still, there is at least a reasonable case for the grounding of objectivity and for being able to draw some distinctions between "is" and "ought."

But even if fact/value boundaries are hard or impossible to make out, that wouldn't meet the problems we have identified: that feminism itself assumes objectivity with regard to power, differentiates oppression from its avoidability and culpability, and sees all of these ideas as extremely clear, simple, and (apparently) ahistorical or transhistorical in nature.

More complicated in a different direction are empirical queries about the human past. These too we can only sketch here. There is reason to view a great deal of feminist conceptualizations of the past as unhistorical—as violations, again, of the historicist sensitivity that is formally part of the feminist creed. To take just one example, feminist views of "patriarchal" religions almost invariably require supposing that the male promulgators of those religions did not sincerely believe them—that claims of religious conviction were mere appearance, thinly disguising parameters of power and control. Doubtless plausible in a great many individual cases, this seems much less so for whole cultures, even for the oppressing male halves of them. Obsessive fear of hell seems to have been all too real and widespread to give much support for the idea of a comfortable male ruling class, controlling and directing their female serfs with bland pieties about God's will.

Another concern about feminist views of human beings is essentially the same as one registered about Aristotle's human nature theory: that they lack depth or three-dimensionality; that these are theories that stay on the surface of things, where it is always daytime, there are no ambiguities or complexities. This is not only or simply the complaint that women are implausibly over-heroized in much feminist writing, though the latter is, I think, the case.[32] If a body of writing systematically implies that the great generality of a category of people has consisted of patient noble martyrs, heroic resisters, or quietly effective agents of daily life and creative struggle, one has reason to believe this is itself symptomatic and revealing. This is an author soothing or cajoling his or her audience, handling it with kid gloves, afraid perhaps that insufficient flattery might puncture that audience's self-confidence or esteem. It is ultimately condescending to the audience; it is elitist, and missionary in spirit, though doubtless well intentioned as most missionary work is.

At any rate, this is not the objection primarily in view here. It is rather that often feminist writing, like Aristotle's, too readily takes people (especially female people) on the emic surface of how things seem to them, or they would say things seem to them. Harris is right: an adequate account of human reality must have an etic and not only an emic dimension. It must make sense of what people are doing not just in terms of the motives and rationale they would offer (and even then certainly not just what they might say to their friends, parents, a social worker, sociologist, or union organizer), but also in terms of an intelligibility in their behaviour that will sometimes, even for heroes, be at odds with the construction they would themselves place on that behaviour.

More than this: there must be a possibility of nuance and complexity, and an attempt at understanding them *whose motivation is not primarily justifying*. We need to recognize "subtextual" motivations

---

[32] This will be found in what is often otherwise some of the most acute, carefully argued, widely informed work, for example Alison Jaggar's book *Feminist Politics and Human Nature* (1983).

in human behaviour that are not only located in demonized or dismissed others (male or female). Much feminist writing does accord multiple motivation to patriarchal males, or females held to be victims of false consciousness. *Their* actions and motivations are not permitted to be taken on their surface, as what their agents would claim they were. But Woman in general, victimized and oppressed, or functioning in the social order however she finds it to be, is always to be taken straight: here appearance and reality always coincide. If the system allows her to, she discovers or creates her values and her identity and then goes out into the world to try to realize the goals she has formulated. She wears *those* clothes, if she can afford it and cares (she may not), because they correspond to her aesthetic values. She meets people and brings to such meetings her projects and values, generally honourably forwarded for possibilities of contractual engagement or mutualities. This is without ambiguity, and therefore without real texture. People do not always know what they want. Indeed, sometimes other people's collisions and coercions nudge or compel one to just this knowing. Sometimes we do have impossible or conflicting goals. More importantly than either, though, sometimes there are layers in the self unknown to conscious agency. It is unclear that feminism can accommodate these facts.

A second criticism of feminist theory of human nature is that it is largely without independent content. According to this view, feminism chiefly consists of two parts, one a social justice issue, the other a set of analyses and claims most of which are either borrowed from pre-feminist theory or are quite implausible, indeed primarily just empty rhetoric. Expanding on this criticism, its proponents identify a genuine and longstanding social justice issue to be found in most human societies. Women have been widely shabbily treated and disadvantaged, disallowed opportunities not merely that men have had but also that women would have wanted whether or not these were the same opportunities as men's. In this respect they have, quite widely and often in human history, been allocated a second-class citizenship akin to that of disadvantaged groups defined by ethnicity, religion, or social class. This social justice issue needs redressing, and in the way of such redress is being seen to imperfectly, patchily, not as quickly as it ought to, but genuinely, in a very wide sector of human societies.

But—this objection continues—as morally important as this matter is, what more is there to say? Is there a distinctive theory of the world or of humanity for every human group that has been unfairly or shabbily treated? No doubt all groups have their own distinctive experiences and perspectives, and potentially everyone may be enriched by knowing about them. But shall we say that there is a special theory (or group of theories) that is implicit in the experiences and perspectives of Jews, homosexuals, gypsies—all three of whom have been the object of literal extermination campaigns—the left-handed, the handicapped, aboriginal peoples, Catholics, Protestants, Armenians, and so on? There have been so many groups of people who have been treated appallingly badly by other groups of people.

Of course, out of unique and distinctive features, felt as important by many or most of the group's members, a special way of seeing things can be designed. But is this yet a theory, something to rival or compare with Aristotle, Freud, or Marx? The suspicions of these critics deepen when they note how much of so-called feminist theory seems borrowed or adapted from non-feminist sources: one has simply to take a common concern about women and their historical and contemporary condition and unite it, in differing measures and degrees, with Rousseau, Mill, Kierkegaard, Marx, Freud, Saussure, Jung, Frantz Fanon, and Wittgenstein, and one will have as much intellectual content as the several feminist views have produced.[33] Anti-Cartesianism—sometimes claimed to be a distinctive feminist contribution—is easily located in several philosophical traditions amply developed before 1949. It is likewise with anti-individualism: common sense and phenomenological perspectives already contain most feminist ideas on knowledge, the body, contextuality, and relatedness. Indeed, what is there in feminism—apart from concerns about women, gender, and justice—that is not to be found at least implicitly in Rousseau and Kierkegaard? (Who in the history of thought has had more developed opposition to analytically detached modes of cognition than Kierkegaard, or more richly articulated ideas of truth as subjectivity?)

Moreover, this dialectic relentlessly continues, where feminism has gone beyond these subjectivist or organicist or social justice-

[33] Ferdinand de Saussure (1857–1913) was the linguist who developed what is called structuralism in linguistics (which played an important role in shaping social constructionism). Carl Jung (1875–1961), once Freud's colleague, formulated his own distinctive variety of psychoanalysis, with emphasis on internal models or archetypes that form the self. Frantz Fanon (1925-1961) was a psychiatrist whose book *The Wretched of the Earth* developed an impassioned analysis of colonialism and the marginalization of the oppressed or silenced.

sensitive roots, the result is typically implausibly exaggerated claims about the social world and the people in it.

This objection to feminism does not deny the reality of women's disadvantage or oppression, or the insufficiency of merely cosmetic or legal/formal measures for its elimination. Nor does it dispute the unique character of female experience, in both positive and negative dimensions, or the fact that its importance for many or most women, and human life and society as a whole, has been under-appreciated, belittled, or wholly ignored. Rather, the objection disputes that there is a distinctively feminist human nature theory, holding that claims to be such a theory disguise the experience of only some, many, or most women as that of all, and represent as feminist ideas that were developed independently of feminism.

Another objection to feminism is a kind of polar opposite to the preceding one. This one acknowledges that there *is* something that feminist analysis and theory has discerned and articulated, with varying degrees of accuracy—perhaps least so in liberal versions, most tellingly in "gender" versions. According to this critical perspective, gender is different from everything else that divides humanity; it is deeper, more pervasive, often almost invisible, and more often still disadvantaging of women. Only, as this objecting view has it, there is no real solution to the "gender problem." There can be mitigation, certainly fairer and more equitable social and economic arrangements, and more elevated and honourable interpersonal relationships between the sexes. But the realization of the feminist dream in any of its more dramatic and revolutionary forms is chimera. That dream, we may say, is that men will be made to give up their greater power or (less plausibly) will voluntarily do so, failing which women will separate themselves from sustained interconnecting with men and live in gynocracy (whether lesbian or with heterosexual periodicity, or a combination of both). Feminists put the dream, and the heart of their analyses, in terms of power, but in fact it seems reasonable to see it as involving also visions of sharing, where not just power would be shared: natures would be, inner sancta, modes and ways of being and behaving, tonalities. (In developed articulation this is what is called the androgynous ideal. But some feminisms that don't advocate that ideal still have sharings of more than power in view.)

The objectors indicated here think that feminism fails to see the degree of female complicity in "genderized" life. They note that, through all the highly articulate and often searchingly detailed analysis of the most focused feminist writing, there is astonishingly little mention of the fact that large numbers of women, probably a majority in every human society, like or love men, and that this is a central and fundamental fact about them, as important for them as wage parity or profession entry or household division of labour. These large numbers of women like or love fathers, brothers, uncles, lovers, husbands, sons, school friends, nephews, neighbours' sons, and men who are celebrities, among other individuals. And very many of them also like or love men as such, in something like the way in which men often are characterized as liking or loving women as such.[34] These facts seem quite obvious from the most basic levels of social experience, and seem to persist through all manner of academic conferences, writing, analysis, revolutionary proposals, demonstrations, or non-negotiable demand. They seem well confirmed when people are young, when they are middle-aged, and when they are old.

Of course, many women don't like men, or their liking is conditional: they will like men only in a rightly ordered world or if they personally have non-negative experiences of genderized life. But the fact of apparently ever-self-renewing heterosexual enthusiasm as the generations proceed seems one of the world's ways. And it does not seem remotely plausible to account for this reality through men's devious management of "the gender system." It over-flatters men to view them as that effective and well organized, and it definitely demeans women to suppose they are that readily and thoroughly bamboozled. And it is also unconvincing, though perhaps a *little* more plausible, that women only seem to like men, or force themselves to like men, because they have to survive in a man's world. Doubtless there is some and even much truth to the latter idea; there have surely been a great many cases of such female adaptation. But even a great many such cases will not seriously detract from the enormously many more instances of enthusiastic interest in intimate linkage with male human beings. This alone will be enough to render implausible views of women or men as classes in anything like a Marxian sense. Having affectional/erotic desires and needs met—for most women, having a favoured man in one's life—is one of the things a class interest is precisely intended to secure, one of the goods of body and spirit. Just where it will fit among desires for children, a secure well-paid job, relations with friends and kin, a satisfactory or pleasing dwelling-place, leisure and leisure activities, security for circumstances of illness or old age, educational and

[34] Which of course doesn't in either case mean all or even most of the opposite sex, and not without all manner of qualifications.

spiritual stimulus, and other desired goods will vary from woman to woman, with time of life and circumstance. One sex may or may not, under different conditions, have an interest in having the company and services of the other accorded a highlighted significance, exaggerating the actual desire/need felt by particular women or men. But the fact of a very deep and wide elemental enthusiasm for getting together with one or more esteemed members of the other sex is evident, and any theory that does not give this a central and non-accidental place in its account of humans is thereby incomplete.

Complicating this centrality, it may be claimed, the relations between the sexes are inherently and inescapably unstable: patterns, recurrent and inextricably intertwined, of attraction and animosity—of Love and Strife, as Empedocles, the pre-Socratic metaphysician, identified the fundamental governing principles of the universe. According to this model there can be no settled, tranquillity-producing contractual arrangement between men and women. Amity is achieved at cost, as, when it occurs, is conflict. To some degree this never-quiescent pattern is, as this view sees it, a matter of divergent interest: men and women to some degree want different things, or they want the same thing but, because that thing is scarce or non-divisible, only one of them can have it. "Mature compromise" is, on this line, illusion; it is usually to do things as the stronger or the more interpersonally skilful prefers. But this line of thinking only partly accurately represents the force of this objection to feminism (in both equality and difference forms), for it neglects the Dionysian extra-rational, passional component of relations between the sexes, the bio-psychic hungering that will not let the one sex leave the other alone. They are bound and determined to "have at it"—a superbly apt phrase meaning both happy, delirious, mutualist sexual coupling and quarrelsome argumentation.

The basis for this kind of objection to feminism may be in beliefs about human biology or in Freudian or other depth-psychological convictions. Some bio-based views see patterns of female feigned indifference to the male and male overt declaration of sexual interest and pursuit as a widely occurring part of attraction and courtship, in not merely primate species. For this position, activities like the "No Means No" campaign for date-rape prevention are colossally dim-witted ideas, guaranteed to ensure large amounts of unnecessary suf-fering. They ignore the textures and subtleties of male-female inter-actions, which will inevitably include elements of sham and pose, trial and (quite certainly) error. On such views, this kind of feminist initiative illustrates well the literalism and surface-level-only complained of earlier. Contrary to their intention, they also diminish the autonomy, inwardness, and self-direction of females and males. For to tell someone who is engaged in the exploration of their own horizons of intimacy that they can and should opt out of the subtlety and uncertainty of such exploration, in favour of police and public tribunal with themselves in the one-dimensional role of accusing victim, with a formula of words they can plant and then ring like a bell, is to tell them to live on the outside of themselves. Of course, people should be able to get out of interpersonal situations that are truly unwanted and unpleasant; and of course genuine assault, sexual or otherwise, must be illegal, able to be established on the testimony of its victim, and punished as serious crime. The exploration of sociosexual horizons (with its possibilities of misadventure) and dangerous, surprising, unwelcome attack are different phenomena, differently coded facets of life in public or social space (which also doesn't preclude the one sometimes crossing over into the other, though rarely if people have been students of themselves and of those spaces).

At any rate, there are more and less Apollonian versions of this general line of objection to feminism. Some of its advocates would see genuine friendship occurring alongside strong sexual involvement as more or less impossible; others would see it as rare or difficult but nonetheless possible, if unstable. Males and females clearly discover genuine friendship with each other independently of sexual involvement; why should the latter preempt the possibility of the former?

On the other side of the matter, if an Apollonian version of the stance referred to here is plausible, and if—as said at the outset—significant degrees of male-female equality in the workplace, in politics, in socioeconomic life broadly, and in private relations are all possible and in the course of becoming actual, then perhaps some feminist dreams would have come true. It may be that a meaningful measure of human happiness, a framework for the self-realization of both men and women individually and interconnectedly, is as realistic to expect and work towards as it is desirable.

Bibliography

Bock, Gisela, & James, Susan, eds. *Beyond Equality and Difference.* London: Routledge, 1992.

Elshtain, Jean Bethke. *Private Man, Public Woman.* Princeton, NJ: Princeton University Press, 1993.

Friedman, Marilyn. "Does Sommers Like Women? More on Liberalism, Gender Hierarchy, and Scarlett O'Hara." *Journal of Social Philosophy* 21 (Fall & Winter 1990).

——————. "'They Lived Happily Ever After': Sommers on Women and Marriage." *Journal of Social Philosophy* 21 (Fall & Winter 1990).

Gilligan, Carol. *In a Different Voice.* Cambridge, MA: Harvard University Press, 1982.

Grant, Judith. *Fundamental Feminism.* New York: Routledge, 1993.

Grimshaw, Jean. *Feminist Philosophers.* London: Harvester Wheatsheaf, 1986. (Published in the United States as *Philosophy and Feminist Thinking.* Minneapolis: University of Minnesota Press, 1988)

Jaggar, Allison M. *Feminist Politics and Human Nature.* Totowa, NJ: Rowman & Allanheld, 1983.

Lehrke, Robert C. "Sex Linkage: A Biological Basis for Greater Male Variability in Intelligence." In *Human Variation,* edited by R. Travis Osborne, Clyde E. Noble, & Nathaniel Weyl. New York: Academic Press, 1978.

Mill, John Stuart. *The Subjection of Women* [1869]. Reprinted in John Stuart Mill, *Three Essays.* Oxford: Oxford University Press, 1975.

——————. *Utilitarianism.* Indianapolis: Hackett, 1979. [1861]

Paglia, Camille. *Sex, Art, and American Culture.* New York: Vintage, 1992.

——————. *Sexual Personae.* New Haven: Yale University Press, 1990.

——————. *Vamps and Tramps.* New York: Vintage, 1994.

Pollitt, Katha. "Marooned on Gilligan's Island: Are Women Morally Superior to Men?" *The Nation* 22 (Dec. 28, 1992). (Reprinted in Pollitt, *Reasonable Creatures*) (see also "Exchange," *The Nation* 256 [March 8, 1993])

——————. *Reasonable Creatures: Essays on Women and Feminism.* New York: Knopf, 1994.

Schapiro, J. Salwyn. *Condorcet and the Rise of Liberalism* (especially Chap. 10, "Feminism"). New York: Harcourt, Brace, 1934.

Sommers, Christina. *"Argumentum Ad Feminam." Journal of Social Philosophy* 22 (Spring 1991).

——. "Do These Feminists Like Women?" *Journal of Social Philosophy* 21 (Fall & Winter 1990).

——. *Who Stole Feminism?* New York: Simon & Schuster, 1994.

Tong, Rosemary. *Feminist Thought.* Boulder, CO: Westview, 1989.

Wollstonecraft, Mary. *A Vindication of the Rights of Women.* 2nd ed., edited by Carol N. Poston. New York: W. W. Norton, 1988.

CHAPTER 13

Marvin Harris ————————

MARVIN HARRIS (B. 1927) HAS APPEARED frequently in earlier chapters, most often as a critic or opponent of other theories. In this chapter we consider his own view of human nature. Harris is a leading contemporary cultural anthropologist. In spite of anthropology's title by etymology and history to be the study of humankind, and hence where we might particularly hope to find ambitious and comprehensive theories of human nature, that discipline has not been especially rich in theory. It has tended to focus primarily on fieldwork studies of small-scale human societies, particularly rural and Third World ones, and has often deliberately (even triumphally) disavowed general theory, rarely aspiring to comprehensive theorizing about human beings. In some cases this distaste for theory has had empiricist or positivist bases—that is, has stemmed from commitments to cautious, ground-level science—but more frequently has had humanist roots, issuing from a glorying in the particularities of human cultural diversity.

Harris therefore stands out, for he has endeavoured over the course of a long career to fashion a highly ambitious, comprehensive, universalist theory—indeed, a science—of human beings. At the same time he has sought accessibility. His many books are relatively informal, good-humoured, engaging pieces of writing. With signal exceptions, they only occasionally and somewhat obliquely reveal the degree of their theoretical underpinnings and the case they mean to substantiate. Harris calls his theory cultural materialism, and *Cultural Materialism* (1979) is the most fully theoretically articulated of his books. He devotes a great deal of attention to attempting to show how the principles of cultural materialism will explain all manner of social and historical development across a plethora of societies and cultures.

Harris's theory is avowedly (historical) materialist, and self-consciously places itself in approximately the same intellectual territory as Marxism. Accordingly, cultural materialism is opposed to all varieties of idealism at least formally, though as with Marxism there is some doubt whether it is as purely materialist as is claimed. At any rate, Harris evaluates at length a wide range of rival positions, both idealist and materialist, endeavouring to show the superiority of cultural materialism. He writes with special vigour and detail about the inadequacies of sociobiology.

Harris is a Darwinian, and accords natural selection the formative creation of human nature, achieved in its present stable form not less than thirty-five thousand years ago. Much of Harris's quarrel with sociobiology is in fact over matters of human biology (and that such a debate, on such terrain, is still possible attests powerfully for the claim that these matters are well short of scientific solidity). As Harris sees it, the problem of reproductive success for our species was solved by our having evolved from forebears who were extremely highly sexed and whose sexuality, in both sexes, was operative at least potentially more or less daily, and thus independent of occasions of ovulation, pregnancy, or lactation (*Our Kind,* pp. 180–183). Our species' shotgun approach guarantees species survival. That same approach divorces our sexual system from a specifically reproductive one. Hence, there is no need to posit specialized reproductive strategies, innate or genetic structures operating as a cunning of reason to maximize the proliferation of our genes. Moreover, Harris holds that there is abundant social and historical evidence against there being such strategies or structures.

Harris calls cultural materialism "a scientific research strategy" (*Cultural Materialism,* p. 6). The subtitle for *Cultural Materialism* is "The Struggle for a Science of Culture." He differentiates science from non-science in reasonably straightforward and orthodox ways, ways that would be shared by most (though not all) of the other theorists in this book. This involves repudiation of allegedly irrationalist critiques of science and scientific method (for example, those of Paul Feyerabend and Thomas Kuhn). Harris is a champion—indeed, a missionary advocate—of science. This is just one of the themes on which he is an engaged and sometimes polemical thinker and writer. At least part of what clearly prompts his advocacy of empiricist science is a set of concerns Harris has about his own discipline of anthropology, which he sees as having been marked by biases against theory, empiricism, and science.

The fundamental principles of cultural materialism can be set out briefly. (Unless otherwise indicated, citations are from *Cultural Materialism.*) "The aim of cultural materialism ... is to account for the origin, maintenance, and change of the global inventory of sociocultural differences and similarities" (p. 27). In addition to an empiricist scientific methodology and epistemology, with a clear commitment to the possibility of objectivity, Harris draws upon

Pike's emic/etic distinction, as noted in Chapter 1. (This contrast, again, distinguishes participants' and observers' perspectives and concepts.) "In the cultural materialist research strategy ... the intent is neither to convert etics to emics nor emics to etics, but rather to describe both and if possible to explain one in terms of the other" (p. 36).

Harris illustrates both concepts, and shows how a cultural anthropologist can seek to utilize them, with the example of the treatment of the so-called sacred cow in India (p. 38). "If the terms 'emic' and 'etic' are not redundant with respect to the terms 'mental' and 'behavioral,' there should be four objective operationally definable domains in the sociocultural field of inquiry." These are emic/ behavioral, etic/behavioral, emic/ mental, and etic/mental. The observing anthropologist in India notes that while farmers declare the sacredness of all cattle, in practice they sometimes allow male calves to starve to death. Harris conceives four distinct conceptualizations for the Indian farmer, expressing what they are doing concurrent with how they see things. These map onto the four theoretical categories. So, on the emic/behavioral level—that is, as the farmer sees what he is doing, in his own terms—"No calves are starved to death." On the etic/behavioral level (i.e., what the observer sees happening): "Male calves are starved to death." On the emic/mental level the farmer's thought is "All calves have the right to life." Finally, on the etic/mental level: "Let the male calves starve to death when feed is scarce." The etic statements are observer's hypotheses, the emic ones supplied by the people observed. Harris thinks etic/ mental hypotheses particularly hazardous, since they involve imputing to someone a thought they may explicitly repudiate. The most secure category, and the one upon which alone a science of culture can build, is the etic/behavioral category (though emics are often useful or necessary for supplying data for these building blocks) (p. 41).

The theoretical principles of cultural materialism are descendants, with important modifications, of Marx's materialist social science.

> The universal structure of sociocultural systems posited by cultural materialism rests on the biological and psychological constants of human nature, and on the distinction between thought and behavior and emics and etics. To begin with, each society must cope with the problems of production—behaviorally satisfying minimal requirements for subsistence; hence there must be an *etic behavioral mode of production*. Second, each society must behaviorally cope with the problem of reproduction— avoiding destructive increases or decreases in population size; hence there must be an *etic behavioral mode of reproduction*.

Third, each society must cope with the necessity of maintaining secure and orderly behavioral relationships among its constituent groups and with other societies. In conformity with mundane and practical considerations, cultural materialists see the threat of disorder arising primarily from the economic processes which allocate labor and the material products of labor to individuals and groups. Hence, depending on whether the focus of organization is on domestic groups or the internal and external relationships of the whole society, one may infer the universal existence of *etic behavioral domestic economies* and *etic behavioral political economies*. Finally, given the prominence of human speech acts and the importance of symbolic processes for the human psyche, one can infer the universal recurrence of productive behavior that leads to etic, recreational, sportive, and aesthetic products and services. *Behavioral superstructure* is a convenient label for this universally recurrent etic sector. (p. 51f.)[1]

There are five major etic behavioral categories, which Harris groups into three larger categories: infrastructure, structure, and superstructure. At the level of infrastructure are the mode of production and the mode of reproduction. A society's structure includes its domestic economy and its political economy. Superstructure has just one etic category, called behavioral superstructure, which includes art, music, dance, literature, games, rituals, and the like—much as in Marxist theory. All mental and emic sociocultural components, in

---

[1] We might note that Harris's theoretical postulates accord a sociocultural system no explicit primary role in the creative challenge of coping with the surrounding physical environment. This seems plainly a deficiency, even if not one with any obvious implications for human nature. Marx's sociocultural theory exhibits the same shortcoming. For a valuable discussion and advocacy of the need to allot the environment a central explanatory and theoretical role in any adequate theory of culture or history, see Richard James Blackburn, *The Vampire of Reason* (1990). Both Marx and Harris give *some* attention to the environment. Thus, Harris's mode of production includes techno-environmental relationships, and ecosystems. But, as with Marx, nature functions here in a largely inert way, from a theoretical point of view. Even if changeable, it is essentially the setting where a usually discrete sociocultural experiment is acted out, rather than a daily and continuous participant in individual and social destiny. On the other hand Harris's individual applications of the principle of infrastructural determinism—for example, the case of Aztec Mexico mentioned below—give the environment a role similar to that in the model provided by Blackburn.

whatever behavioural category they are found, are grouped together as mental and emic superstructure.

Harris acknowledges Marx as having anticipated his principles, with one important exception: Marx's neglect of the critical and independent infrastructural role of the mode of reproduction. Harris enunciates his own fundamental assumption:

> The cultural materialist version of Marx's great principle is as follows: The etic behavioral modes of production and reproduction probabilistically determine the etic behavioral domestic and political economy, which in turn probabilistically determine the behavioral and mental emic superstructures. For brevity's sake, this principle can be referred to as the principle of infrastructural determinism. (p. 55f.)

As Harris elaborates this principle, he indicates that the idea is that this formula of infrastructural determinism serves to guide investigation and explanation in the social sciences. The principle's claim of mere probabilistic determinism will always allow that, in exceptional circumstances, something will occur that wasn't fully materially caused or conditioned.

Infrastructure—the modes of production and reproduction—includes, Harris explains (p. 52), technology of subsistence, techno-environmental relationships, ecosystems, work patterns, demography, mating patterns, fertility, natality, mortality, nurturance of infants, medical control of demographic patterns, and contraception, abortion, infanticide. Infrastructure "is the principal interface between culture and nature, the boundary across which the ecological, chemical, and physical constraints to which human action is subject interact with the principal sociocultural practices aimed at overcoming or modifying these restraints" (p. 57).

The principle of infrastructural determinism operates upon human nature. Harris identifies a set of "human bio-psychological selective principles," which he holds apply to most other primates as well as humans, namely:

1. People need to eat and will generally opt for diets that offer more rather than fewer calories and proteins and nutrients.
2. People cannot be totally inactive, but when confronted with a given task, they prefer to carry it out by expending less rather than more energy.

3. People are highly sexed and generally find reinforcing pleasure from sexual intercourse—more often from heterosexual intercourse.

4. People need love and affection in order to feel secure and happy, and other things being equal, they will act to increase the love and affection which others give them. (p. 63)

The broad picture is that natural selection operated over the many millions of years that produced fully modern *homo sapiens,* from earlier primates to not later than thirty-five thousand years ago. Around that date, in a relatively short period of about ten thousand years, fully formed human societies—cultures—appeared. From then on, cultural selection, essentially the principle of infrastructural determinism, has been the primary factor shaping and governing human development, experience, and history (*Our Kind,* pp. 126–128).

Harris undertakes to show how cultural materialism and its principles will make sense of, explain, every sort and kind of social and cultural phenomenon. Providing such explanations is in fact the central content of his semi-popular books (among them *Cows, Pigs, Wars and Witches: The Riddles of Culture* [1974], *Cannibals and Kings: The Origins of Culture* [1977], and *Our Kind* [1989]). Harris attempts to explain the origins and continuity of sexism, racism, warfare, and different sexual, familial, religious, and dietary patterns and activities—always by reference to the principle of infrastructural determinism. The institutions and practices of simple tribal societies, contemporary industrial liberal democracies, and every variety between are investigated. So too are patterns of historical development and now-departed historical societies like the Aztecs of Mexico, who Harris argues (*Our Kind,* pp. 432–436) became a cannibal culture of massive proportions, caused to be so by a depletion of protein sources in the Valley of Mexico region, with this response to their environmental constraints then superstructurally validated by the creation of a religion whose pantheon required the practice.

I will not evaluate the success of Harris's cultural materialist analyses of specific cultural phenomena. They rest on a considerable body of empirical data, some of which is contestable, and sometimes he seems to generalize, implausibly, beyond the base of his evidence.[2] On the whole his explanations carry some weight,

---

[2] For example, in his attempt (*Our Kind,* pp. 378–380, 388–390) to derive state-societies in general from a "big man" phenomenon known in a num-

frequently appear entirely persuasive, and are almost always fascinating. *Our Kind* expands the cultural materialist base to seek a broad understanding, in its terms, of human behaviour in general and not just social institutions and practices. The theoretical and methodological framework is fundamentally the same, and the results claimed are, again, chiefly sociocultural. A new principle is added to the repertoire, that of exchange: "Giving and taking, or exchange, is the glue that holds human societies together" (*Our Kind,* p. 190).

Harris's theory of human nature may be, overall, the most plausible materialist theory of humankind yet produced. It remains to be determined how successfully it weathers extended reconsideration and how plausibly it predicts future patterns of cultural and historical development.[3]

Some of the weaknesses in Harris's cultural materialism, as a theory of human nature, stem from the specially social and cultural character of its claims. That is to say, the theory has little or nothing illuminating to say about individual differences within a cultural or economic group when they do not have obvious economic/material causes. Why is this individual fastidious, careful, punctual and that one none of these things, even where both are in the same sociocultural condition? Why is this one drawn to gambling and that one quite uninterested? (In both cases one might be talking of siblings.) Harris has nothing to say about this.

But neither, perhaps, should he. He is an anthropologist, which is to say, a certain kind of sociologist. His unit of focus is the whole society or culture, not its individual parts or members. Only sometimes is the science of culture he aspires to, and claims, held also to be a whole reckoning of being a human. (But he *does* sometimes claim this much, and it is as an entire theory of human nature that cultural materialism is before our view.)

ber of Pacific and North American tribal societies.

[3] Cultural materialism has received very extensive discussion and evaluation from Harris's fellow anthropoligists, some of it favourable, some of it pointedly (if not always convincingly) critical. For some of this criticism, see R. N. Adams, "Natural Selection, Energetics, and 'Cultural Materialism,'" *Current Anthropology* (1981) (with comments by D. T. Campbell et al., and Adams' replies); P. J. Magnarella, "Cultural Materialism and the Problem of Probabilities," *American Anthropologist* (1984); D. Western, "Cultural Materialism: Food for Thought or Bum Steer?" *Current Anthropology* 1984).

There are also weaknesses from the other side of the spectrum, and there are arguable difficulties or over-simplifications to which anthropology in general seems professionally prone. These are difficulties in accounting, or accounting adequately, for interactions between societies or cultures. In the anthropological scheme of things, it often seems, societies appear as if hermetically sealed from each other, beavering away in their isolated habitat. There is sometimes, to be sure, a "neighbouring tribe" with whom periodic warfare or some other form of interaction occurs; but this is really part of the same artificial phenomenon, another part of the imposed script. Many anthropologists in recent decades, not particularly Harris among them,[4] have worried about the role of the observing anthropologists themselves—whether it may slant the findings or have ethical dimensions. And there is also (almost always for small tribal societies in the contemporary world) the fact of a huge imperialist macroculture, almost invariably menacing.

But the character of cultural interactions has extended far beyond the kinds indicated—isolated tribe, tribal conflict/symbiosis, tribe plus one or two alien observing social scientists, or tribe plus the whole weight of aggressive, engulfing western Christendom. Indeed, there is good reason to believe that for very large portions of humanity historical experience has consisted essentially and not just interstitially of what W. H. McNeill calls "troubling encounters with strangers"[5]; and hence with world-views and behaviours that contain ongoing elements of adaptation to such encounters. They may therefore also, let it be said, contain adaptation strategies for such encounters that would not be successful, and so not achieve Harris's level of techno-economic rationality.

Harris's methodological assumption of cultural economic rationality is in general surely a plausible and productive one. That is, he assumes that, all else being equal, what a particular group of people are doing makes sense, and that the sense it makes is a function (generally discoverable) of the constraints and possibilities of their habitat. Their cultural mode—hence, who they are—will be the result and the expression of a certain kind of attempt to achieve a satisfactory level of group well-being in that habitat (including its fluctuations). But things are quite often not equal, more often perhaps than Harris's theory can comfortably accommodate. People in groups

[4] Although he *discusses* the matter in *Cultural Materialism,* p. 45.

[5] McNeill, *Mythistory and Other Essays* (1986), p. 37.

can, without being killed, dispersed, or enslaved, develop "cultural strategies" that are either maladaptive or, if as good as circumstances permit, not obviously the expressions of economic rationality Harris will attempt to construe them as.

There is finally what he himself is sometimes prepared candidly to conceive as an idealist residue. By his own acknowledgement (*Our Kind,* p. *xi*), Harris has little useful to say about the fine arts (and especially music and dance). He ought also to acknowledge that he has nothing more useful to say about the material conditions that yield advanced intellectual culture: neither the fact of mature western scientific culture at large nor—still more glaringly—specific and frequently incompatible contents of scientific culture. What are the material constraints that enabled Harris himself to formulate culture materialism and recognize its truth? Which companion constraints prevented his idealist and sociobiological colleagues from achieving the same outcomes? Indeed, mere enabling cannot be sufficient in any of these cases, for there would then still be a chasm for free creativity to leap beyond, to truth and error respectively. What constraints—features of geography, technology, and material culture—bestow cultural materialism upon Harris but withhold it from other members of the American Anthropological Association? Can Harris seriously hold that extensions of his theory will in future, or in principle, produce answers to such questions?[6] It would seem not.

Let me conclude this brief discussion of Harris's cultural materialism on a more favourable note. Far more striking than the theory's inadequacy in the face of "high culture" is the extraordinarily broad range of phenomena, commonplace and institutional, for which cultural materialism offers fertile and suggestive explanation, including a very large part of the spiritual lives of human individuals and communities. Attempting cultural materialist avenues of understanding for what "our kind" does and is seems never misguided or inappropriate. There will be, I think, an "idealist" residue that forever eludes such probing, and it will include at least a core part of the probing itself. Theoretical rationality—philosophy, broadly—may supervene upon the practical/economic rationality from which it was historically emergent. Furthermore, theoretical rationality may or may not be able to operate transversally upon our circumstances, either at odds with or leaping beyond habitat-triggered

---

[6] It should be noted that one other naturalistic "reductionist" theory, Freud's, tries to explain theoretical predispositions and commitments as reflections of personality type.

rationality. (The hope that it will is expressed and affirmed in the unmistakably idealist concluding sections of *Our Kind*.) But the kind of base from which and with which Harris advocates that the investigation of humans be undertaken—the methodological assumption of a principle of sufficient material reason—seems to have a good deal to commend itself, since it appears quite often, at least, to lead to convincing results about human life.

Bibliography

Adams, Richard N. "Natural Selection, Energetics, and 'Cultural Materialism.'" *Current Anthropology* 22, no. 6 (1981) (with comments by Donald T. Campbell et al. and Adams' replies).

Blackburn, Richard James. *The Vampire of Reason.* London: Verso, 1990.

Harris, Marvin. *Cannibals and Kings.* New York: Random House, 1977.

—————. *Cows, Pigs, Wars and Witches.* New York: Random House, 1974.

—————. *Cultural Materialism.* New York: Random House, 1979.

—————. *Our Kind.* New York: Harper & Row, 1989.

—————. *The Rise of Anthropological Theory.* New York: Harper Collins, 1968.

Magnarella, P. J. "Cultural Materialism and the Problem of Probabilities." *American Anthropologist* 84 (1982).

McNeill, W. H. *Mythistory and Other Essays.* Chicago: University of Chicago Press, 1986.

Western, Drew. "Cultural Materialism: Food for Thought or Bum Steer?" *Current Anthropology* 25 (1984).

CHAPTER 14

Conclusion ———————

WE BEGAN OUR ENTERPRISE WITH THE IDEA AND the ideal of a science of humankind, originating in the Enlightenment and successively spun in diverse directions in the three centuries following Newton. This Enlightenment idea provides a useful way to compare our eleven theories, some of which claim to realize this grand project while others explicitly or implicitly challenge its possibility.

In the first group are certainly Marx, Freud, the biological theories, Harris and, in their different way, the non-self theories. Somewhat more tentatively we may also place liberalism and Rousseau under this umbrella, for both, with their shared conviction of fundamental human goodness, envisage possibilities of filling in the ledger of human nature in ways that make for enlightened understanding and a social world conducive to human flourishing. This may seem more obvious in the case of liberalism, with its commitment to scientific knowledge and rationality, than with Rousseau. But both theories think it possible to realize conditions in which human beings can be genuinely (not merely negatively) free, and both see this being achieved principally through enlightened methods of education. And though he lived long before Newton, Aristotle, *il maestro di color che sanno* ("the master of those who know"), as Dante called him, will also belong here. Aristotelian science does not clearly fit post-Newtonian models, but the fundamental and ubiquitous imperative of all of Aristotle's work—also identified as one of the central human traits—is open, rational curiosity, the desire to understand. Aristotle is committed to the possibility of systematic and comprehensive knowledge of human beings; indeed, as we have indicated, he thinks he himself has achieved it.

Feminist views are divided. One constituency, evidently the less numerous, believes in the rational investigation of the world along more or less empirical and objective lines. Such investigation is thought to disclose a considerable though not limitless plasticity, and a basic equality, of nature within and between the sexes; or differences due to a history that need not determine, or be repeated in, the future. Another constituency, probably a current majority within the academy, challenges the idea of a science of humanity in anything like the mainstream or received sense, either because no science of anything is possible, or because a science of humans (or of women) is impossible, or because received science is masculinist and hence incapable of being the neutral, or reasonably neutral, objective enterprise it purports to be. In the latter case it would remain open and perhaps negotiable whether an investigation freed of masculinism might show us in some comprehensive and illuminating way who we are.

Conservative individualism also appears to bear a complex relationship to the Enlightenment project. Some conservatives are drawn to biological theories of human nature, often sociobiology, and will thus be aligned with the systematic scientific knowability of humanity. But there is a note of anti-intellectualism sometimes met with in conservatism, or, less tendentiously, a stand that takes the world as it finds it and does not suppose significant illumination will come from probing. We find people thus and so; it is an unexplored and possibly unexplorable mystery why they are so. Something similar may be said of Christians, even modern ones: although science will have its say and its uses, there remain enigmas, parts of our makeup that link us to the unseen spiritual world.

There are other commonalities among the eleven theories. Some see a considerable gap between humans and the rest of animate nature; others don't. That is, some of the theories stress our identity as an animal species, or more accurately, their survey of us fails to register marked discontinuities between ourselves and other living creatures. Other theories, by contrast, are unmindful of other animals and don't think our animality a matter of primary importance. Obviously Darwin's and the post-Darwinian biological views (sociobiology and Lorenz) are in the bio-focused group; but so, I think, are Aristotle, Freud, and Harris. So also are the non-self theories, though in the case of cyberneticist views of humanity the science-fictional possibilities (that may or may not become realities) of non-living, artificially produced, or extraterrestrial intelligent information-processing systems seems to distance this image from our biological background.

By contrast with all these views are those that take human beings just as ourselves, generally without reference to our origins. Although he does discuss those origins, Rousseau belongs on this side of this divide; for his anthropological speculations are ungrounded scientifically and serve chiefly to prompt the notion of the natural human who can then be juxtaposed with Rousseau's civilized human. The "naturalness" of any other species is a thing quite unknown to this view. Rousseau does not wonder what it is like to be a bat, but does know (or thinks he does) what it is like to be several kinds of human being. Christianity too sees us as special, ourselves as ourselves (if also for God). And in spite of his historical materialism and avowal of rootedness in science (including Darwinian science), Marx also really belongs here: our conscious being is what is important about us, even if it is created and then transformed by materially determined social relations. The spirit of feminism, as also of liberalism, is the declaration of human autonomy from wider or larger nature. Finally, conservative individualism, with its insistence on human darkness—though this is often suggested by or claims support from our animal nature and background—also takes people only as people.

Still another axis of comparison for our eleven theories assesses them in terms of their view about the malleability of human nature. One of the old aphorisms of folk belief is that "you can't change human nature." How do our eleven theories stack up regarding this adage? Some are clearly and incontestably on its side: conservative individualism, Rousseau, Freud, and the biological views all affirm a universality and essential stability in our fundamental condition and prospects. (Although Darwin himself, and Lorenz, do accord culture some independent causal importance for human life, thereby suggesting a greater openness to change than might be supposed of a bio-based view.) Non-self views too suggest a more or less fixed nature, with the important proviso that connectionist stances seem compatible with the idea of our "software"—our genetic and other information-processing structures—being rewritten, at least in principle. Christian theory straddles the fork between its Whig and Tory branches. On both we have genuine free will; but in the Tory branch at least we trudge through life saddled with dispositions that will not go away, whatever our uses of our rational agency. The Whig variety of Christian theory also does not seem to envisage a fundamental rewriting of the species' script. As with Rousseau, we are basically good on this view but also capable of bad, and each individual life will be a new but archetypally similar human venture.

This leaves five of our theories. All permit some or considerable malleability in the human clay, dividing interestingly along a fault line of the source of change. For two of the theories what fashions the form we take in the first place and on every subsequent occasion is something other than ourselves, individually or corporately. These are the views of Marx and Harris, which assign to material/social conditions and relations the architect's role in the arrangements and rearrangements that are made of us. The Marxian human is more open-ended than Harris' human: the possibility of a communist utopia seems to point to a Marxian freedom from biology that Harris does not share. Marx is a kind of dualist—in this respect somewhat like Aristotle—for whom while in and of nature, we stand also apart. For Marx more than for Harris, then, there is considerable alterability in human possibilities—only it is not we ourselves who can take advantage of this fact (at least not in the more materialist version of Marx we have focused upon). For Harris we are nonetheless significantly alterable: culture is learning, and we can learn to redirect our pathways if our cultural and natural habitats jointly prod us to.

For Aristotle we are free and have considerable powers of initiatory agency. Yet we are also an animal species, and we have a nature, which can be perverted or frustrated, and also depends on education for its optimal unfolding. Feminist theory divides between a kind of Marxian variant, with socially created sex natures that may be not significantly alterable in fact though they certainly are in theory; and a liberal variant. This last, like liberalism generally, accords us possibly the greatest degree of autonomous self-altering agency of any of our theories.

I will, in concluding, make no prediction of the future of human nature theory. Human self-interest, meaning both preoccupation with ourselves and what tends to our benefit, together with human ingenuity and curiosity, will continue to provide interesting and, surely, some quite new models of our identity. It might be supposed that the great variety of theories about human nature—all with universalist claim, many at least plausible and substantively grounded, and most incompatible with each other—point to an unending future odyssey of self-exploration. However, even this does not seem a safe or probable bet. For as we also affirmed when we began, we may already have achieved the essentials of the truth about human nature: we may know, but just not know that we know.

Index ─────────────────────

Pike, Kenneth 10, 18
Plato 29, 33, 36, 38, 45, 56, 59, 110, 231
Plutarch 113, 118
Pollitt, Katha 215f, 219, 242
positive/negative liberty 74, 210
postmodernism 22–25, 112, 138
Poulain de la Barre, François 211
private property 125, 136
proletariat 126, 133
Protestantism 42, 47f, 112
psychology 170, 177
Pythagoras 1

Quakerism 46

racism 144–46, 148f, 233
Rand, Ayn 90, 146, 221
Rawls, John 33, 57, 80–82, 88
recognition 130, 132
ressentiment 11f, 229
Rivera, Diego 179
Robespierre, Maximilien de 47
Rochester, Earl of 66, 68
Roosevelt, Franklin D. 76
Rorty, Richard 112
Rose, Steven 20, 28, 156, 163
Rousseau, Jean-Jacques *ix,* 33, 48, 101–19, 121–26, 132, 160, 223, 225, 229, 237, 255–57
Rumelhart, D. 201f, 207
Russell, Bertrand 1, 66, 84
Ryle, Gilbert 203

Saint-Simon, Claude-Henri de 121, 124–26, 132
Sartre, Jean-Paul 20f, 28
Saussure, Ferdinand de 237
Schindler, Oskar 210
Schopenhauer, Arthur 81, 83, 165f, 181, 191
Sellars, Wilfrid 39, 41
Shakespeare, William 180, 189
Skinner, B.F. 134
Smith, Adam 89, 132, 157
social activism 46
social constructionism 118, 122, 161, 193

social contract, contractarianism 33, 80–82, 107
social Darwinism 143, 146f
social justice 211f, 236f
Socinianism 51f
sociobiology 83, 138, 143f, 153–58, 162, 193, 245, 256
sociology 120, 170, 177
Socrates 132
Sommers, Christina Hoff 219, 228f, 243
Spencer, Herbert 57, 144, 146, 181
Spinoza, Benedictus 2, 54, 83, 110, 165, 177, 230
Stoics 29, 45, 110

Tacitus 113
telos 31, 77, 80, 102, 118, 125, 175, 221
Thatcher, Margaret 221
Thoreau, Henry David 105
Tong, Rosemarie *ix,* 22, 28, 191, 243
Tönnies, Ferdinand 5
Tories 45, 48, 63
Toynbee, Arnold 187
Trinity 51
Turgot, Anne Robert 132

unnatural 32f

Vaihinger, Hans 204
Vico, Giambattista 89, 126, 132, 137
Voltaire, François Marie Arouet de 73, 84, 98, 225

Wallace, Alfred Russel 139f
Watson, J.B. 196–99, 207
Weber, Max 5, 48, 68, 131, 137
Weiss, Penny 117, 119
Whigs 45, 48, 210
Wilson, E.O. 143, 153–55, 164
Wittgenstein, Ludwig 112, 203, 207, 237
Wollstonecraft, Mary 46, 211–13, 230, 243
Wrightsman, Lawrence S. 9, 18

Xenophanes 66